THE COMPLETE IDIOT'S GUIDE® TO

Franchising

by James H. Amos Jr.

ALPHA

A member of Penguin Group (USA) Inc.

ALPHA BOOKS

Published by the Penguin Group

Penguin Group (USA) Inc., 375 Hudson Street, New York, New York 10014, U.S.A.

Penguin Group (Canada), 10 Alcorn Avenue, Toronto, Ontario, Canada M4V 3B2 (a division of Pearson Penguin Canada Inc.)

Penguin Books Ltd, 80 Strand, London WC2R 0RL, England

Penguin Ireland, 25 St Stephen's Green, Dublin 2, Ireland (a division of Penguin Books Ltd)

Penguin Group (Australia), 250 Camberwell Road, Camberwell, Victoria 3124, Australia (a division of Pearson Australia Group Pty Ltd)

Penguin Books India Pvt Ltd, 11 Community Centre, Panchsheel Park, New Delhi—110 017, India

Penguin Group (NZ), cnr Airborne and Rosedale Roads, Albany, Auckland 1310, New Zealand (a division of Pearson New Zealand Ltd)

Penguin Books (South Africa) (Pty) Ltd, 24 Sturdee Avenue, Rosebank, Johannesburg 2196, South Africa

Penguin Books Ltd, Registered Offices: 80 Strand, London WC2R 0RL, England

International Standard Book Number: 1-59257-329-0
Library of Congress Catalog Card Number: 2005925415

07   06   05   8   7   6   5   4   3   2   1

Interpretation of the printing code: The rightmost number of the first series of numbers is the year of the book's printing; the rightmost number of the second series of numbers is the number of the book's printing. For example, a printing code of 05-1 shows that the first printing occurred in 2005.

Printed in the United States of America

Note: This publication contains the opinions and ideas of its author. It is intended to provide helpful and informative material on the subject matter covered. It is sold with the understanding that the author and publisher are not engaged in rendering professional services in the book. If the reader requires personal assistance or advice, a competent professional should be consulted.

The author and publisher specifically disclaim any responsibility for any liability, loss, or risk, personal or otherwise, which is incurred as a consequence, directly or indirectly, of the use and application of any of the contents of this book.

Most Alpha books are available at special quantity discounts for bulk purchases for sales promotions, premiums, fundraising, or educational use. Special books, or book excerpts, can also be created to fit specific needs.

For details, write: Special Markets, Alpha Books, 375 Hudson Street, New York, NY 10014.

Logos that appear on the front cover are registered trademarks of their respective companies as follows:

H & R Block	Mathnasium LLC
Bally Total Fitness Corporation	Cinnabon, Inc.
Doctor's Associates, Inc. (Subway)	Uno Restaurant Holdings Corporation
1-800-Flowers.com, Inc.	Ramada Franchise Systems, Inc.
United Parcel Service of America, Inc.	Days Inns Worldwide, Inc.
Snap-on Incorporated	RadioShack Corporation
7-Eleven, Inc.	McDonald's Corporation and Affiliates
Sona MedSpa International, Inc.	Molly Maid, Inc.

To the many friends and colleagues who have contributed to my education in the extraordinary world of franchising in the past 30 years, and in particular those who have traversed the globe many times with me as part of the International Franchise Association. Thank you for your entrepreneurial vision and courage, qualities that have made franchising the most powerful economic engine in the world today. You are my franchise family.

Contents at a Glance

Contents

Foreword

This book does not answer the most often-asked question, "What's the hot franchise?" But it does answer the two most important questions for your future, "Is a franchised business right for me?" and "How do I go about finding the best franchise for me?" Jim Amos has been in the trenches and in the towers of franchising for nearly 30 years, which gives him a truly unique perspective in delivering solid, actionable information for anyone considering owning and operating their own business.

And that's the first question Jim helps answer, "Are you committed to owning your own business?" If the answer is yes, then the next thing you must decide is whether a franchise business is the right choice for you. This book lays out the pros and the cons in a straightforward way that will help any aspiring business owner decide between a franchise and going it alone. It raises the right questions that need the right answers for you and your future. Important issues—ranging from the financial to interests, skills, and quality of life—all play a part in determining the right answer.

Read this book from cover to cover and then ask yourself whether a franchised business is the right choice for you. Even if you don't choose a franchise, your time will be well spent because this book will be your most valued resource for "how to" information in tackling any business endeavor. You will especially benefit from the useful and unique insights into the heart and soul of business ownership, the issues surrounding ethics, integrity, and quality of life. You'll also get the unvarnished truth about some of the challenges arising out of a franchise relationship from a balanced perspective of both the franchisee and the franchisor. There is no gilding of the lily between these covers.

A very special aspect of this book is Jim's perspective as the former CEO of one of the most successful franchise brands in the world, Mail Boxes Etc. MBE was bought by UPS and rebranded as The UPS Store, so Jim has dealt with every single issue discussed in this book and then some. His successful strategy for managing the people and business issues inherent in any franchise system is reflected in the pages that follow. Equally important are Jim's deep beliefs about relationships, values, and doing the right thing in life as essential ingredients of franchising success or for that matter, any success—business or personal.

Almost every book on franchising written in the last decade has crossed my desk during my tenure as president of the International Franchise Association and Jim's book has a definite edge. This is not only a great book for the uninitiated; it's a terrific read for the seasoned franchising pro. Few "how to" books connect the rudiments of business with the elements of success. Those elements often have more to do with attitude, perseverance, integrity, and quality of life issues than we may think. Jim connects the dots through investigation, decision-making, and ultimate success in a way that I have not seen done in any other book written on this great world of franchising. If you do choose a franchise, you'll be way ahead of those who came before you without the benefit of this book.

Don DeBolt

Former President of the International Franchise Association, and publisher of *CEO Update.*

Introduction

In this book, you'll find almost everything you need to know about becoming involved in the franchising community, whether you want to be a franchisor who develops a new system, a franchisee who opens up a new franchise outlet, or a supplier or investor who wants to learn more about this business system.

I have chosen to use eagle symbolism throughout this work on franchising, just as throughout my life and career I have embraced the eagle as both a personal and business metaphor for excellence. First in the Marine Corps and later in franchising, the eagle has represented, for me and those that I have been privileged to work with, both aspirational and inspirational values. I and all of my associates, including my colleagues at Mail Boxes Etc. and now at Sona MedSpa, have always worn an eagle pin on our lapels to make a statement that we believe and support those values. Let me take a few moments to explain why.

Perhaps no symbol has been more prevalent in history and culture worldwide than the eagle. An important part of the literature and history of nations for both the warrior and the poet, a bird of unsurpassed power and majesty, the eagle has often been referred to as the lion of the air.

Eagles are strong of heart, responsible, and stable. They soar. But soaring never just happens. Soaring is a result of strong mental and physical effort. It requires clear thinking and a bold, confident, positive attitude. To soar we must embrace the eagle in our mind.

The pastor Chuck Swindoll once reflected that we live in a negative, hostile world that says the glass is half empty, not half full. Society focuses only on what's wrong instead of what is right; ugliness instead of beauty; destruction instead of construction; the impossible instead of the possible; the hurt instead of the help; what we lack instead of what we have. Our society seems to be engulfed in cynicism and mediocrity, where excellence is lost in the shuffle.

To break this cycle of cynicism, I believe that we should adopt the philosophy of "eagle excellence" to develop the steadfast character that gives a business, a family, and a nation its purpose and pride. To do this we should embrace the eagle in our mind.

The first step in this process is becoming a person of "eagle vision." The eagle, with visual cells eight times denser than a human's, can see a dime in 6 inches of grass from a height of 600 feet. The person with eagle vision can see the goal far off in the distance.

People of eagle vision see what others would miss. Eagle vision people have faith and positive attitudes, refusing to sink into cynicism and doubt. They believe in the long haul. They soar, because they are people of dreams. Dreams, not desperation, move people and organizations to the highest level of performance.

One of the lesser-known attributes of the eagle is about the hope and power and challenge of renewal. When the eagle's mighty wing feathers become heavy with dirt and oil and its beak becomes calcified and brittle, it retires to a cave or rock out of the reach of predators and experiences a time of renewal. With its great beak the mighty wing feathers are plucked one by one and then each claw is extracted. Finally, the beak itself is smashed against a rock until it, too, is gone. Defenseless for a time, this magnificent metaphor patiently mends until its beak, talons, and feathers reemerge, larger, stronger, renewed, and restored, to climb to even greater heights than before.

So, in life and business, embracing the eagle in your mind means setting priorities and pursuing them with conviction and determination. It means understanding that choices determine how high you soar, and knowing that you are accountable for your actions. Embracing the eagle in your mind means separating the lasting from the temporary, the short term from the eternal, and is the quality that produces greatness.

I cannot think of a better way to pursue the eagle in your mind than by embracing a life or career in franchising. As many have before you, you can soar to heights only limited by your vision and dream. Two thousand years ago Solomon said, "The way of the eagle in the sky is wonderful." Isaiah reflected that because of the strength, swiftness, vision, and freedom from earthly ties, the eagle was a metaphor for God's care for his children. He would go on to write, "But they that wait upon the Lord shall renew their strength; they shall mount up with wings as eagles; they shall run and not be weary and they shall walk and not faint." For all of these reasons, it is my hope that this guide will assist you as you contemplate participating in the most powerful economic engine in the world today, franchising.

What You'll Find in this Book

In this book, I've collected almost everything you'll need to know to get started in franchising. While most of the information is meant to help prospective franchisees evaluate the many choices and opportunities ahead of them, other readers will find much information to be of use to them. If you're a small business owner and you're thinking of turning your business into a franchised one, you'll learn how you can do that, too. And if you're thinking about investing in a franchise, you'll find how you can separate the best franchises from those that still have room to improve.

I've organized this book into six parts:

♦ In **Part 1, "Feathering the Nest,"** you'll learn the basics of franchising, which industries have franchise businesses, and what the International Franchise Association, the leading organization for members of the franchising community, is all about.

♦ In **Part 2, "Building the Nest,"** I'll help you explore the opportunities that are right for you. I'll also explain the financial disclosure information that every franchisor must offer, as well as how you can develop the right attitude that will help you become successful in franchising.

♦ **Part 3, "Learning to Fly,"** will have more nuts-and-bolts information about setting up your franchise unit. It covers everything about financing your venture, what you'll encounter in a training program, how you can pick the best location for your business, and how you will supply your store.

♦ Once you're up and running, you can fly like an eagle. In **Part 4, "Flying Like an Eagle,"** I'll cover how you can market your business, make friends within the franchising community, and hire and manage the best people for your venture.

♦ In **Part 5, "Soaring to New Heights,"** you'll learn how to grow your business, acquire more units or another franchise brand, take your business public, renew your franchise agreement, or, if you have your own business, become a franchisor.

♦ **Part 6, "Using Your Eagle Vision for the Future,"** explores how you can be a part of franchising's future. These chapters will look at the globalization of franchising and trends, as well as what some of the leading experts in franchising have to say about this remarkable type of business model.

Last but not least, I've included resources that any prospective franchisee will need: the Federal Trade Commission's guide to buying a franchise, the International Franchise Association's code of ethics, and an opportunities guide developed by the staff at the International Franchise Association.

Bonus Information

In addition, this book will feature a number of extra bits of wisdom throughout its pages.

Eagle Eyes

To help you develop your personal "eagle vision," the information in these side-bars will help you see opportunities and then take action.

Franchise Facts

These items clear up the myths and misunderstandings about franchising as a whole as well as the franchises you do business with everyday.

Definitions

In case you are new to business or franchising, I define some terms you may not have encountered.

Aviary Alert

Since no business venture is without risk, these sidebars will help you foresee potential problems.

Franchising Eagles

I also share personal stories of those who have made a positive impact on the franchising community and beyond, people who I call soaring "franchising eagles." Their stories are both inspiring and informative.

Acknowledgments

Nothing worthwhile is ever accomplished alone. As some wag once said, if you are walking through the woods and come across a turtle on a stump, you can make one certain assumption: he didn't get there by himself. This work is testimony to that assumption. So in that light, I would like to acknowledge the folks who have been so supportive and helpful in completing this book.

First to Jessica Faust of Bookends, who approached me with this project over a year ago; I am grateful for her vision and persistence. To Lisa Kaiser, an outstanding writer and editor in her own right, this book would simply not have happened without her assistance. I'd like to thank Mike Sanders, my editor. Thanks to the staff at the International Franchise Association for their assistance and particularly to my friend and colleague, Don DeBolt, who recently stepped down as chairman of that fine organization.

Thanks to all the soaring Franchising Eagles who made themselves available for this project: Heather Rose, Russell Grove, and Kurt Schusterman. The International Franchise Association staff created the opportunities guide you'll find in this book, and I'd like to thank Scott Lehr, Catherine Marinoff, Debra Moss, and Terry Hill for their efforts. And, thanks to all of the contributors to Chapter 23 all of whom are my friends, consummate professionals, and true franchising heroes and stars. I begin with Eileen Harrington of the Federal Trade Commission, Gary Charlwood, Doc Cohen, Cheryl Babcock, Bill Hall, Dick Rennick, Lewis Rudnick, Steve Siegel, Jo Anne Shaw, Ken Walker, Peter Shea, and Matt Shay.

Finally, I offer humble thanks to all those that have made my 30 years in franchising so rewarding and worthwhile. Of course, this includes mentors like Bill Rosenberg and so many others that forged the way before us but most of all the friends. What a rich and rewarding life this has been to be able to pursue so many dreams with family and friends. To all of you, I say thank you, thank you.

Special Thanks to the Technical Reviewer

I owe a special debt to Don DeBolt, who served as the technical editor for this book. Don is an extraordinary individual whose professionalism and leadership guided the International Franchise Association into its status as the worldwide clearinghouse for franchising information. Everyone in the franchise community—and Don has seen to it that we see ourselves as part of a community—owes him a debt for his vision and integrity. He has provided us with a wise example to follow, and his insights have made this book a better one. Thank you, Don.

Trademarks

All terms mentioned in this book that are known to be or are suspected of being trademarks or service marks have been appropriately capitalized. Alpha Books and Penguin Group (USA) Inc. cannot attest to the accuracy of this information. Use of a term in this book should not be regarded as affecting the validity of any trademark or service mark.

Part 1

Feathering the Nest

If you want to be a franchisee, you'll be required to make an agreement for the next 10 or so years—and you'll have to pay an initial franchisee fee to get started. If you want to be a franchisor, you'll have to offer your franchisees a full range of services that go far beyond just having a great business concept. You definitely want to go into franchising with your eyes wide open. You'll also want to make sure that you've got the right mind-set for franchising.

In this section, I start at the beginning, so that you can feather your nest. I explain what franchising is all about, where and how it started, and how it impacts the economy and individual families. Then I look at some of the opportunities you'll find in franchised businesses. I also introduce you to the International Franchise Association, the trade organization that includes franchisors, franchisees, and industry suppliers.

1

Learning About Franchising

In This Chapter

- ◆ Exploring franchising
- ◆ Taking a trip back in time
- ◆ Understanding licensing and franchising
- ◆ Building business opportunities
- ◆ Distributing products

Franchising works. According to a 2004 study done by the consulting arm of PricewaterhouseCoopers for the International Franchise Association Educational Foundation, more than 9.7 million people in the United States work in the world of franchising. Franchising is found in almost every industry, from the most visible—the fast-food industry—to hotels and motels, educational services, home repair and remodeling, health and wellness services, and business-support services. According to the IFA, some industry analysts indicate that sales through franchises businesses have grown faster than the gross domestic product. And over 50 percent of retail sales are made at franchised shops.

So if franchising is such a powerful economic engine, then what's driving it, and how can you get involved?

In this chapter, I explain what franchising is, how it got started, and when it got its start. I also tell you how to differentiate between a franchisor and franchisee, briefly explain the legalities of licensing and franchising, and discuss the two key types of franchises: business format and product distribution. As you read through this book, you'll find out if franchising is for you, and how you can be a part of it.

What Is Franchising?

At its most basic level, *franchising* is a business relationship. In fact, in my opinion, franchising is the most relationally intense business concept that exists. This relationship links a company that wants to distribute a product or service and an entrepreneur who wants to run his or her own business. In both types of franchises, the company that sells the rights to distribute a product or use a business format is called the *franchisor*. The businessperson who buys those rights is called the *franchisee*.

The company that owns the product or service grants a limited *license* to the person who wants to sell or distribute that product or service. There are two types of franchises that exist today: *product distribution* and *business format*. Product distribution franchises involve an agreement between the manufacturer and entrepreneur granting the rights to sell the manufacturer's product, but do not operate under the name of the manufacturer.

Definitions _____

A right granted to a business by a company to use the company's name and sell or rent its products and services is called a **franchise**.

A **license** grants permission to engage in a particular business activity.

The right to use a brand name and distribute a product is a **product distribution franchise**.

The right to use a brand name and distribute a product plus the systems needed to operate the local business is a **business format franchise**.

The company that sells the right to offer its product or service to a businessperson is the **franchisor**.

The businessperson who buys the right to sell the product or services of another company is the **franchisee**.

The more common type of franchise today is called business format franchising; the company offering the franchise provides not only the product or service, but also licenses the entrepreneur, who wants to start the business, an entire system for running that business.

I discuss more details about both types of franchises in a following section, but first let's take a brief step back in time to look at how this type of business relationship started.

Franchising: The Early Years

Historians credit two different groups of people for the early stages of franchising. Some historians believe the pope is responsible for the first franchising system when, centuries ago, he was in charge of tax collection. Certain people were selected to serve as tax collectors and were given a geographical area over which they would collect the money. The collectors kept a sizeable portion of the money they collected and then gave the rest to the pope.

Other historians believe that franchising began in the Middle Ages, when local sovereigns or lords granted rights to local businessmen to hold markets or fairs, operate the local ferry, or hunt on sovereign's land. Kings offered franchises for most commercial activities, ranging from building roads to brewing ale. Basically the king gave some businessman the right to a monopoly for a particular type of commercial activity. Regulations developed regarding these franchises, which are still part of European Common Law today. The actual term *franchise* comes from an old French word meaning privilege or freedom. I find it very interesting today that for many who have pursued the franchising dream, the word *freedom* has been the ultimate objective.

The concept of franchising as it is known today dates back to the 1840s in Germany, when major ale brewers gave the exclusive rights to sell their products to certain taverns. But the true guru of modern franchising is Isaac Singer, who in 1858 built the market for Singer sewing machines using franchising agreements similar to those found today.

Singer's method of franchising, the product distribution method, was picked up by many manufacturers, including Coca-Cola, which expanded its product throughout the United States by shifting the burden of manufacturing, storing, and distributing its soda to local businesspeople through the process of selling them bottling rights. Car manufacturers found they could shift their distribution and selling costs to local businessmen who wanted to run car dealerships. Oil companies saw the light, too, and shifted their distribution and retail costs to local businessmen who ran convenience stores, gas stations, and car-repair shops.

Franchise Facts

Isaac Singer faced two problems when he wanted to get his sewing machines to market in the 1850s: training and money. His customers needed to be taught how to use the machines before they would buy them. He also needed a great deal of money to build his manufacturing facilities. Rather than hire a huge staff of trainers and raise all the capital himself, Singer decided to sell the rights to local businesspeople, whom he trained to teach customers how to use the product. In exchange for the right to sell the product, the businesspeople paid Singer license fees, which Singer used to help fund his manufacturing costs. The language, format, and contractual franchise agreements Singer used are very similar to those still being used today.

After World War II, when millions of U.S. servicemen and women returned from the war needing jobs, the concept of business format franchising took hold. Many of these veterans decided they wanted to run their own businesses, but didn't necessarily have the knowledge or capital to develop a business concept from scratch. In addition to the need for jobs, there was also a dramatic need for the rapid expansion of service industries, such as hotels, motels, and fast-food restaurants.

Franchise Facts

McDonald's has often been referred to as the king of the business format franchise. It all started when Roy Kroc, a milkshake machine salesman, discovered a successful drive-in restaurant in San Bernardino, California, run by the McDonald brothers. Kroc bought the rights from these two brothers to sell their method of running a restaurant as a franchise. Today McDonald's systemization has developed into an idiot-proof system for every aspect of running a fast-food business—from specifying how many seconds french fries should be cooked to scripting exactly what employees should say when they greet customers. McDonald's training program teaches every franchise manager how to implement its systems so that each restaurant will be run the same way 100 percent of the time. If the franchisee doesn't adhere to McDonald's high standards, McDonald's has the contractual power to terminate the franchisee.

These two forces drove the creation of the type of franchising that dominates the sector today—business format franchising. Companies that developed an ideal business model for running one of these types of service businesses sold their business model to local businesspeople who wanted to run that business in their own area. Unfortunately, at that time not all franchise businesses were legitimate, and many people who bought the rights to franchise found out the person who sold it to them did nothing more than take their money and run.

Both the industry and the government stepped in to clean up the franchise industry to save the concept of franchising. The International Franchise Association, which I discuss in great detail in Chapter 3, was founded in 1960 and has since worked to enhance the professionalism of the industry. The IFA is now the world's largest clearinghouse and voice of franchising.

The U.S. Congress gave the Federal Trade Commission the responsibility for developing federal regulations. The FTC developed the rules behind the Uniform Franchise Offering Circular (UFOC) in 1979, which must be given to all businesspeople interested in buying a franchise before the company selling that franchise can accept any money. I talk more about the UFOC in Chapter 2 and get into the gory contract details in Chapter 6.

> **Franchising Eagles**
>
> "The boom in business format franchising is a result of … the shift in the U.S. economy from production of goods to the providing of services. In particular, services that fill the needs of life styles."
>
> John Naisbitt, author of "Megatrends," in a 1989 study he conducted for the International Franchise Association

Franchising Today

Today the FTC specifies that three key elements must exist in order for there to be a franchise business relationship:

- The franchisor must grant limited rights to use the company's trade name, service mark, logo, or other advertising symbol.

- The franchisor must sell the rights to use systems or methods associated with operating the core business.

- The franchisor receives a payment in return for granting the rights mentioned in items 1 and 2.

When the franchisor is also a manufacturer, the relationship can be different in the FTC's eyes. When the franchisee is purchasing the rights only to distribute specific products without using the company's name and identity, then different elements comprise this segment of franchising, called product distribution franchising. The most common companies using this type of franchising are beverage companies, oil companies, and automobile companies. For example, when a dealer sells Saturns or Saabs, it uses the car names on its dealership, but it doesn't promote itself as a dealer for the General Motors Corporation.

Franchising vs. Licensing

In the early years of franchising, when the concept was just being developed, companies sold licenses and took licensing fees when they granted a local businessperson the right to sell its products. Today, licensing has a much different meaning than franchising.

Companies, like soft drink bottlers and distributors, that only license products or services today are more passively involved in the sale of their product or service. They supervise the proper use of their license and collect license fees, but they do not get involved in the actual business operations of businesspeople who buy the licenses. Instead, they are more concerned about limiting the ability of a businessperson to modify the trademark or reduce the value of the licensed product or service. They monitor the sale of their product or service to be sure the licensee offers the product or service in the way specified by the licensing company.

That's a very different role than the one taken by franchisors. Franchisors do license the use of their trademark, but they take a much more active role in how the franchisee actually operates his or her business using that license. Franchisors put limits not only on the way the franchisee sells the product or service, but also on the way the franchisee operates his or her business. How far that active involvement will go depends upon whether the franchisee is buying business format franchise or is just buying the rights to distribute the product. I explain the differences next.

It's All About Brand Recognition

When you buy a business format franchise, you can expect that the franchisor will supply you with training, marketing materials, and operating systems, as well as a manual for how to operate that franchise. This will include extensive management systems to help make your business venture a success.

The franchisor is not giving all this to you solely to help you succeed. If you don't run the business according to the systems the franchisor has designed, your business will not match those of other franchisees. To maintain the company's image and provide customers with expected products or services worldwide, each franchisee must run his or her business in the same way. Imagine how disappointed you would be as a customer who expects a certain type of hamburger prepared in a specific way when you walk into a McDonald's and you don't get what you expect.

That's true for any type of business format franchise, whether you are buying fast food or looking to mail a box at a UPS Store, or having your hair removed at a Sona MedSpa. The name brand you see on the door is what you depend on to get the product or service you want. You don't know the franchisee. You do know the brand.

Franchisees get lots of advantages for buying into the system, including the following:

♦ National advertising that helps bring in more customers

♦ Combined purchasing power that comes with being part of a large national—or even international—operation

♦ Proven marketing techniques that have worked for others

♦ Operational systems that include tools, controls, and procedures to help make a business a success

♦ Name-brand awareness

If the franchisee doesn't offer the product or service in the way customers have come to expect from that brand name, it won't only reflect badly on the franchisee, but also reflect poorly on the brand as a whole. The entire franchise is at risk when even one franchisee doesn't live up to the expectations of a franchisor.

Most of this book will focus on the elements of buying and running a successful business format franchise, from helping you determine if you are cut out to be a franchisee to figuring out which franchise to buy and how to run it successfully. In Chapter 19, I even discuss how you can franchise your own business.

Getting Rights to Distribute a Product

Only someone who has access to thousands, and in most cases millions, of dollars to buy a distributorship can get involved in product distribution franchising. Most of these types of franchises are sold to people who are already running one for the manufacturer. For example, a Buick dealer might decide to buy the rights to open a Saab dealership from General Motors.

Other top dealerships include gas stations for the major oil companies or bottling distributorships for the major soda manufacturers. I don't spend a lot of time talking about these types of franchises because most of you won't be considering this type of purchase. If you are, then you'll definitely need to do additional research about this type of franchising.

The Least You Need To Know

- ◆ Franchising involves putting together a business relationship between companies that want to sell a product or service and businesspeople who want to offer that product or service on a local level.

- ◆ There are two types of franchises: product distribution franchises and business format franchises. The majority of franchises available today are business format franchises.

- ◆ Franchising started centuries ago, but the modern-day business format franchise did not become popular until after World War II.

- ◆ The power of brand recognition offers franchisees an advantage over individual entrepreneurs, because more people are aware of and depend on their franchise's products or services.

- ◆ Some companies license their brands, but are not structured as franchise systems.

Chapter 2

Exploring the Opportunities for You

In This Chapter

- Identifying high-growth industries
- Evaluating brands
- Understanding franchise agreements
- Who becomes a franchisee?
- Exploring opportunities

You've decided you want to start your own business, but don't really know where to go from there. You've built a lifetime of skills and would like to put them to work for you instead of someone else, but you're not really sure what the best model is for helping you achieve your dream.

Franchising might be just the thing for you. Most people think of fast-food restaurants, like McDonald's and Wendy's, when they think of franchising, but in reality there are many types of industries in which franchises can be awarded to qualified candidates.

In this chapter, I explore the types of industries in which businesses are already operating and which industries are growing. I talk about the advantages of working under the umbrella of a known brand through franchising, and introduce you to the basics of franchise agreements. I also discuss franchisee profiles and talk about how you can match your skills to the opportunities available.

Discovering the Industries

If you think that franchised businesses are limited to fast-food and retail establishments, think again. Almost every industry includes franchised companies—that's why franchises are such powerhouses in the economy. Franchises exist in the hotel and motel industry, manufacturing, the high-tech and telecommunications sectors, health care, clothing, and many more sectors. Many business-to-business (B2B) companies and work-at-home ventures are franchises as well.

Although most industries are growing, some categories are growing especially quickly. Just like the larger economy, the fastest growing franchises are found in the service sector. They include everything from dating services to auto repair, real estate sales to temporary help agencies, to high-tech concepts such as laser therapies. With the boom in home ownership comes an increased need for repair services, cleaning, lawn care, and remodeling. Business-support services such as mail processing, advertising, accounting and bookkeeping, package wrapping and shipping, and printing and copying are especially well positioned for growth. And more personal services—such as hair salons, health aids, tanning centers, educational products, laser hair removal, and skin rejuvenation centers—also fall into this expanding category.

> **Eagle Eyes**
>
> When evaluating industries and brands, look at the performance of the company leadership and management as well as the industry. Even a booming industry won't always include successful brands.

Franchises are especially well suited to the service industry because they combine entrepreneurship with reliability. Customers can depend on the high standards of a nationally recognized company, while the franchisee can meet the unique needs of his or her community.

Discussing the Brands

You may be surprised to find that many of your favorite brands are franchises. In fact, without realizing it, you most likely do some sort of business with a franchise every day. You've eaten at Baskin-Robbins, Cinnabon, Dunkin' Donuts, KFC, Pizzeria Uno, and Carvel Ice Cream Bakery. You've relied on experts to calculate your taxes at H&R Block, to ship packages at The UPS Store, and to repair your car at Midas Auto Service Experts. You've bought shoes at The Athlete's Foot, stocked up on vitamin supplements at General Nutrition Centers, had your hair removed or skin rejuvenated at a Sona MedSpa. And you've no doubt purchased just about anything and everything at your nearest 7-Eleven. All of these corporations are built on franchises.

Franchise Facts

Can you identify a franchise business? Yes—if you see an "independently owned and operated" sign on the premises, the establishment is most likely a franchise.

Many of these companies are not restricted by national borders. Just as the American economy is going global, so are franchises, which is why so many recognizable brands are found all over the world. For example, The Medicine Shoppe, a retail pharmacy chain, operates more than 200 stores outside of the United States. One Hour Martinizing, the world's largest dry cleaning franchise, operates almost 200 franchises outside of North America. And World Gym International is living up to its name as it adds fitness centers around the world.

The brand name—and its familiar and reliable service or product—is what hooks people. For example, before selling Mail Boxes Etc. (MBE) to UPS, I was president and CEO of that franchise company, so I know it very well. You could find a Mail Boxes Etc. in any city you visited, and more likely more than one. You knew what services would be offered and had a good idea of the prices for those services. If you needed to mail a package, would you be more likely to look for a Mail Boxes Etc., or stop by a local store that mailed packages with a name you didn't know? Most people would go to a store with a name they knew because they trusted the service. That's the power of brand identification—and not just in the United States. MBE had a thousand stores in other countries.

A franchise's brand is a very valuable asset. Franchisors know that customers will decide whether or not they want to walk into a store in the franchise system or use the services of a franchisee based on the reputation of the brand name. Unless you happen to be a personal friend of the person who owned a Mail Boxes Etc., you probably had no idea who the owner was and probably didn't care. You just wanted to go to a place that you knew could be trusted to mail a package for you and that you knew would be in there the next day or next week to help you track the package if it got lost.

Remember that although franchise establishments are independently owned and operated, they still maintain the high standards of the franchisor and the uniformity that contributes to brand recognition and reliability. That's why a tasty treat at a Mrs. Field's in Maine will be just as tasty at a Mrs. Field's in Arizona—or in another part of the world.

A franchisor's advertising and marketing efforts benefit the franchisee as well. After you choose your franchise and become part of a system, you should be able to depend on the franchisor to continue advertising and marketing that brand so that you won't have to. That ongoing advertising and marketing will continue to bring new customers into your door.

> **CAUTION**
>
> **Aviary Alert** _____
>
> Just as too many cooks can spoil a meal, too much success can ruin a franchise. As you evaluate franchisors, ask yourself: Is the company growing too quickly? Is it too young? Does it have enough staff and resources to support its growth? Make sure the company you're looking at has been established long enough to have solid procedures and steady growth as well as seasoned leadership and management.

Not all franchises have national name recognition, though. You may decide to get in on the ground floor of a franchise that still needs to build its brand. That's especially true if you have only a small stash of cash to invest. The large, well-known franchises are usually bought only by a group of investors, *or* individuals who have a higher net worth, or someone who already owns and runs at least one other unit in the franchise.

If you find a franchise opportunity that interests you but is not a name brand you recognize, there's a good chance most people won't recognize that brand name either. That doesn't mean it isn't a good opportunity, but you do need to be sure you understand what the franchisor will do in your community to help you build the brand, as well as what the franchisor is already doing to build a national brand name and reputation.

Franchise Agreements

When you buy into a franchise system you sign a franchise agreement that spells out precisely what you are buying. You could be buying one franchise store or possibly the right to build several store locations. You also may be looking to buy the rights to own all the stores in a particular geographic area. If you really want to think big you not only can buy the rights to a geographic area, but you can also buy the rights to sell franchises to others in your geographic area.

Each of these structures involves a different type of agreement. The offers to buy a franchise must comply with the *Federal Trade Commission's* standards for a *Uniform Franchise Offering Circular (UFOC)*, which I discuss in detail in Chapter 6, but even under the rules of the UFOC there are different types of franchise agreements you can be offered. These agreement types include single-unit franchises, multiple single-unit franchises, area-development franchises, and master franchises. The following sections briefly review each type.

Definitions

The **Federal Trade Commission** is the federal agency that oversees franchises. The **Uniform Franchise Offering Circular (UFOC)** is the extensive disclosure document a franchisor must present to any potential franchisee.

Single-Unit Franchises

If you just want to own and operate one store or franchise unit, then you would sign an agreement for a single-unit franchise. This is the simplest form of franchise ownership. Not all franchises are storefronts. For example, service franchises, such as Chem Dry (a carpet-cleaning franchise) or Maid Brigade (a house-cleaning franchise) are usually run from someone's home without any storefront at all. The most common way customers find these franchise owners is through advertising in the telephone book or in local newspapers. Again, the brand name is the selling point.

Multiple Single-Unit Franchises

Successful franchisees often look to buy more than one franchise unit from the same franchisor. For example, that GNC retailer of nutritional supplements at your local mall may also own the GNC in the mall a few miles away. It's not unusual for a franchisee whose first unit proves profitable to sign a second agreement with the same franchisor for another location. This would be called a multiple single-unit franchise agreement.

Because the business owner is already familiar with the operation and the people involved, she fully understands the potential for another similar franchise unit and can get that second (or maybe third) unit up and running much more quickly than trying to buy a different type of franchise. Both the franchisee and the franchisor benefit from the quicker start-up with less initial costs and time for training. What's more, the operator may be able to promote some of her current staff to management roles in the new unit and get it off the ground more smoothly.

However, even though the agreement and method of operations for the franchise will be nearly identical, there could be some differences in the terms for each new unit. As franchises grow and become more popular, you will usually find fees are higher, different equipment may be required for start-up, or initial investment requirements could increase. Although the franchisor might not require its older franchisees to upgrade to state-of-the-art equipment, there is a good chance the franchisor would require the franchisee thinking of buying another unit to sign a new agreement that includes any new provisions.

CAUTION

Aviary Alert

If you sign a multiple single-unit agreement, watch out for a clause called a cross-default. This common clause states that a franchisee who is found to be in violation of a franchise provision at one of his single-unit stores will be considered in violation for all of his agreements. Be sure you understand how the purchase of another franchise unit from the same franchisor might impact your current successful unit. Don't ever sign a franchise agreement without the review of an attorney who specializes in franchise contracts.

Area-Development Franchises

Some successful franchisees decide they'd like the right to build more than one unit at a time. They've determined that this is the right franchise system for them and they don't want to risk the possibility that another franchisee opens a unit in their area.

To avoid the possibility of someone else invading their turf, the successful franchisee can negotiate an area-development agreement. Instead of signing just a single-unit agreement each time he's ready to begin his next development process, the franchisee can protect his rights to build a number of units in a particular geographic area by a set date and time. As the franchisee gets ready to develop each of his units, he will still need to sign a unit-development agreement, which governs the terms for how each unit will be run and the franchise fees for the unit.

For example, the franchisee could promise the franchisor that he will develop 10 units in the Atlanta metropolitan area within five years. The area-development franchise agreement would include a schedule for building those units. If the franchisee can't maintain that schedule, he will likely lose the rights to develop all the units and probably lose his development fee. Most franchisors have a provision in the area-development agreement that specifies it can cancel the agreement if the franchisee fails to meet the specified development schedule.

Franchisees pay a fee for area-development rights. Many times a portion of this fee is credited toward each unit fee as the units are developed, but that's not a guarantee. Each franchise system deals with the fee structure differently. Some require that you still pay the initial franchise fee in full, even if you've paying an area-development fee. Others offer a reduced fee for each unit if you hold area-development rights. Remember, each franchise system is a unique business and can determine its own terms for operating. I can't emphasize enough how important it is for you to seek professional guidance from an attorney who specializes in franchise law before entering into any franchise agreement.

> **CAUTION**
>
> **Aviary Alert** _____
>
> If you're thinking of entering into an area-development franchise, be sure that the fees you are paying for that right include a promise of market exclusivity. Otherwise the franchisor could enter into other single-unit or area-development franchise agreements and undercut your overall market building plans for the area you've selected.

Master Franchises

The highest step on the rung for a franchisee is a master franchise agreement. With this type of agreement the franchisee not only gets the right to develop a certain number of units within a geographic area, he also gets the right to subfranchise or sell the franchise to other franchisees.

The master franchise agreement is similar to the area-development agreement. The master franchisee agrees to develop a set number of units in a particular geographic area within a set time period. The key difference is that the master franchisee won't likely develop all those units himself. Instead, he will find others to develop some of the units. In fact, some master franchise agreements require the master franchisee to find others to develop individual units.

Most master franchise agreements require the master franchisee to open and operate at least the first single unit themselves, and in most cases require the master franchisee to own and operate at least two of the units in his area. Once he has those up and running, he then gets the right to sell additional locations in his area to other franchisees, which are called subfranchisees.

Master franchisees pay a fee when they sign the master franchise agreement. Then as the franchisee either opens his own units or sells units, he will need to pay additional fees. Just like the area-development agreement, the structure for these fees will vary depending on the terms set by the franchisor. The most common arrangement is that the master franchisee will share the income from the single-unit franchise fee with the franchisor as each franchise is sold. The percentage each gets varies widely from franchise system to franchise system.

These subfranchisee agreements can be structured in several different ways:

◆ An agreement may be signed directly between the master franchisee and the subfranchisee.

◆ An agreement may be signed directly between the subfranchisee and the franchisor.

◆ The franchisor may hold the right to approve all subfranchisees.

◆ The master franchisee may hold the right to approve all subfranchisees.

◆ Training may be provided by the franchisor, or the agreement may specify the master franchisee has full responsibility for training, or there could be a shared responsibility for training subfranchisees.

◆ The fees for the single-unit agreement may be paid directly to the franchisor, directly to the master franchisee, or the payment of the fees may be split, with some going to the franchisor and some going to the master franchisee.

Eagle Eyes

The International Franchise Association's pamphlet, "Investigate Before Investing," is a must-read for potential franchisees. Go to www.franchise.org for more information.

Again, I must remind you to contact an attorney before entering into this most complex type of franchise agreement.

You probably won't find many master franchise agreements available in the United States because most franchisors prefer to have a direct relationship with each of its franchisees. However, you are more likely to find master franchise agreements for international development. Franchisors who seek to develop franchises in another country do prefer to designate one master franchisee to develop the units in that country. They realize that cultural, political, and economic differences make it critical to have someone lead their franchise unit development in each country who has significant experience developing businesses in the target country. So if you've lived and worked for a long time in another country and think there is potential for a franchise system there that doesn't currently exist, this might be your best opportunity for developing an international business operation.

Exploring Franchisee Profiles

As you can see, there is a wide variety of franchise industries, brands, and agreements. And there is a wide variety of people who become franchisees. Some franchisees want independence. Others like the security of being connected to an established corporation that provides training and backup. Still others just like to grow a business without having to come up with the idea for that business.

You're probably wondering whether you match the profile of the perfect franchisee. Well, there really isn't an ideal franchisee, because so much depends on the industry in which you want to work and your background and experience in that industry.

Yet, you will find some common characteristics that fit all franchisees. The most important character trait you must have is the ability to balance the needs for being your own boss versus being an employee.

Franchise Facts

You don't need to be an expert to be a franchisee. Most franchisors train their franchisees if few technical skills are required. Some prefer that franchisees have little industry experience—but have some basic business skills and a lot of motivation to learn.

In reality all franchisees play both roles. They must manage their people, but they also must comply with the rules of their franchise system. While a franchisee runs his or her own business, that business must be run according to the system and rules dictated by the franchisor, who has already perfected the business, or at the very least wants a consistent national image and method of operation for the business. All franchise systems are constantly being tweaked and updated to respond to changes in the marketplace. You could find that taking directions from the franchise's headquarters is a drag and not what you had planned when you started the business. Successful franchisees learn to keep a proper balance between maintaining the franchise system rules, taking direction from the higher-ups at franchise headquarters, and being able to delegate responsibilities to employees who work for them.

No matter what franchise system you choose, one thing is guaranteed: In the initial years you must be willing to work long hours (in the initial years, you must be willing to work 60 to 80 hours per week) and you can't expect to earn much money in the first two years as you build your business.

I talk more about how you can test whether you are cut out to be a franchisee in Chapter 4. Chapter 5 focuses on how to pick the right industry and system. Chapter 6 reviews the legal stuff you need to understand as you start exploring opportunities as well as how to evaluate the financial potential for the opportunities that interest you.

Matching Franchisees with Opportunities

If you think you would make a good franchisee, the next step is finding franchisors that offer opportunities that match your skills and interests and fit your budget and financial needs. This requires a fair amount of research. After all, buying a franchise is a very big purchase and your livelihood will depend on it. Extra care during the research phase of selecting a franchise will definitely pay off down the road.

Fortunately, franchisors want to find you as much as you want to find them, so if you think they're hard to find, they're just hiding in plain sight. Franchisors can be found in a number of ways.

First, franchisors are organized professionals, so seek out the International Franchise Association (www.franchise.org) for its member listings. The IFA is the world's largest clearinghouse on information about franchises, so if you can't find a franchisor through this organization, beware. You'll also find easy-to-use online tools to evaluate its members, too. The IFA does much more than this, but you can start your search with its data.

Franchisors are also listed for sale with business brokers. These intermediaries can match you with businesses for sale. However, they earn a commission on sales, so they may put their own interests before yours just to make the sale. The brokers FranChoice, FranNet, and Entrepreneur Source are examples of sound brokers. Each promotes itself as a consultant. The good brokers do their best to recommend good solutions for you and their franchisor client. Use of a broker can be helpful because the ultimate cost of the franchise should be no more expensive than initially dealing with the franchisor directly. The franchisor pays the commission to the broker, just like the home seller.

Franchisors often have websites, so a thorough Internet search will turn up franchises you may have overlooked. You can also find supplemental information about your targeted franchisor on its corporate website.

Franchises for sale are often advertised in the classified section of your local newspaper, and also in publications such as *USA Today, Franchise Times, Franchising World,* and *The Wall Street Journal.* In any mature franchising system, there will be new franchises to be offered as well as existing ones that need to change owners. But be sure that you know exactly why the current franchisee is selling—and if location or product is a problem, beware.

Franchisors often find franchisees through expos or franchising shows. While these can oftentimes be overwhelming, you can make contact with many franchisors at one of these events and become aware of options you may have overlooked.

These are some of the ways you can find potential franchisors. But remember—these are your first steps, and it's in your best interest to examine every aspect of the franchisor and your agreement. I cover the following steps in the remaining chapters so that you have thoroughly investigated every potential upside and downside of your deal.

Before I get into those details, I first want to introduce you to the premiere resource for information about franchising today in Chapter 3—the International Franchise Association. The IFA's resources can be used before you take the leap and become a franchisor and after you've bought your first franchise.

The Least You Need to Know

- Franchises exist in almost every industry, but the fastest-growing industry is the service sector.

- Franchise systems exist in more than 200 industries with over 1,200 franchise systems available for purchase by franchisees.

- There are four distinct types of franchise agreements—single-unit franchises, multiple single-unit franchises, area-development franchises, and master franchises.

- Franchisees must be good at balancing being a boss to their employees and following the franchise systems rules, which is in a sense also being an employee at the same time.

Chapter 3

Seeking Information About Franchising and the IFA

In This Chapter

- Discovering the economic power of franchising
- Understanding regulations
- Developing a code of ethics and the ombudsman program
- Getting political
- Participating as a franchisee
- Continuing your education

I'm sure it's easy to feel overwhelmed by the opportunities presented by franchising. Not only are there many industries and brands to choose from, but there are also more personal issues to consider, such as why you're considering becoming a franchisee or franchisor and when and how you can make your move.

That's a lot to think about. Fortunately, a professional organization has gathered together franchisors and franchisees, studies and statistics, contacts and educational programs. This organization is the International

Franchise Association, otherwise known as the IFA. The IFA, which was established in 1960, serves 28,000 members in 75 industry categories. The IFA's members include franchisors, franchisees, and suppliers. It commissions studies and surveys, and lets Washington know about the power of franchising. The association's mission to protect, promote, and enhance franchising helps maintain a positive climate for franchising's growth. In this chapter, I help you understand how you can make use of the IFA's many resources.

The Power of Franchising

As you know, franchising encompasses an enormous number of people and companies, and when you're starting to think about getting involved in this way of doing business, you need to be well informed. The IFA has commissioned studies of franchising to help you understand what it's all about and what franchising can do.

A recent study commissioned by the IFA Educational Foundation was conducted by PricewaterhouseCoopers and was published in March 2004. Its findings were astounding. Titled "The Economic Impact of Franchised Businesses in the United States," it found that franchises provide close to 10 million jobs with a $229 billion payroll and operate 760,000 franchised business units. But the impact of this business goes much further, because franchises stimulate the rest of the economy with their mighty purchasing power and awesome output. They generate $1.53 trillion of economic output, greater than the gross domestic product of China.

The study also found that franchised businesses operate in every state and every congressional district, which can be a factor when lobbying the government regarding legislation that can affect franchising. It also found that the most jobs and greatest payrolls from franchising were in California, Texas, Florida, and Illinois. Franchising had the greatest impact on the economies of Nevada, Arizona, New Mexico, Florida, and Mississippi.

Definitions

Business services comprise a sector that includes everything from photocopying services to package delivery—anything that helps a business to continue running.

Quick-service restaurants encompass fast-food restaurants and fast-casual restaurants.

Information about the industries affected by franchising was also obtained. The study stated that "*business services* accounted for more establishments, met a greater payroll, and generated more output than any other single line of business. *Quick-service restaurants* hired more people." It also found that franchising had the most significant impact on the sectors of quick-service restaurants, lodging, retail food, and table/full service restaurants.

Franchising Regulation

Despite franchising's great reach in the United States, it wasn't long ago that this way of doing business had a less-than-stellar reputation. That's because with so much opportunity came opportunists—those who abused relationships and left investors and customers holding the bag.

During the 1970s, 14 states—California, Hawaii, Illinois, Indiana, Maryland, Michigan, Minnesota, New York, North Dakota, Rhode Island, South Dakota, Virginia, Washington, and Wisconsin—enacted laws requiring franchise companies to file or register their franchise offerings with a state agency. In 1978, the Federal Trade Commission adopted the FTC Franchise Rule setting out more uniform disclosure requirements. The presale disclosure document is known as the Uniform Franchise Offering Circular (UFOC). The most important part of the UFOC rules is the presale disclosure, which was designed to protect investors by requiring that franchisors provide detailed information about the business to the prospective franchisee before any agreements are signed or fees are taken.

Franchise Facts

California was the first state to develop franchising regulation. In 1972, that state enacted the first law for franchising, requiring presale disclosure to prospective investors.

I discuss the UFOC at length in Chapter 6, but for now, know that the UFOC contains information from the franchisor regarding its finances, principals, and other franchisees. This disclosure document is intended to help potential franchisees investigate the company they're buying into. It requires franchisors to put their claims on the record.

In addition to their availability from individual franchisors, these disclosure documents can be obtained from the various states for a modest copying fee. California has established a public website, www.corp.ca.gov, where many of the franchisor disclosure documents can be viewed at no charge.

These restrictions help ensure that the franchisor and franchisee enter into an honest relationship. After all, at the heart of franchising is a business relationship, and if this relationship lacks integrity, the reputation of franchising will suffer. If franchisors don't adhere to their agreements, their brands and business will suffer. And if prospective franchisees aren't secure in their agreements, they won't buy new units and deliver the goods to their customers. And if the customers can't count on getting their package delivered, finding a clean comfortable hotel room, or repairing their home through a franchised business, they'll shop elsewhere—and the franchising model will sink.

To maintain high standards, the IFA has developed self-regulation programs that apply to its members. These programs are seen as an alternative to onerous legislation and expensive litigation. The system consists of the following:

◆ A code of ethics

◆ A streamlined code enforcement mechanism

◆ The ombudsman program, which is an endorsement of the National Franchise Mediation Program

◆ New educational programs and comprehensive compliance training programs endorsed by the Federal Trade Commission

The IFA believes that if these programs are utilized, franchisors and franchisees will thrive.

Code of Ethics

The IFA code of ethics is intended to establish a framework for the implementation of best practices in the franchise relationships of IFA members. The code represents the ideals to which all IFA members agree to subscribe to in their franchise relationships. The code isn't intended to establish standards to be applied by third parties, such as the courts, but to create best practices that will lead to healthy, productive, and mutually beneficial franchise relationships.

The code includes components that members must adhere to. First, members make a commitment to trust each other, to be honest, and to share information and communicate in truthful, clear, and direct terms. They must have mutual respect and reward for all members and business partners. They aim to have open and frequent communication. They pledge to obey the law, including all applicable federal and state franchise regulations. They recognize their means of conflict resolution, the establishment of a method for internal dispute resolution. This includes the IFA's ombudsman program, which I discuss later in this chapter, and the use of the National Franchise

> **Eagle Eyes** _____
>
> In addition to finding franchising-related data at the IFA's website, www. franchise.org, you can also locate information at the FTC (http://ftc.gov or 1-877-FTC-HELP).

Mediation Program (NFMP) when a more structured mediation service is needed to help resolve differences.

This code isn't just an empty promise—it's actively enforced by the IFA. Whenever the IFA becomes aware of a possible violation of the code by an IFA member, the IFA president may call for an investigation. The IFA Executive Committee then reviews the allegations and determines appropriate sanctions, such as reprimand or suspension or termination of the company's membership in the IFA. These are heavy penalties to pay, so IFA members do their best to adhere to the code. A list of IFA member companies who agree to abide by this code can be found on IFA's website, www. franchise.org.

The Ombudsman Program

Another component of the IFA's self-regulating system is the ombudsman program, which was designed to facilitate dialogue between franchisees and franchisors when disputes arise in their relationships.

The ombudsman is independent and acts as an impartial source of assistance to all parties and has no vested interest. The ombudsman process is confidential and non-binding. More information about this program can be found at www.ifaresolve.com.

Public Policy Advocate

You already know a little bit about the awesome economic power of franchising, and about its reach throughout the United States and, increasingly, around the world. With this economic stake comes an obligation to educate public policy makers—the regulators and legislators—about the positive contributions franchising makes to our economy and our society. Educated policy makers will avoid laws and regulations that could impair franchising's current success and future growth. A watchful eye helps protect the investment of those currently in franchising.

To be a public policy advocate for franchising, the IFA has created a political action committee called FranPAC. This PAC allows IFA members to contribute to candidates who understand the concerns of franchisors and help promote

Franchise Facts

In the 2002 federal election, the IFA endorsed and FranPAC supported 33 candidates—31 of which won. In 2004, 71 of 74 FranPAC-supported candidates were elected.

franchising-friendly legislation and policies. These candidates are generally supportive of small business, free enterprise, and franchising, and want to limit government
regulation of small businesses. Overall, FranPAC increases the visibility of the IFA
and franchising, and educates legislators about the importance of franchising to our
economy and local communities.

FranPAC also encourages get-out-the-vote initiatives via its Franchising Votes! political education website. It provides contact information for IFA members' representatives, information about issues concerning franchisors, and data about candidates.
Members can get voter registration information, secure absentee ballots, and find
their polling place through this site. In addition, through an agreement with the
U.S. Chamber of Commerce, IFA member companies can set up their own voter
education websites at no cost. You can find more information about it at www.
franchisingvotes.com.

Franchisee Inclusion

In 1993, the IFA expanded its membership to include franchisees in its organization,
and now has 26,500 franchisees who are either direct members or have membership
through their franchisee association's membership. This has helped franchisors
understand the concerns of franchisees. This development has dramatically strengthened the organization.

Eagle Eyes

I've been involved in franchising for 30 years, and I've been associated with the
IFA for about 25 of those years. I even had the privilege of serving as the IFA's
chairman in 2001. I have great respect for the organization's work on behalf of
its members, but on a personal level I would like to note that the IFA is like a family within a family. Just as franchising is about its relationships, the IFA is centered
on people, too. When you get involved with the IFA you'll see what I mean.

According to the IFA's website: "Franchisees are actively involved in all IFA committees, programs, and activities and a number of franchisees serve on IFA's Board of
Directors." In 2002, Steve Siegel, then a Dunkin' Donuts franchisee, became the first
franchisee to be elected chairman of the IFA.

Forums

One of franchising's strengths is its numbers of motivated, connected people. A franchisor or franchisee is not in this alone—thousands of colleagues have dealt with the same or similar issues. Networking is invaluable to gain information and support.

The IFA operates the grassroots Franchise Business Network (FBN) in 27 cities, where it brings together local franchisors, franchisees, and vendors to discuss business issues. Topics are suggested at the national level to bring some uniformity to the meetings, but members can talk about anything they're facing.

The IFA's Women's Franchise Committee is also dedicated to bringing people together. The WFC holds an annual leadership conference, maintains a mentoring program, and presents an award to exceptional women in franchising. The Women's Franchise Network also has local chapters for women dedicated to succeeding in franchising.

Helping to connect the franchising community is the Internet, where millions of people can make contact on discussion forums and bulletin boards. More than 200,000 visitors each month utilize the vast resources of IFA's website, www.franchise.org.

Franchise Facts

The FBN grew out of an initiative by Fred DeLuca, founder of Subway Sandwiches and Salads. DeLuca wanted to bring together the franchising community in his area, and the 2nd Tuesday program was born. Now renamed and expanded into the FBN, it's an important component of the IFA's programs.

The IFA operates a number of these online forums, where you can post questions or concerns, make note of interesting developments, or learn from those who have walked in your shoes. The IFA's forums are moderated, and some can e-mail you their daily digests. No matter what your concerns, you'll probably find someone out there who's shared your experiences.

The IFA's forums include Go Global Community, about international franchising; Franchise Finance Forum, about money issues; Franchise Administrator's Network, which provides networking opportunities; Franchise Development Community, for those who want to establish or grow their own franchise system; Prospective Franchisee Discussion Forum, for newcomers; Tech Forum, which answers questions about the role of technology in the franchised workplace; and Women's Franchise Discussion Forum, developed by the IFA's Women's Franchise Committee.

Educational Opportunities

An important arm of the IFA is the Educational Foundation, which was formed in 1983. This tax-exempt organization has a mission: "increasing the knowledge and professional standards of all members of the franchising community; educating the next generation of franchising practitioners; increasing recognition of franchising's key role in the free enterprise system; and providing comprehensive information and research about important developments and trends in franchising."

To accomplish this mission, the Educational Foundation has set up a number of online courses for both franchisees and franchisors. Anyone can work his or her way through these courses and receive a certificate of achievement at the end. I highly recommend these courses—knowledge is power, and in business, it's mandatory.

The IFA's online courses include the following:

♦ Franchise Basics is targeted to those who are interested in becoming a franchisee. It explains the process as well as what the franchising relationship is all about. It also helps potential franchisees evaluate whether this choice is truly for them.

♦ Franchise Sales Compliance is more technical and is geared toward executives, franchise sellers, paralegals, and lawyers who are involved in the sales of franchises. It helps them understand the legal and business issues that go into franchise sales.

♦ Practical Financial Management for Growing Business offers tools to enhance financial analysis and management.

> **Eagle Eyes**
>
> The IFA's Minorities in Franchising Committee provides educational programs to IFA members and potential minority franchisees. If you qualify, check out the minority section at www.franchise.org.

♦ Diversity Today educates franchisors about the importance of creating and maintaining a diverse workplace. The course is made up of four sections: What is Diversity?, Workplace Fundamentals, Marketplace Fundamentals, and Developing a Diversity Plan for Your Company.

♦ Selection and Development of Top Performers is a Caliper Course that shows how the best people can be recruited for franchises, whether they work in the boardroom or at a franchise.

The IFA also administers the Franchise Sales Law Enforcement Program in partnership with the Federal Trade Commission. Through this program, franchisors can learn more about franchise regulations and potential violations. Participation is voluntary, but, again, I highly recommend it. Franchisors who have committed technical and minor violations of the FTC rule may be given an opportunity to undergo the training in lieu of an FTC enforcement action.

In addition to all of these great programs is IFA-University.com, which offers courses to IFA members. Successfully completing the courses earns members credits toward the Certified Franchising Executive (CFE) designation. The courses at IFA-University.com include: business and accounting; communications; diversity management; franchising courses; free courses; HR and recruiting; industrial skills; IT and technology; management skills; negotiating; OSHA compliance; personal skills, growth, and interest; project management fundamentals; project management professional; sales and customer service; and team performance. There is a fee for these courses and proceeds go to the IFA Educational Foundation.

As you can see, the International Franchise Association is hard at work for its members, from studying the economic power of this type of business model to offering courses on how to get started in franchising. I believe that anyone connected to franchising should get involved in this great organization.

The Least You Need to Know

- ◆ The International Franchise Association serves 28,000 members of the franchising community—franchisors, franchisees, and vendors.

- ◆ Franchises exist in every state and every congressional district.

- ◆ IFA members participate in a self-regulating program to maintain integrity in the community.

- ◆ Anyone can participate in online IFA courses and forums.

Part 2

Building the Nest

If you're serious about franchising, you'll need to build a solid foundation, the nest that you'll return to as you begin to realize your dream.

Like the twigs, strings, and other materials that eagles use to build their nests, you will need certain elements to create the structure of your franchise. First, you need to find the right franchise opportunity for you, one that's going to grow and needs your skills and drive. You also need to understand the UFOC, the financial disclosure document that franchisors must give to their prospective franchisees, and the franchise agreement that seals the deal. You also need to take a long, hard look at your attitude. A winning attitude often determines an individual's success. In addition to these elements, you need to gauge your chance of success—and ask the right questions before signing your franchise agreement.

Chapter 4

Are You Cut Out to Be a Franchisee?

In This Chapter

◆ Do you fit the profile?

◆ Your advantages as a franchisee

◆ The drawbacks of being a franchisee

◆ Assessing the risks

◆ Building on your dream

If you've read through the overview of franchising and the legal and ethical structures and regulations and you've still got this book in your hand, you're probably still interested in becoming a franchisee. You aren't alone. Thousands of people have been able to build a business through the franchise system, and many of them share common character traits with you. It's up to you to find out which skills and assets you bring to a franchisor, and how you can make it all work out for you.

In this chapter, I explore what it takes to become a successful franchisee, as well as the pros and cons of entering into this relationship. I think of this as the beginning of the "building the nest" phase, the time when you're picking out pieces and putting them together to build a brighter future. You'll soon know if franchising is part of your future.

Fitting the Profile

The franchising industry has incredible variety—roughly 85 categories of businesses have franchising relationships, including everything from pet care to real estate. And with this variety of products and services come a variety of people. You'll find all sorts of people have become busy and prosperous because of their franchised businesses.

But a few traits do stand out, and a profile of a successful franchisee has been developed. These people are comfortable with long-term commitments, have the support of their families, have some business skills, are willing to learn new skills and procedures, and have enough cash reserves so that they can pay the franchising fee and still have enough money to finance a certain amount of time in business before cash flow is positive. They aren't putting their family's future at risk simply because they want to run a franchise. They can balance being a boss and being an employee. They're determined to see things through, even when times are tough. They're passionate about their franchise and willing to make sacrifices for their business, employees, and family. They also appreciate the many benefits of franchising, too, and are proud of their successes.

In addition to these common traits, franchisees must also have some traits specific to their chosen industry. Some businesses require franchisees to work with the public, and great social skills are an asset. Other industries require technical knowledge, such as knowing how to repair a car or cut and style hair. Some franchisees will need to use specific software, be highly proficient at math, or know how to manage people.

Aviary Alert

> Your franchisor will be evaluating you as much as you will be checking them out. If they aren't concerned about your skills, financial background (other than your ability to pay your start-up costs), and long-term goals, beware. If they think you're "perfect" before they've gotten to know you, be doubly cautious. They may be more concerned in selling you a franchise than in helping you to become a successful franchisee.

Demographic trends are affecting this franchisee profile. Minorities, women, and veterans are becoming more involved in franchising in recent years and have been attracted by the opportunities presented by this business model. Minorities are finding that franchising offers them what they traditionally lack—business experience and capital. In fact, minorities are being encouraged by the IFA to take the franchising route to financial independence. Women are more visible in franchising, both as franchisees and as executives at corporate headquarters. Veterans benefit from the IFA's VetFran program, which provides assistance for veterans who want to become franchisees. Every veteran with a dream of owning his or her own business should investigate the VetFran Program through the IFA. You can find out more about VetFran at www.franchise.org.

So as you can see, if you're driven to succeed, you can find something interesting in the many franchise opportunities available to you.

Take the Franchisee Quiz

To help you evaluate yourself as a potential franchisee, I've developed this quiz. Be honest with yourself. If you find that you won't be a terrific franchisee, you may find that you're more suited to being an independent business owner, consultant, or fantastic employee for a new company. You may even find that you're just fine right where you are.

1. Why do you want to be a franchisee? Which aspects are most appealing to you? Which are the least appealing?

2. What are your financial goals? Do you require a large annual income? Do you need to turn a profit right away? Do you need help in coming up with the initial fees?

3. How does your family feel about your decision to become a franchisee? Are their reservations valid?

4. Can your family survive without your current income for 6 to 12 months? Are you putting their future at risk? Will they be insured and have funds for college? Can you pay your monthly bills without your income?

5. Have you put together a business plan? Have you crunched the numbers—realistically? What do you still need to investigate, and what makes you feel uncomfortable?

6. What technical skills do you possess? Which industries or businesses need your skills? What kind of technical skills are required to be a franchisee in your targeted industry? If you don't have them, how can you acquire them? What business skills do you possess? Do you require more training?

7. Do you know any franchisees? How do they feel about their business? What are their reservations?

8. Are you comfortable with conforming to established rules and standards? Can you take instruction from authority figures? Can you ask for help?

9. Can you go without a vacation—or many days off—in the foreseeable future? Can you put in long days and work weekends? Can you call on your friends and family for help?

10. Are you comfortable with technology, both in doing business and in researching your business and potential clients?

Looking through your answers, evaluate your responses to determine your strengths and weaknesses. If you are interested in becoming a franchisee but have identified some weak spots, figure out how you can strengthen them. Perhaps you require more technical training or more cash reserves. You may need to win over your spouse. If you've found that you would be a good franchisee, but not right now, that's fine, too. And if you've realized that franchising just isn't for you, that's a perfectly acceptable answer, too.

 **Eagle Eyes** _____

If you're having a hard time answering these questions, your difficulty may tell you something about your ability to be realistic about your plans to become a franchisee. You may like the idea, but not the reality. Ask a trusted friend for help in answering these questions—and then brainstorm about your career options. This quiz may help you explore other alternatives you may have overlooked.

Advantages of Being a Franchisee

Obviously, I'm a big fan of franchising. I've seen many people thrive in business as franchisees—and franchisors—and I'm proud to be a part of this innovative business arrangement. And I have no problem listing the many advantages for being a franchisee. Some of the advantages include the following:

♦ The business has been tested. You're buying into a company with a proven track record, established system of operating, and recognizable brand. Even if your brand or service is relatively new to the market, the franchisor has done the hard work of developing the product or service and overall vision.

♦ You don't have to come up with a new business idea. Business procedures and the format have been developed, so you don't need to start from scratch.

♦ Franchises inspire trust. Consumers are comfortable with a familiar, recognizable brand that they can rely on, especially when they're far from home or flipping through the Yellow Pages.

Franchise Facts

In a 1996 IFA-commissioned Gallup Organization survey, about 64 percent of franchisees say that they would be less successful in the same type of business on their own, and not as part of a franchise system.

♦ High standards ensure quality, uniformity, and predictability—and this increases the consumer's comfort level with your brand's product or service.

♦ You've got a helping hand. Ongoing support from your franchisor and other franchisees in the system helps you get through the start-up phase and the rough patches you may encounter. Everyone in the system has a vested interest in your success. A failed franchise is a black mark on the entire system.

♦ Training and preparation. You and your staff will be well trained, both in business procedures and technical requirements.

♦ You've got integrity. Federal—and sometimes state—regulations help assure you and your clients that your franchise is legitimate.

♦ Pride of ownership. It's an old but true idea that you will work harder for yourself than for a boss. There's nothing like knowing that you are "independently owning and operating" your own establishment.

♦ You have more tools at your disposal for investing in a franchised business, including the requirement that you receive the names and phone numbers of current and former franchisees.

♦ Start-up costs are fairly predictable and you can verify actual experiences by talking to current and former franchisees.

When looking at the many advantages of the franchise system, you may wonder how many entrepreneurs make it without the help of a strong franchise relationship. Franchises truly are powerhouses.

Disadvantages of Being a Franchisee

For every advantage of the franchise system, there seems to be a disadvantage. This will turn off some of you, but, again, that's fine. It's better to realize now, before you've committed to a franchise, that it just doesn't suit you. But, even if you do go ahead with buying a franchise, you should be fully aware of the disadvantages of being a franchisee. These disadvantages include the following:

♦ **Loss of independence.** Although some franchisees may be comforted by their franchisor's rules and procedures, others will chafe against these constraints.

> **Definitions**
>
> The **franchise fee** is the nonrefundable purchase of the franchisor's format or business system, the right to use the franchisor's name for a given amount of time, and ongoing assistance.
>
> You may have to pay the franchisor a percentage of your income during the duration of your partnership. This is the **royalty payment.**

♦ **Start-up costs may be a burden.** According to a recent IFA survey, 88 percent of franchisors charge an initial *franchise fee* of $40,000 or less. But this fee doesn't cover other expenses such as real estate, payroll, equipment, insurance, and other needs. But these are usually the same type of expenses you would experience in starting your own business from scratch.

♦ **Franchising requires a long-term commitment.** Think of franchising as an arranged marriage for about 15 to 20 years. Can you make this relationship work in the coming years? Will you resent paying *royalties* through the term of your partnership?

♦ **Room for innovation is limited.** If you have a great idea, your franchisor may want to hear it. But you may not be able to act on all of your ideas.

♦ **Ongoing support may be less than promised.** Determine the level of support you'll get from the franchisor and if it's ongoing or just during the start-up phase.

♦ **Expansion may be restricted.** Your agreement with your franchisor will spell out if, when, or where you can acquire new units within your company or with another company.

♦ **The franchisor is the final decision maker in an unequal partnership.** While you are the owner and are fairly autonomous, you are in a partnership with someone who is bigger and more powerful than you—and often has the last word on disputes and disagreements as defined in your franchise agreement.

- You must be open about your finances. You'll have to open your books to the franchisor, and you may feel that your privacy is being invaded.

- Another franchisee can affect your business. A good franchisor will terminate its agreement with a substandard franchisee, but bad service at one unit can make customers think twice about patronizing yours.

- You'll give up control over many issues, including—possibly—the site of your establishment, your vendors, the services and product you offer, and your territory. Expect to be vetoed at times.

Eagle Eyes

Franchisors are currently required by law to give you 10 business days to look over your agreement before signing. This cooling-off period was created for a reason—so that you won't be pressured or pumped up by the franchisor's offering. Go over the advantages and disadvantages of franchising one more time while you've got the time.

If you have read all of the disadvantages I've just listed, but believe that they're worthwhile tradeoffs for the right to represent a particular product or service, you may be on the road to becoming a franchisee. Continue thinking about the pros and cons of franchising, and if you still feel comfortable, you could make a good franchisee.

Looking at the Risks

Quite simply, franchising diminishes risk. Established brands have credibility with consumers. Nationwide chains have brand awareness and visibility that has sometimes taken years to develop. Established business and operating systems help franchisees hit the ground running. And federal, state, and IFA regulations ensure that franchisors are legitimate and honorable. All of these factors give franchisees a head start over an entrepreneur who wants to start his single-unit independent business.

Still, life in general is risky, and franchising, like everything else, isn't a completely sure bet. There are always unknowns, and sometimes things don't work out as well as planned, even by the best business plan. Even with the safety net provided by a sound franchise system, there are risks.

Buying a franchise is a huge purchase. Many franchisees have put up what for them is an enormous amount of money with the hopes that they will have a return on their investment. For some franchisees, the ability to work for themselves is worth it. But for others, especially those who want to make a lot of money quite quickly, they won't be satisfied by their franchising relationship.

Franchises are also subject to business trends, and these are sometimes unpredictable. You may buy into a franchise system that sells this year's gotta-have-it widgets, only to find that next year's widget craze makes yours obsolete. The next fad diet may claim that your confection is entirely off limits, and your customers may flee you. Or a new technology may crop up that leaves your service looking primitive. Despite these changes, you'll still own the franchise, and without some serious marketing or research and development efforts by your brand, your business may suffer.

Another risk relates to earnings. When investigating your franchisor's UFOC, you may come across their earnings claim in Item 19. But make no mistake: this statement is no guarantee of earnings. This is merely a report of what other franchisees have earned. It doesn't say that other franchisees in your area have earned this, or that they did so in their first year of business. It doesn't say that every franchisee has earned this amount. Just like everything else about purchasing a franchise, this statement requires some investigation. The FTC does not mandate providing an earnings claim, so not all UFOC's contain this information.

In addition, remember that as a franchisee, you aren't in business alone. You're taking a risk by entering into relationships with a franchisor, your employees, and your customers. And anything to do with relationships is always full of risk. We humans are always full of surprises. In business, disputes and disagreements will sometimes come up, and you'll be forced to solve them. You'll also need to communicate with your contacts at headquarters, so this relationship is also an unknown. And you'll most likely need to hire employees, smooth things over with customers, and become a credible leader for your employees and in the community. You'd best be ready for these challenges.

Lastly, remember that in a sense, your friends and family are taking this risk with you. Hopefully, they're there to support you as you take this great leap. But they may try to talk you out of your plans or put up a fuss when you're busy with your new enterprise. They may resent that you aren't contributing to the household income for a time, and they may worry about their own futures, too. That's why I feel that if at all possible, you must have the full support of your loved ones as you take on the responsibility of owning a franchise. If not, be single-minded and focused, and don't let anyone steal your dream.

Beginning and Ending with Your Dream

Over the years, I have seen many amazing success stories in the world of franchising. One common denominator is that each individual began with a dream. It's important to remember that everything begins with a dream. As I wrote in *Focus or Failure: America at the Crossroads*, published by Executive Books:

> Everybody wants something. Cars, homes, peace of mind, happiness, recognition, a place to belong, the list is endless. Because of this, desire is at the foundation of all effort. It is from desire that persistence grows because what attracts you can activate you to action. It is this attraction or desire or dream, if you will, that is the beginning of faith. Faith is actually a reaction to a dream, and dreams are God-inspired. The dream not only predates goals, but it encompasses and transcends them inspiring people with a spiritual energy. Napoleon once said that the only way to lead people is to show them the future and the future is encompassed in the dream, pursued in faith, and inspired in hope. This is why I would exhort you to get a new hold on your dream.

As we go forward, I will introduce you to people I call "Franchising Eagles" who share in their own words the pursuit of their dream and how they were able to soar high.

Yes, everything begins and ends with the dream.

The Least You Need to Know

- ◆ Successful franchisees are long-term thinkers who can handle risk and celebrate rewards.

- ◆ Minorities, women, and veterans are increasingly involved in franchising.

- ◆ Franchisees are able to learn from others in their franchise system, a strong advantage over those who are starting from scratch.

- ◆ Franchisees must be able to give up some independence in order to work well within their system.

- ◆ While franchising diminishes many risks, it doesn't guarantee success or a certain level of earnings.

Chapter 5

Determining the Right Model

In This Chapter

◆ Identifying the right opportunity for you

◆ Examining your skills and businesses

◆ Looking at franchise listings

◆ Starting your own franchise system

◆ Team player or loner?

If you've found that you fit the model for being a franchisee, the next step is to sift through the many industries and companies that offer franchise systems. The franchise community is a vast one, and one franchise system is sure to be right for you.

In this chapter, I show how you can sift through the many options and target a few industries or companies that would be right for you. I also discuss how you can surround yourself with supportive partners. Remember, at its heart, franchising is about partnerships as much as it's about business.

Exploring Your Options

Franchised businesses permeate our economy and culture and franchising opportunities can be found in almost every industry. So when you're beginning to look at where you fit in, you may feel either shut out or totally overwhelmed, and that your options are either everywhere or nowhere.

I think it's a good idea to take a look at your skills, and which industries need them. Then you can identify which of those industries are needed in your area. Although this does require some soul-searching, which at times can be difficult, this time is well spent.

A Quick Skills Inventory

Let's start with a quick inventory of your skills. If you've ever held a job, you have marketable skills. And even if you haven't worked outside the home, or haven't done so in a while, you've got skills that you probably don't even know you have but are needed in today's economy.

To take an inventory of your skills, answer the following questions:

- Which skills do you use in your current or previous job?

- Which computer programs can you use? Are you comfortable browsing the Internet?

- Are you proficient at math?

- Can you write e-mails, letters, or other types of correspondence without assistance?

- Can you talk to people in a professional manner? Have you ever made a sales call or worked with the public?

- Can you operate office equipment, a cash register, or a credit card machine?

- Have you ever managed people or worked as part of a team? Do you prefer to work alone?

- Which skills would you like to acquire?

- What do you like to do? What are your hobbies?

- What do you want to do?

After you've answered these questions, you should be able to put together a list of all of your skills. If there are any that you possess that haven't been covered by these questions, add them, too.

Franchising Eagles
"I made a [resolution] … that I was going to amount to something if I could," Ray Kroc of McDonald's said. "And no hours, nor amount of labor, nor amount of money would deter me from giving the best that there was in me. And I have done that ever since, and I win by it. I know."
Kroc also said something else that impressed me. This fabulously wealthy man once said: "All money means to me is a pride in accomplishment."
Spoken like a true Franchising Eagle.

Industry Survey

Now that you've got a full list of your work skills, it's time to look at the industries and companies that need someone like you. To discover this, you'll have to answer these questions:

- Which industries can you envision yourself working in and feeling passionate about?

- Which industries do you have experience in?

- Which companies, services, or products can be found within these industries?

- Which industries, according to your local newspaper's business section or classified ads, need your skills?

- Which industries are on the rise?

Hopefully these questions will help you get ideas about which industries, products, or services are your best opportunities. Make a list of your top three or four industries.

For example, let's say that you're a fitness buff, you've done customer service, you've worked retail, and you enjoy working with people. You

Eagle Eyes

If you're having a hard time identifying industries, products, or services, check out IFA's alphabetical listing of industries on its website, or flip through the Yellow Pages for ideas. You're sure to find something that interests you. Even if you have identified some industries, check out these resources anyway. You never know what you may have overlooked.

know a little bit about standard business procedures and bookkeeping. You're totally comfortable with computers and gadgets, and you don't like having a boss looking over your shoulder but you like knowing that you can get help if you need it. You decide that your top targeted industry is fitness and your second-place industry is health care.

At this point, you have a lot of information. It's time to take the next step: determining the need for your service.

Determining the Need

You're now ready to explore the need for your targeted industries or services. Answer the following questions about your top industry, and then move onto the other industry on your list. You may need the phone book or a quick tour of your local mall to get this information.

◆ Which businesses in your industry can already be found in your area?

◆ Which services or products are needed in your area?

◆ Which services or products do you, as a consumer, need?

◆ Have you read anything about this industry in the newspaper or business magazines? What does it say about the future for this industry?

◆ Who would be your customers or clients?

◆ Do you think that this industry will be healthy in 5 or 10 years? What makes you think that?

In addition to answering these questions, you may want to discuss the industry with your friends who have knowledge of it. How do they react to your interest? Are their positive reactions sincere? Do they have any reservations about the long-term growth of this industry?

CAUTION

Aviary Alert

You may be interested in an industry that has a seasonal market. Although most businesses have high and low seasons, some businesses—such as tax preparation and lawn care—have a more dramatic cycle. To succeed, ask about ways to smooth out the cycle, either by offering a more diverse mix of products or services that will be used throughout the year or by being flexible about staffing or hours of operation. Of course, you could always move your frozen yogurt franchise from Alaska to Miami, too.

If you've found that your local market is saturated with companies within your industry, move on to the next industry on your list.

Let's go back to the fitness example. During your research, you went to a few gyms in the area in which you want to locate your franchise, but you weren't terribly impressed by them. You ingested a few energy bars and drinks because you know that they're pretty hot right now. By talking to friends who work out regularly, you think that people want more limited gyms right now, ones that cater to their specific exercise requirements. You also think that people like the personal touch of smaller fitness centers. You think that clients don't want to be intimidated by the instructors or other personnel.

You can keep a record of all of your ideas by jotting them down in a notebook or by tape recording yourself as you brainstorm. That way, you won't forget insights that can help you in the future.

Finding the Franchises

You're now ready for the final step in this exercise: finding franchises. As you know, there are franchise businesses in almost every industry, and franchises provide almost every product and service you can imagine—and probably a few more, too.

You can find many franchise listings online. I'm partial to the IFA's listing on its website, which contains its members, a little bit about their businesses, necessary qualifications, and contact information. You can also find listings through other websites and publications, such as *The Franchise Opportunities Guide, Bond's Franchise Guide,* and others. As you look through the listings of companies, determine what makes each one unique, and how each one could serve both your needs and your community's.

When you seek out information about franchises, you'll often come across types of business models that are sometimes franchises, but not always. Some of these business types are *turnkey operations, multilevel marketing programs,* and *business opportunities.* It's a good idea to get acquainted with these terms.

Definitions

A business that is already operating and is to be turned over to a new owner is a **turnkey operation.** This can be a franchise, but it doesn't have to be one.

Often confused with a pyramid scheme, **multilevel marketing programs (MLM)** are direct-sale businesses that include "uplines" and "downlines," ways to profit from others' sales.

A **business opportunity (biz op)** is an idea, product, or service that is being offered for sale that will help someone start his or her own business.

Remember, you aren't making a commitment at this point. You're just gathering information on what's out there and what might be a good fit for you.

To go back to the fitness example, you would want to look at which gyms or fitness centers are available as franchises. You'd probably also want to check out if there are any franchises that sell products that fitness buffs would be interested in, such as supplements, gear or equipment, clothing, and so on. Then you can seek out more information on these companies to find out if any are suitable for you.

Why Not Start Your Own Franchise?

After taking a look at your own skills and the industries that interest you, you may be bursting with ideas. One of those ideas may be for a new company or product that's needed, but not yet brought to market. And, what's more, you think that it would make a great franchised business. Instead of becoming a franchisee, and working in someone else's system and pitching their product or service, you'd like someone to do that for you. You want to be the franchisor, not the franchisee.

Great. I won't stop you. But you'll need to start small, develop your business, and then think about franchising. It won't happen quickly, nor will it happen alone. Also, keep in mind that while franchising is an effective way to grow, not every business concept should turn into a franchise. Focus on your core business, then see if franchising is the best way to expand your business.

To become a franchisor, you must have a solid product or service. It must be good, original, and fill a need. It can't merely duplicate another product or service that's already out there. It should be successful and profitable, so that you don't leave your prospective franchisees—or your customers—in the lurch.

Then you must have an original way of delivering this product or service—through your own company, for example. And, what's more, other people should be able to duplicate this method, too. It can't just be built on your personality or by making things up as you go along. Your business should look and feel distinct, but you should be able to train people to set up shop just like you, too.

Lastly, you should have a product or service that will stand the test of time. After all, you'll be issuing franchise agreements that will last a number of years—10 to 20, typically—and you'll want demand for your business to be strong at least a decade from now.

These are the bare minimum requirements you'll need to become a franchisor. If you want to know more about becoming a franchisor, I cover this topic in depth in

Chapter 19. If you have a great idea but don't think you want to take on the responsibilities of becoming a franchisor, consider setting up your own business, and take it from there.

Acquiring an Existing Franchise

While discussing which industries and franchises you should explore further, I've almost made it seem that you must start from scratch by launching a franchise unit where none currently exist. But this isn't the only way you can become a franchisee. You can also buy an existing franchise from an owner that wants to sell it. This can happen when the owner wants to strike out in a new career direction, or when he or she wants to retire from business altogether. This can also happen when the franchisor wants to sell a company-owned unit to a franchisee and blend it into the franchise system.

Although the franchise outlet is up and running, you'll still need to thoroughly investigate it just as you would if you were establishing your own outlet. You'll need to fit your skills and interests to the business. You'll need to determine why the owner is selling and what the franchise is all about. You'll need to look at the long-range health of the business and sort out any problems that are currently plaguing the unit or the system as a whole.

On the other hand, you will also have a lot of information that you can use to your advantage. Instead of working with estimated numbers—earnings and annual sales, for example—you'll be able to see the actual financial statements before buying. You'll also, one assumes, have an existing customer base that is familiar with your brand. You won't have to introduce your business to the community.

Acquiring an existing franchise unit is an option you can explore while seeking out information on units you'll buy directly from the franchisor and set up in a new location.

Team Player or Loner?

You may think that franchising means striking out on your own. But franchising enmeshes you in a long-term relationship. No franchisee—or franchisor—is an island. Therefore, I've found that team players do best in the franchising community.

Being a franchisee—or a franchisor—will challenge your social and communication skills more than you probably realize right now. Think about all of the people you'll encounter while working in franchising. You're entering into a relationship with your franchisor and the units in your system. It's competitive, of course, but a healthy competition. Success at one unit will increase your brand's name recognition, which ultimately helps you. And your clients and customers will no doubt patronize your fellow franchisees and get the same great service available from you.

Therefore, it's a good idea to consider whom you'll encounter in your franchise system. Do you respect the leaders and where they're taking the company? How involved will they be in your day-to-day business? How clear are the training manuals and program, and what kind of support staff is on hand? Are they concerned about systemwide communications by scheduling regular conference calls, meetings, conferences, or workshops? How do they utilize technology, such as video cameras and the Internet?

> **Aviary Alert**
>
> I think it's a good idea to check out your prospective business partners as closely as you'll investigate your prospective franchisor. Know his or her business experience, credit history, legal problems, and personal characteristics. A bad partner can bring you down, so prevent that from happening by being cautious at the beginning.

> **Eagle Eyes**
>
> The IFA offers an online course about finding and retaining great managers and employees. It's called "Selection and Development of Top Performers" and can be found at www.franchise.org.

Another important person to consider is your business partner, if you're investing with one. There are a few kinds of partners—some want to be equal, while others are passive investors who don't want to be part of the day-to-day operations but will help you put up the money that you need. Business partnerships can be tricky. A great one is worth its weight in gold, while a problematic one can sap your business and your spirit.

Some very important people are your employees. If you've ever managed people, you know how important it is to have a good staff—they, too, can make or break your business. They'll need your leadership—they'll look to you for answers, even if you're feeling clueless. In addition, make sure that there are available employees in your area who will work for the pay that you will offer.

Your clients or customers will rely on you, too, for professional service or well-made products. Think about whether you'll be comfortable with your clients. If you aren't comfortable with sales, make sure that someone on staff is. If you thrive on interacting with people, make sure you can network as much as possible.

Last, but certainly not least, some of the most important people who will be affected by your decision to go into franchising are your family members. Not only will they have to cope with your decision, but sometimes they'll go through the experience with you. Many franchisees go into business with their spouses and have achieved great success. But others have strained their relationship. If you do plan on working with your spouse, make sure that you have clearly defined roles and responsibilities, and talk about your goals and how you can create enough personal space so that you won't feel overwhelmed by the challenge of living and working together.

The Least You Need to Know

- You'll increase your chances of success by matching your skills to industries that need them.

- You should consider industries that show chances of growing in the long term, not just those that are hot right now.

- Seasonal businesses can smooth out their dramatic highs and lows in demand by varying the products or services they offer.

- A franchisor must have a distinct product or service and an easily replicated operating system.

- Buying franchises that already exist allows you to review actual financial documents and not rely on estimates.

- While many successful franchisees go into business with their spouse or relatives, doing so can strain relationships.

Chapter 6

Signing a Franchise Contract

In This Chapter

- ◆ Why rules and regulations protect you
- ◆ Picking apart the disclosure statement
- ◆ Analyzing the franchise agreement
- ◆ Making changes to the agreement

At the heart of the franchising system is the franchise agreement. This document states the terms of the partnership between the franchisor and franchisee. The franchisor drafts this document, so, not surprisingly, it dictates the terms. However, that doesn't mean that the franchisee is powerless. Thanks to the Uniform Franchise Offering Circular (UFOC), a statement that discloses much financial information about the franchisor, the franchisee can go into this partnership with eyes wide open.

However, getting to that point requires attention and a willingness to read through and understand two important statements: the UFOC and the franchise agreement. In this chapter, I discuss these documents point by point. I also explore which terms can usually be negotiated, and how you can get professional help for this process.

Rules and Regulations

As I've explained, franchising used to be a highly unregulated system. Almost anyone could set up a franchising system, get people to invest in it, and then pocket the money and move on. And since there was so much money to be had, a lot of well-meaning people got had.

The government stepped in, and the franchising' sales process is the second-most regulated industry. Only the sales of securities have more regulations.

To begin with, the Federal Trade Commission defined what, exactly, a franchise is. A franchise must have these three components:

1. The franchisor must grant limited rights to use the company's trade name, service mark, logo, or other advertising symbol.

2. The franchisor must sell the rights to use systems or methods associated with operating the core business.

3. The franchisor receives a payment in return for granting the rights mentioned in Items 1 and 2.

The FTC also forces franchisors to follow certain protocols before, during, and after selling a unit to a franchisee. A part of that is giving a prospective franchisee a Universal Franchise Offering Circular (UFOC), and then entering into a franchise agreement that, if all goes well, will be signed, sealed, and legally binding.

Some states have additional regulations placed on franchises operating in their jurisdiction. In addition, as I mention in Chapter 3, the International Franchise Association maintains a self-regulation program that its members must follow. The IFA believes that this will ensure the integrity of the franchise system without having to rely on the government for direction.

> **Franchise Facts**
>
> A whopping 33 different agencies regulate franchising, so there's considerable oversight of this business system.

> **Aviary Alert**
>
> Although the franchisors are responsible for putting together these agreements, it's up to the franchisee to evaluate them. You must do your homework before signing. You must have an experienced franchise attorney working with you. After the franchise agreement is signed, there's no going back.

> **Eagle Eyes**
>
> Anyone thinking about reading and signing a franchise agreement should hire a franchise lawyer to help him or her through the process. This attorney must be experienced with franchising—another type of lawyer won't do. You can find one through your local bar association and IFA's website.

This setup gets to the heart of franchising—a way to attain freedom. Informed businesspeople are able to enter into agreements without over-regulation from the government. The franchisor must be honest in its disclosure documents, and the franchisee must be making an educated decision. As long as all parties remain true to that ideal, the system will survive.

Examining the UFOC

I've referred to the UFOC many times in this book, but only in passing. Now, you're ready to dive into it and examine the contents of this disclosure agreement.

There's a lot of information contained within the UFOC. However, even though it's filled with a lot of names and numbers, you'll still have to gather information on your own, by, perhaps, speaking with other franchisees in the system or going outside of the system by reading newspaper and magazine articles about the company, doing library or Internet research, or talking to those who have done business with a particular franchise. First things first: let's look at the UFOC.

When you become interested in a franchise system and want to get serious, you will receive a UFOC from a representative of the franchisor. This document contains background information about the company and which state's laws will govern the agreement. It then lists 23 items that cover just about everything you'll need to know about the franchise.

The introductory pages contain warnings about the contents of the document. It states that the FTC hasn't verified the data and warns franchisees to take time reading it and perhaps show it and the franchise agreement to a qualified lawyer or accountant. It also encourages franchisees to seek out and abide by franchising laws in their state.

It also declares which state's laws will govern the agreement, where the franchisee can sue the franchisor, and if the parties may use an arbitrator to settle disputes.

> **CAUTION**
> **Aviary Alert**
> Although the UFOC contains a huge amount of information, remember that you should consider the source—the franchisor. The franchisor can provide information that makes it look good and omit some information it isn't so proud of—for example, in the earnings statement. That's why you should examine the UFOC with a critical eye.

Items in the UFOC

At this point, the 23 items commence. Here they are, point by point.

Item 1: Franchisor. In this item you'll find the name of the franchisor, its predecessors, and its affiliates; the name the company does business as; the company's address; and the state of incorporation. It also states the aim of the franchisor's business and the experience of the franchisor.

Eagle Eyes

A thorough Internet or library search can help you dig up more information on the franchisor's executives. Don't merely rely on the biographies given in the UFOC.

Item 2: Business experience. This item gives you information about the officers, directors, and executives of the franchisor.

Item 3: Litigation history. You'll find if there's any relevant criminal or civil litigation regarding the company or its management.

Item 4: Bankruptcy. If the company or its managers have declared bankruptcy, you'll find that information here.

Item 5: Initial franchise fee. At this point, the franchisor will start to talk about money. This is one of the most attention-grabbing items in the UFOC. It contains the amount franchisees must pay to acquire the franchise, if all franchisees must pay this amount, and how the franchisor settled on this amount.

Eagle Eyes

Initial franchise fees are usually nonrefundable. This is yet another reason why you must investigate, investigate, investigate before signing—and then investigate some more.

Additionally, a low initial franchise fee isn't always a bargain. Look at the bang you get for your buck. What kind of support will you get from the franchisor? Will you receive supplies? If you have to pay extra for many of your franchisor's services, you aren't getting a bargain.

Item 6: Other fees. The initial franchise fee isn't the only fee that the franchisee must pay. He or she is also responsible for other payments, such as royalties, training fees, advertising contributions, and transfer and renewal fees.

Item 7: The initial investment. This item contains a table with other payments the franchisee must make to set up the business, as well as when and how to make these payments. Some of these items may include the initial franchisee fee, real estate, equipment and supplies, signs, various license fees, advertising, and capital. It also provides a grand total for the initial investment, much of which is paid to third-party suppliers or providers other than the franchisor.

Item 8: Business restrictions. In this item you'll find restrictions on suppliers, products, equipment, or services that are related to the franchise. If the franchisor wants you to use a specific supplier, or if it earns revenue off of your purchases, you'll find that here.

Item 9: The franchisee's obligations. This item is rather wide-ranging, and includes information about what the franchisee is required to do. This varies according to the type of business the franchise system is in, but some items may include initial and ongoing training, fees, insurance, advertising, noncompetition terms, customer service standards, and much more. As with everything else in this document, read this item closely.

Item 10: Financing. If the franchisor offers financing, the terms will be set out here.

Item 11: The franchisor's obligations. Here you'll find what the franchisor is offering. Like Item 9, this varies with the franchise system and type of business. Some items may include what the franchisor will do before and after opening, site location rationale, training program, and advertising.

Item 12: Territory. This states if the franchisee will be granted exclusive rights to a territory and whether the franchisor can set up another unit within it.

Item 13: Trademarks. This sets out the franchisor's trademarks, service marks, and trade names that will be used.

Item 14: Patents, copyrights, and proprietary information. This contains information on which of these the franchisee may use, and how.

Item 15: Participation. If the franchisee must be a hands-on owner, or if the franchisee may be an absentee owner, you'll find that set out here.

Item 16: Product or service restrictions. This delineates the products or services the franchisee may sell.

Item 17: Renewal, termination, transfers, and dispute resolution. This is made up of another table setting out the terms of the agreement—the length of the term, renewals, termination reasons, *transfer rights*, and other items.

Definitions

Transfer rights are the franchisee's right to sell the unit to another person with the approval of the franchisor.

Aviary Alert

Just as you should be concerned about how you will get into franchising, you should be concerned with how you will get out of it. In Item 17, make sure you clearly spell out your rights to terminate, renew, and transfer ownership of your franchise. Your attorney can help you understand and clarify these issues.

Item 18: Celebrities. If any public figures are involved in this venture, details of that celebrity's agreement are presented here.

Definitions

Company-owned outlets are the individual units many franchisors operate in addition to maintaining those in the franchise system.

Item 19: Earnings claims. This is another attention-grabbing item. This statement contains what other franchisees have earned. Some franchisors leave this item blank, for good reason. I cover this item in depth later in this chapter.

Item 20: Other units in the system. This provides information about other franchisees, *company-owned outlets*, the estimated number of franchises to be sold in the next year, and other information.

Aviary Alert

Item 20 contains a lot of contact information that you can use. Go ahead and introduce yourself to franchisees listed in Item 20, and find out all you can about their experiences. But be warned: some may be less than honest. Some may feel pressured to put in a good word for the franchisor, while others will want to dissuade you from buying your unit. They may want your territory for themselves. And it's safe to assume that you'll talk to at least one disgruntled franchisee. Every system has at least one, so find out why he or she isn't happy in business.

Item 21: Financial statements. You'll find the past three years of the audited financial statements for the franchisor here. Once again, you can find a host of interesting information if you know what to look for.

Item 22: Agreements. The actual franchise agreement is attached. If you must sign any other agreements, you'll find them here.

Item 23: Confirmation. You must sign a receipt stating that the franchisor provided you with the UFOC. This is necessary, because you must have the UFOC for 10 days before signing it. This gives you a chance to investigate the company's claims and think over your decision.

After you have read the items in the UFOC, you can start investigating the company's claims. I recommend that you use an experienced franchise lawyer and an accountant to help you out. I cannot stress enough the importance of having good counsel. Although many people believe that they can skimp on this expense, I've found that not getting appropriate legal representation saves them nothing. In fact, I've found that some people believe they've bought into a franchise system, only to find that they haven't—they've been taken by a shark preying on their lack of knowledge. Remember, after you're in business, you're only as good as the quality of your professional services. Receiving poor advice can invite complete disaster.

Eagle Eyes

If the franchisor is a publicly held company, you can obtain its filings from the Securities and Exchange Commission. This will give you more information about the company's finances, management, and strategy. Go to www.sec.gov for more information.

The Franchise Agreement

Although the franchise agreement and the UFOC may seem like the same thing, they aren't. The franchise agreement is a section of the UFOC, which you'll find in Item 22 of the UFOC. This is your contract, so read this carefully. This is what you—and the franchisor—will be held to in the years to come. If you have discussed some terms with the franchisor's representative, but they don't appear in this agreement, make sure you get those promises in writing. If some of the information in the rest of the UFOC conflicts with what's in the franchise agreement, your lawyer should inquire about it. Again, a seasoned franchise lawyer can help you out.

The law states that you must have the franchise agreement for five days before signing it so that you won't be pressured into signing a contract that you haven't read and digested thoroughly. This is much like the 10-day period you've got to evaluate the UFOC. Although the five-day franchise agreement period can be conducted during the 10-day UFOC period, you may want to take the extra time to think over your decision. Unless you've got a lot of competition for a franchise you know you want to buy into, the time will be well spent.

Evaluating Earning Potential

I'm sure you didn't miss Item 19, the earnings claim. After all, you're going into business, not signing up for a new hobby, and you want to make some money. You're putting up a significant amount of money, too, so you're definitely interested in making a return on your investment.

Item 19 doesn't tell the complete story about earnings. In fact, some franchisors don't fill out this item. If they don't promise anything, they can't be held accountable for it. However, other franchisors do fill out this item, although they may do so in different manners. This has significance for you.

Earnings claims can be calculated or crunched in a number of ways. They may be averaged, but you may not be the average franchisee. It doesn't state what you'll likely earn during your first years in business, which is where you're starting. It doesn't state what the franchisees in your area earned, or how franchisees with units like yours earned. It may simply be that the franchisor doesn't have current information for all of its units—or that the numbers are so bad that they don't want to report them.

I should also warn you about "off the record" claims made by the franchisor's representatives or brokers. These are not earnings claims, and you should treat them with care. Unless the number is in the UFOC, you can't trust it. And even then, you should investigate it.

Another thing to remember is that you'll be looking at a snapshot of the company. You won't get the entire dynamic history in the earnings claims or the impact of various brother or sister franchisees. And the attitude and contribution of the franchisees is one of the most significant factors in becoming successful.

Negotiating Terms

The UFOC is an official statement from the franchisor, and the franchise agreement contained in it is a formal document given to all prospective franchisees. However, that doesn't mean that the terms are carved in stone. Many of the items can be negotiated, although some franchise systems are less amenable to this than others. Still, you can try to tweak your schedule, for example.

However, I must warn you that most franchisors do not significantly alter the franchise agreement for individual franchisees. After all, the power of franchising comes from its ability to be duplicated with other people and in other places. The franchisor has stated out the terms that it has found to work best, and, obviously, its franchisees agree. In addition, how would you feel if you knew that a fellow franchisee got started with an advantage that wasn't offered to you?

Franchising Eagles
One of franchising's brightest success stories is that of Subway, a submarine sandwich shop that was founded by a 17-year-old kid who was just trying to make some extra money for college. Fred DeLuca, the young entrepreneur in question, took a suggestion—and $1,000 in seed money from family friend Dr. Peter Buck—to open up a sub shop in Bridgeport, Connecticut, in 1965. The two opened Pete's Super Submarine and launched another one a year later, which made them realize that two factors would help them build their business—marketing and visibility. They changed the name to Subway and created the distinctive yellow logo. The next piece in the puzzle was franchising, a strategy that helped them build brand awareness and one that would also allow other people to own their own business. The first Subway franchise was opened in Wallingford, Connecticut, in 1974. In August 1995, Subway celebrated 30 years in business and witnessed the opening of its 11,000th restaurant. In 2005, there are more than 20,000 Subways around the world.

Another important reason why franchisors don't significantly change the franchise agreement is that each big change means that the UFOC must be refiled in the various registration states, which is costly and time consuming. And this means that the terms of the agreement must be disclosed and, again, discrepancies can cause problems and create more work for little gain.

The Least You Need to Know

◆ The franchising sales process is one of the most heavily regulated business activities in our economy.

◆ The UFOC and the franchise agreement are two different documents, but the terms should be the same.

◆ Read the UFOC and the franchise agreement carefully, because once you sign it there's no going back.

◆ An experienced franchise lawyer and accountant are indispensable to prospective franchisees.

◆ Earnings claims, if made, do not guarantee you that amount of income or profit.

Chapter 7

Assessing Your Attitude

In This Chapter

- The impact of your attitude
- Developing a winning attitude
- Examining integrity
- Building good relationships
- Your attitude's influence on your planning, vision, and mission

Other than my eight-year stint in the Marine Corps, which I take great pride in, my entire professional life has centered on franchising. In this time, I've seen a number of people come and go, pursue their dreams, or be deeply disappointed. What I've found is that no matter how good a deal appears to be on paper, something more intangible is more critical to success in franchising. And that is attitude, and having the right one.

In this chapter, I explore why attitude determines success, and how you can cultivate the right one. I also look at how the right attitude can impact your relationships, planning, vision, and mission—factors that are of great importance in your franchise business.

Your Attitude and Its Impact

I've said many times that the relationship between the franchisor and franchisee is the most people-intensive *synergistic* relationship I've seen. It's up there with marriage. Think about it: these two entities enter into a partnership that links them financially, personally, competitively, and with their dreams. They are linked in the day-to-day stuff, such as how to best run the business at the everyday level, to the loftier stuff, such as how to define success and achieve it in the long run. The relationship changes as the franchisee develops more experience and independence and as the franchisor develops new strategies and direction.

This is a terribly intimate relationship, and with this intimacy comes conflict. In franchising, conflict is inevitable and if you look for it you will not be disappointed.

However, I don't think that the inevitability of conflict should turn off a prospective franchisee or franchisor. In fact, I think that conflict can be an opportunity for achieving something greater. It allows us to come up with solutions and develop leadership skills that recognize the importance of people, not spreadsheets. And this will only strengthen the franchising community and elevate the level of *integrity*, values, motivation, and performance.

What matters is one's *attitude*. I firmly believe that one's attitude is an individual's greatest asset or greatest liability. It determines our present disposition and our future actions. It is the foundation of our lives. Although many would agree that knowledge is the prerequisite to success and sustained effort helps us get there, attitude is the foundation upon which everything else rests. All of the knowledge in the world will not overcome a bad attitude.

Definitions _____

Synergy occurs when people or organizations act together; the results of their efforts are greater than what they could have achieved individually.

Integrity is a steadfast adherence to a strict moral or ethical code to achieve unity or completeness.

An **attitude** is a complex mental state involving beliefs, feelings, and values that predispose an individual to act in certain ways.

That's why I believe that all of us—franchisors, franchisees, and those who aren't in business—must develop the right attitude toward life and business. Attitude is greater than appearance, competence, or skills and has the capacity to make or break any enterprise, deal, negotiation, alliance, or circumstance.

Developing a Winning Attitude in Life

So many times the term "attitude" is portrayed negatively, as expressed in the statements "You've got an attitude problem" or "I don't like your attitude." However, these statements only refer to people who have bad attitudes, people who think negatively, act negatively, and feel negatively about everything. And you know this type of person. He or she is dried up like a prune, appearing to have been weaned on a pickle.

Attitudes can be positive—winning, successful, or optimistic. A positive attitude can help us overcome any obstacle in our path and can even determine which path we follow (or blaze).

An attitude takes time to develop, though. Whether good or bad, an attitude isn't created instantly. Little by little, like icicles that form on the eaves of your house during a winter freeze, our attitudes are developed. If the water that freezes to form the icicle is clear and free from pollution, then the icicle itself becomes pristine and clear. But let a little dirt or mud foul it and the icicle becomes opaque or splotched and not very attractive.

Just like the icicle is made up of drops of water, our attitude is made up of a few components. First, our attitude is made up of our thoughts. I believe that what we think becomes our future. Second, our attitude is made up of our feelings. A thought that is combined with emotions and feelings is on its way to becoming a belief. Third, our attitude is made up of our actions or behavior, which comes from our emotion-tinged thoughts. It has integrity, because it is based on the whole. This last component reflects our real attitude. It isn't what we say or think or even feel that determines results. Ultimately, it is what we do. We may say that we have hope, or faith, or love, but unless that translates into action, those are empty words. When this happens, we lose integrity.

Franchising Eagles

"Colonel" Harland Sanders was a Franchising Eagle that almost everyone on the planet can recognize, even if his 11 herbs and spices are still a secret. Sanders opened his first restaurant, Sanders' Café, in 1929 in Corbin, Kentucky. That first café grew into more than 600 Kentucky Fried Chicken restaurants by 1964, when he sold the company for $2,000,000, a lifetime salary of $40,000, and a seat on the board of directors. He remained an active spokesman for the chain—and his "finger lickin' good" chicken—until his death in 1980.

"Don't be against things so much as for things," Sanders was quoted as saying, and I completely agree.

After you understand how these three components combine to create your attitude, you can start to identify your attitudes, and then change the ones that are problematic. Be warned that this won't happen overnight. Changing one's attitude (and habits) is a process, typically sparked by a crisis. I think of the process as looking something like this:

- Problem: Something is wrong.

- Crisis: We realize that something is wrong.

- Action: We begin to do something about it.

- Change: When we change our thoughts, feelings, and behavior but no one believes it.

- A new attitude: Our attitude is one of respect for others and ourselves.

For example, let's say that the holidays are approaching and you must tell your employees that they must work longer hours to accommodate your customers. When you draw up the new schedule, nobody is pleased—but you aren't budging. Your attitude is that everyone must pitch in equally and work as a team. Fair is fair. Some of your employees complain because they want to spend more time with their families. Some are students and need to work on their term papers and study for exams, and working for you is a lower priority.

At this point, you have a problem. Something—the holiday schedule—is wrong. It becomes a crisis when your employees begin complaining among themselves and their negativity affects their work. Some even call in sick at the last minute, leaving you in the lurch. And to make matters worse, they don't care. They expect you to cover for them even though you're stretched thin.

You realize that you must take action. You must find a better way to fill your holiday schedule. You think about your options. You feel that you've been unfair to those who have too many responsibilities at this time of the year. And then you decide to change your actions. You begin by talking to some of your most critical employees to get their input. Although they distrust you at first, they eventually warm up to you. Then you talk to others who seem to be willing to work more hours. And then you begin to change the schedule. Although everyone won't be contributing equally, they are contributing as much as they can. And in this way, the crisis is resolved, your attitude about fairness has changed, and you and your employees have a new respect for each other. You've achieved success—and acted with integrity.

Your attitude has a huge effect on your involvement with franchising. Your thoughts, beliefs, and actions combine to help you succeed or find nothing but difficulties and limitations.

Through my years in franchising, I've noticed that some people share a common attitude that always spells trouble. This attitude is that franchisors and franchisees are opponents who have different goals that come into conflict. These people believe that franchisors want to get rich at the expense of the franchisees, who do all of the hard work and make things happen. They blame each other when things go wrong and take the credit when things go right.

But I've found that this attitude is all wrong, and thinking this way just sets the stage for failure.

I think that those in the franchising community can and should develop the right attitude, one that's based on achieving the greater common good, one that's based on achieving integrity. The units in each franchising system play a role in its success, and people are at the heart of this system. Therefore, I believe that the right attitude is a people-focused one. This attitude is based on the following elements:

- Putting people first. Remembering that franchising is based on relationships between people. Each interaction should be based on this recognition.

- Ethics and honor. Recognize the importance of values and ethical actions. Franchising means trusting that your partners will treat you fairly and honorably, just as they trust you to do the same.

- Interdependency. Franchisors and franchisees need each other. Franchisors develop the overall strategy and brand development. Franchisees benefit from brand recognition. They also deliver—day in and day out—on the promise of the brand.

- A focus on solutions. The franchise community should be solution oriented, not conflict oriented. Problems should be dealt with early, before they spiral out of control or infect the entire system.

- Opportunities. When conflict does occur, it should be seen as an opportunity for growth and mutual understanding. It helps people identify differences, find common ground, and discover solutions.

- Respect for the process. The process is more important than the result. The process is about communication, which, when done openly, can achieve the right result.

- Adherence to the culture. The culture of the organization holds it together. It reflects the values and beliefs of the people in the organization. The leadership establishes the culture, but it is executed with the permission of the members of the community.

- Leading. Leadership is important at every level of the organization. Whether it's developing overall strategy, or dealing with the details at the street level, franchising requires great leaders throughout each organization.

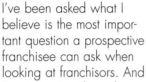

Eagle Eyes

I've been asked what I believe is the most important question a prospective franchisee can ask when looking at franchisors. And that question is: are these the people I want to be in business with 10 or 15 years from now? People are more important than the product or service one will offer through the franchise.

The Franchising Eagles portrayed throughout the book, as well as those interviewed in Chapter 23, are excellent examples of people who conduct themselves with a high level of integrity.

Banking on Integrity

Integrity is the foundation of the franchise relationship. It permeates all of the relationships found within the system, from the board of directors to the daily interactions between the franchisee, his or her employees, and the customers.

Integrity is defined as steadfast adherence to a strict moral or ethical code; the state of being unimpaired, soundness; the quality or condition of being whole or undivided, completeness. In franchising, integrity has many implications.

When people act with integrity, their attitude—their thoughts, emotions, and actions—are all in alignment. This sense of integrity means that they don't believe one thing and do another. There exists a completeness in who a person is, what he or she believes, and his or her behavior. A person with integrity speaks words that mean something, and his or her thoughts are focused on solutions, success, and values.

At the most basic level, integrity means that all members of the franchising community will treat each other with respect. This also includes customers, suppliers, and vendors—anyone who comes into contact with the franchise.

Integrity also means that the business will be conducted ethically. Leaders won't cash out early and selfishly. Rather, they'll make good on their commitments and seek out long-term gain. In addition, it means that financial statements will be honest and realistic. Investors in the franchise will feel that they've purchased something of value, while those who make decisions about these investments do so for the good of all.

Integrity is also extended to the product or service provided by the franchise. It will deliver on the promises made by its advertisements and will benefit its customers.

> **Aviary Alert**
>
> It's amazing how your instincts come into play when looking at prospective franchisors or franchisees. That's because purchasing or selling a franchise is an emotional event as much as it's a business deal. Oftentimes you can tell yourself to overlook numbers that seem unrealistic or you may feel pressured to sign a deal because your emotions are being manipulated. However, when you encounter others who act with integrity you don't need to be talked into anything. It'll feel right and you'll know it.

Integrity also means that leadership qualities will be cultivated at every level of the franchise system. All members will follow through on their promises and take responsibility for their actions. In this way, the franchise will maintain high standards—even raise them—and become a good workplace.

Lastly, integrity means that members strive to remain united in the system. If there are weak links, that will affect the entire franchise. That's why all voices should be heard and respected. Remember: by becoming involved with a franchise, you're representing that brand for many years. You have to ask yourself if you'll be proud to be a part of that system, and if they will appreciate your efforts on behalf of that franchise community.

At the end of the day, integrity will keep the relationship intact. Although you'll sign an agreement that will set out the terms of your relationship, I think that in a strong franchise system made up of dozens—or even hundreds—of relationships, you won't need to rely on the legalities of your agreement. In the best-case scenario, you'll trust that your partner, whether it's the franchisor or another franchisee, has everyone's best interest in mind.

In this way, the franchise agreement is like a prenuptial agreement. Before the marriage you'll hash out who owns what and who will be entitled to what if the marriage breaks down. In a true marriage, that document won't dictate the terms of the relationship. If you have to run back to the prenup to establish the ground rules of your marriage, then I believe that you are not in a true marriage.

The same can be said about franchising. If you have to constantly refer back to the terms of your franchise agreement to reinforce the definition of your relationship with your franchisor, then you don't have trust, and you don't have integrity.

Building Good Business Relationships

It's imperative that franchisors and franchisees build good relationships and then nurture them. Although the intensity of this relationship may be challenging, ultimately, it can be rewarding.

A great deal of time, energy, and money is put into creating the legal papers and structure that defines the relationship. Be sure you have legal counsel and sound documents, because they have the power to affect your entire business—and even your personal life, too. However, the contract shouldn't drive the relationship. Like a prenup, the moment the contract drives the relationship, it's over.

Eagle Eyes

You'll know a franchisor is serious about franchisee relations if it has employees that are dedicated to working with franchisees in the system. By doing so, this kind of franchisor will earn its franchisees' respect.

I believe that communication is key to building good business relationships. When a problem arises, you can work through it, instead of hiding it until it blows up in everyone's face. When you're successful, you can share your techniques so that others can learn from you, and you can also celebrate the good times together. Recognizing stellar performers—what I call "franchising eagles"—at conventions and workshops is a great way to motivate people and let them know they're appreciated.

I also believe that each side must earn each other's respect. Both franchisors and franchisees must exhibit leadership qualities by making good on promises and showing initiative. Both sides must be able to withstand the scrutiny that should come before the franchise agreement is signed. And both sides should be comfortable with a long-term relationship by avoiding short-term solutions that are supposed to fix longstanding problems. In my experience, these quick fixes just make matters worse. Although it may be tempting, and may please your shareholders, sometimes the more difficult long-term solution is the one that will actually do the trick in the long run.

Overall, though, franchisors and franchisees must realize that they're in it together and must make the best of it. Strained relationships will always show, whether it's in the year-end statements or on the front lines of the business.

Supporting Your Plan, Vision, and Mission

Your attitude, sense of integrity, and relationships will have a huge effect on the success of your franchise. If you enjoy your work and see a brighter future for yourself, that attitude will impact your business. If you operate ethically and are backed up by a system that has integrity, your customers will know that they can rely on you. If you have built and are nurturing strong relationships with those you encounter, you'll have a support system for you whenever you need it.

All of this will affect your plans and vision for the future. If your overall dream is to own your own business, earn enough money to live on, and enjoy your work—a common dream in franchising—you can make decisions based on achieving this dream. However, if you don't have integrity, you will make decisions that will work against you. You may become sloppy or lazy and neglect the "little" duties that you think are beneath you but are terribly important, and this will affect your profitability. Or you may resent coming to work every day and your negativity will affect everyone around you, or you may quit when things become difficult or a little boring or routine and you decide to "check out" early.

However, if you have integrity, you can achieve your dreams. You will hang in there when your business is dull or difficult, and you will know your business inside and out because you feel responsible for the quality of your product or service. You'll motivate your employees because you truly love your work. And you won't need to have pep talks to do it—your attitude and actions will get your message across loud and clear.

In this way, your attitude and sense of integrity will be vital to the realization of your dream. And nothing in life is more important than that.

The Least You Need to Know

- The franchisor-franchisee relationship is naturally full of conflict, but a win-win attitude will help solve problems.

- A winning attitude is based on thoughts, feelings, and emotions that have integrity.

- Integrity is important in any endeavor, since it helps an individual act on his or her beliefs, and not get stuck in self-defeating behavior.

◆ The most important question a prospective franchisee can ask when looking at franchisors is: are these the people I want to be in business with 10 or 15 years from now?

◆ Franchisors and franchisees must earn each other's respect everyday through actions and the adherence to the company's vision.

Chapter 8

Gauging Your Chance of Success

In This Chapter

♦ Naming the keys to franchising success

♦ What makes a franchisor great

♦ Asking the right questions

♦ The three most important strategic issues

♦ Why franchises fail

This section of the book is titled "building the nest" for good reason. In the past few chapters you've had to gather information about your dream to own a franchise. Like twigs, string, and other materials eagles use to build their magnificent nests, you'll take this information and put the pieces together to build your own safe space. All of this knowledge will give you a sense of security. As you continue going forward in franchising, you can return to this nest as you begin to fly upward and onward toward your dream.

In this chapter, you'll build the foundation for your franchising venture. I give you the tools to gauge your chance of success in franchising. You'll learn the most basic questions that must be answered before you become part of a franchise system, as well as which answers should satisfy you. I also cover some of the strategic or tactical issues you should be aware of as well as the reasons why franchises fail.

Your Keys to Success

Over the years, I've seen many franchisees—and franchisors—succeed and realize their dreams. And I've found that they share common features that help them become what I call "Franchising Eagles." These elements include …

♦ **A win-win attitude.** Franchising Eagles know that what benefits the franchisor benefits the franchisee, and what helps one unit helps the entire system.

♦ **Self-knowledge.** Success comes from knowing one's skills, habits, goals, and limitations.

♦ **A cohesive team.** The franchisor, franchisee, suppliers, business partners, investors, professional advisers, employees, and one's family and friends work together in a supportive way.

♦ **A quality brand.** Quality will attract and retain customers and give you a sense of pride in your business.

♦ **A growing industry.** Growth isn't based on trendiness, and there's still some room to increase one's market.

♦ **A suitable workplace.** Whatever the location, one's workplace is organized, inviting, and represents the brand.

♦ **A head for business.** Knowing how to operate and manage a business will help prevent fraud and waste.

> **Eagle Eyes** _____
>
> A hunger for knowledge is vitally important not only in franchising, but in life. To me, the search for knowledge conjures up the idea of the "eagle renewal." Every so often, an eagle will retire to a high cliff or aerie, where it will break off the calcified portions of its beak or talons. It will also pull out some feathers, too. This leaves it quite vulnerable. When it heals and leaves this aerie, though, it'll be able to soar to new heights, thanks to its renewal. Keep this image in mind as you learn new skills and information, no matter what the context.

◆ A hunger for knowledge. Franchising eagles make the most of their training and networking opportunities and realize that there's always more to learn. In fact, learning must become a lifelong quest. Remember: a stream does not rise higher than its source, so fill yourself with knowledge and you'll lift yourself up.

◆ Social skills. Franchising will challenge your ability to create and maintain working relationships with your franchisor, *brother or sister franchisees*, customers, and vendors. This is paramount and one of the prerequisite skills you'll need to succeed.

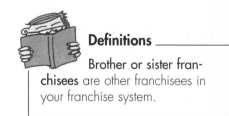

Definitions

Brother or sister franchisees are other franchisees in your franchise system.

◆ A nest egg. Those who are successful have enough capital to grow the business and take care of living expenses at home.

◆ Courage and stamina. Opening or taking over a franchise is hard work, especially at the beginning.

◆ Long-term vision. Franchise agreements typically last between 15 and 20 years, so you must be in it for the long haul.

◆ Motivation. You may get into franchising for your own, unique reason, but whatever it is, you should be motivated to succeed.

◆ A dream. I've never seen anyone succeed without a dream and the desire to make it come true. Everything begins with a dream.

Look over this list one more time—these ideas can't be stated often enough. These keys to success will have a big impact on how well you do in franchising, and how well you do in franchising will have a big impact on your life.

Characteristics of a Successful Franchisor

When you're looking at prospective franchisors, you need to know what to look for. Keep these characteristics in mind as you do your research.

Well-managed franchisors have …

◆ A good product or service with a high reputation. The brand must be built on something solid.

◆ Broad geographic appeal. Your brand is worth more if more people across a wide area recognize it.

◆ Broad market appeal. The brand shouldn't depend on a narrow or elite customer base.

◆ Growth potential. Sales and development shouldn't be maxed out as you buy in.

◆ Utilization of trends, not fads. The brand must capitalize on upward trends, not fleeting fads.

◆ A well-developed support system. It's in the franchisor's best interests to see that each unit within the system is supported properly.

◆ Money. The franchisor must have enough capital to develop the system securely and at a healthy pace—and still keep an eye on trends and market enhancements that can increase the value of the brand.

Aviary Alert

One of the primary reasons for both franchisee and franchisor failure is undercapitalization. In the franchisor's case, it doesn't have enough money to support its existing franchisees, develop new franchisees, and sustain a healthy system. A franchisor should never be dependent on the fees from franchise sales to offset the cost of operational support. Royalty income should cover the basic operations of the franchisor unless the system is dependent on product sales instead of royalties. Enough working capital should be there to support the system well before these two lines converge.

◆ Excellent training and ongoing support. Training and support are how franchisors convey their mission, operating system, and culture to their franchisees.

◆ Continual research and development. The franchisor is committed to offering the most up-to-date products and utilizing innovations within the system.

◆ A concern for individual unit economics. The franchisor should be committed to assist each unit to perform at its peak and attain profitability.

I've set the bar pretty high, but successful franchisors will be able to meet these standards for most franchisees. (But remember—both franchisees and franchisors must do their part.) Look for these criteria when you're looking at franchise systems to buy into. If you're thinking about turning your own business into a franchise, make sure you've covered these points, too.

Asking the Right Questions

The questions one can ask about franchising are endless, and I've already posed many of them in previous chapters. However, there's a reason why I've done so. Getting information up-front, before you sign a franchise agreement, is critical. You need to go into business with your eyes wide open, both about the franchise and about your personal situation.

Questions About the Franchisor

There are many questions the franchisee can ask about the franchisor. They can be addressed directly to the franchisor, other franchisees, or both, since what is promised by the franchisor (or what the franchisee assumes the franchisor has promised) may not be what the franchisor delivers. The answers may also be in the UFOC. Regardless of where the information comes from, the prospective franchisee should answer these questions before getting serious about signing on. Some of the most basic questions you should ask about the franchisor are …

- What experience does the franchisor have?
- Does this experience lessen the risk of starting a business?
- How will I be trained, and by whom?
- Who are my suppliers, support staff, employees, and customers?
- How will the company support the development of my business?
- How are my franchise fee and royalty payments utilized by the franchisor?
- What advantage do I receive from the brand recognition and development?
- Who will select the site?
- Can I relocate my franchise?
- How can I renew my agreement or terminate it?
- How can I transfer the rights to my franchise?

Questions to Ask Current and Former Franchisees

Since you must be well informed about all aspects of investing in a franchise system, it's a good strategy to contact other franchisees within the system. You'll find their phone numbers and addresses in the UFOC, and you should contact at least 10 of them for their take on the franchisor. This type of personal input is essential for making a wise decision about the future course of your franchise career.

- Did the franchisor do everything promised?

- Were your financial expectations met?

- Was the total initial investment about what you planned?

- How long was it before your revenue covered all your expenses and reasonable compensation for yourself? Was that what you expected?

- Are you thinking of opening additional units? Why?

- Have you closed any units? Why?

- If you had it to do all over again, would you invest in this franchise?

As I said, there are endless questions you can—and should—ask about a franchisor before becoming involved with it. If you aren't happy with some of the answers, make note of your reservations and continue doing your detective work. With so many franchising opportunities out there, you can find the right system for you, one that makes you feel confident and proud to be associated with it. You don't have to settle for a franchise system that you aren't completely comfortable with.

Questions for Oneself

Prospective franchisees should ask themselves these questions—and should answer yes to all of them:

- Can I work within and conform to an established system?

- Can I follow rules?

- Am I comfortable with taking this risk?

- Am I ready for this long-term commitment?

- Do I like the people I'll work with?

- Have I talked to other franchisees?

- Do I have sound legal and financial advice?

- Can I afford to do this?

- Will I want to do this in 10 years?

- Will I enjoy this?

- Does my family support my ambitions?

- Do I have a dream?

If you have reservations about any of these issues, think about how you can overcome them. In some cases, you just haven't found the right opportunity yet, or perhaps the timing just isn't right. Keep looking and working toward your dream—you'll get there, even if it is later rather than sooner.

Strategic and Tactical Issues

In addition to the questions that address the franchisor's track record and your own attitude, you should be aware of the more long-term strategic and tactical issues that affect the franchise business. Although some issues may be unique to a particular industry—such as how to deal with various regulations—others will apply to most franchise systems. For example, every franchise system wants to capture its market and increase its market share. Franchises within an industry may go about this in different ways, but they will be—or should be—following a specific strategy with effective tactics.

Franchising Eagles

Dave Thomas was the founder and chairman of Wendy's Old-Fashioned Hamburgers, a fast-food restaurant franchise that specializes in hamburgers. But perhaps Dave doesn't need an introduction. He was the public face of Wendy's in his more than 800 commercials for his business. At the beginning of his career, Dave was a franchisee who owned four Kentucky Fried Chicken franchises. He opened his first Wendy's in Columbus, Ohio, in 1969, and the rest is history. At the time of his death in 2002, there were more than 6,000 Wendy's restaurants operating in North America.

I think Dave had the right idea when he said: "It all comes back to the basics. Serve customers the best-tasting food at a good value in a clean, comfortable restaurant, and they'll keep coming back."

Dave Thomas was a true Franchising Eagle. He was committed, personable, and focused on the right stuff—the basics.

In my nearly 30 years in franchising, with the last 11 years as a chairman and CEO, I've followed a very simple leadership strategy that has three basic components.

First, I hire the right people and put them in the right places in the company. I try to hire people who are smarter or stronger than me in areas in which I'm limited, and I try to learn from them. The entire system benefits when the best and the brightest are allowed to work without interference. People selection is always first and foremost; systems do not run people, people run systems.

Second, I allocate the right resources to the right places. If the research and development department needs more cash, I'll approve it. If more people are needed to staff the field support operations, I'll allow more workers to be hired. At its basic level, strategic planning is simply resource allocation. This means adding gas in the form of resources to the right engine.

Third, and this should come as no surprise to you if you've read this far, I keep the company's vision and mission out there, front and center, all of the time. This helps everyone in the company—including myself—understand what they're working for and why. It also helps build integrity, which is how companies with diverse functions and workers build cohesion. And it also reinforces the company's value system, a message that can't be conveyed too often.

So, find out what your franchisor's strategy is to build the system and maintain high levels of quality. Make sure that its tactics are honorable and effective, as well. Although this may seem to be a daunting task, remember that you are interviewing them just as they are interviewing you. Do not be shy about asking questions about vision, values, and execution. These folks will recognize a leader when they see and hear one: you.

Why Franchises Fail

Just as there are endless questions to be asked before committing to a franchise, there can also be endless reasons why franchises fail. However, I believe that there are three major reasons why some go out of business long before they should. This in my opinion applies to all businesses, not just franchises.

> **Definitions**
>
> **Servant leadership** is having others' best interests at heart, being willing to do more for them, and serving them. This is true leadership.

The first factor is a judgment error. This can be anything from having too little capital to stretching resources too thinly to hiring the wrong people. This type of error is sometimes reversible if caught in time, but not always. And after the negative repercussions become apparent, it's usually too late to do anything about it. As Robert Greenleaf writes in his work on *servant leadership*, leaders should become more "aware" than others. This means you are constantly doing the environmental scanning necessary to make the right moves at the right time.

A second primary reason for failure is a development that affects the entire industry—and dooms it. Today, this often is referred to as "being disintermediated." This tends to come from technological shifts that make some products or services obsolete. Imagine being in the cassette tape–manufacturing business when CDs hit, or in the buggy-whip business when autos arrived. You'd have to change the entire company on a dime or go bust, two options that are less than desirable. The rise and acceptance of the Internet and other technologies have produced countless ripple effects that businesses must contend with to prevent becoming obsolete.

The third primary reason why franchises fail, as I see it, is a lack of integrity and values. A successful franchise has a solid foundation and all of its parts work together. The parts—and people—are interdependent, not independent or working at cross-purposes. A strong sense of values also runs through the system and affects decisions ranging from how people will be treated to how money will be invested. This integrity ultimately shows up in the individual franchises as a solid product or service, great customer satisfaction, and happy, motivated employees—and franchisees.

I suspect that had these kinds of foundational values been fully understood in the boardrooms of Enron, ImClone, and other corporations, a host of recent spectacular meltdowns might have been avoided.

The Least You Need to Know

- One of the primary reasons for both franchisee and franchisor failure is under-capitalization.

- Every prospective franchisee should ask a lot of questions before getting involved in a franchise. Seek out information from the franchisor, other franchisees, those who have done business with that brand or industry, and other sources. Doing some soul-searching will help, too.

- My simple leadership strategy is to hire the right people for the right positions, allocate the right resources to the right places, and continually convey the vision of the business.

- Businesses generally fail because of a judgment error, having one's product or service become obsolete, or a lack of core values.

Part  3

Learning to Fly

To get your business off the ground, you need to learn how to fly. In franchising, you'll go from being a private individual to being a member of a larger franchising system that's set up to build brand awareness and deliver superior products and services to your customers.

In this section, I explain what you need to breathe life into your franchise unit. You need to fund your business, because many new business owners fail when they don't have enough capital to keep the business running until it can turn a profit. I also discuss a significant aspect of franchising, one that gives franchisees an advantage over independent entrepreneurs—the franchisor's training program. In addition, I explore how you can evaluate sites for your business and what your franchisor will have to say about it. Finally, I look at how you can supply your business so that you can deliver great goods and services to your customers.

Getting Creative with Your Financing

In This Chapter

- ◆ Calculating the costs
- ◆ Finding funds
- ◆ Developing a business plan
- ◆ Talking to financers
- ◆ Can franchisees predict their income?

I know I've written about dreams and soaring eagles and integrity and trust when discussing franchising. These ideas point out the fact that franchising is a business relationship between people, and this relationship must be recognized and nurtured throughout the course of the partnership.

However, franchising is also a business, and being fully aware of the financial details is absolutely important. It's hard to nurture a relationship if you've risked your life savings—and then some—and are working like crazy to make a return on your investment. So you've got to take care of your business because after all, it's *your* business. You are the owner and you're responsible for making it work.

In this chapter, I cover some of the financial issues you need to know when starting out in franchising, and how they affect you throughout your enterprise. I look at the costs, how you can come up with money to launch your venture, and why a business plan is so important. I also discuss income issues and how to avoid going into debt.

However, this is just an overview of the numbers you need to know. Just as I believe that you need an experienced franchise lawyer on your side when looking at the UFOC and franchise agreement, I believe that you need an expert accountant to help you decipher the financial issues involved in franchising.

What'll It Cost You?

Every franchise relationship contains an exchange of money. The franchisee pays an initial franchise fee for the right to operate the business, while the franchisor hands over the business model and support that will enable the franchisee to get started and create a successful business.

However, the initial franchise fee isn't the only cost to the franchisee. In addition, other fees, training expenses, and start-up costs will have to be paid. The amount of the initial investment should be listed in the UFOC and franchise agreement. These numbers should be analyzed closely; although they're estimates, they should be based on hard facts and figures.

As you read through these fees and expenses, remember that you'll need to cover them—or at least cover a portion of them, and finance the rest—and then have something to live on while your business takes off. I generally advise that you have 6 to 12 months of your living expenses saved up, but this depends on your personal situation and what type of business you're running.

Eagle Eyes

The Federal Trade Commission's publication "A Consumer Guide to Buying a Franchise" provides a good overview of the financial issues prospective franchisees face. You can find it in Appendix C, but it can be downloaded at www.ftc.gov/bcp/conline/pubs/invest/buyfran.htm.

You'll find the initial franchise fee in Item 5 of the UFOC, and I'm sure this number popped out at you when you read it. This fee allows you to purchase the right to do business as a franchisee of a specific company. This is the price of admission to the game, and nothing more. You may be impressed by a low franchise fee, but be warned: an inexpensive franchise fee may not be a bargain. You must determine what you'll get for your buck. If you have a low fee, but have to pay extra for a host of other services, you aren't getting a bargain. And note, too, that this fee is, most often, nonrefundable. If you have buyer's remorse after signing your agreement, you must still go ahead with your plans.

> **Eagle Eyes** _____
>
> Initial franchise fees can vary considerably. An established franchise outlet in a mature system will be more expensive, while building your own unit in an up-and-coming system will generally have a less expensive initial franchise fee. If you have limited funds to invest up front, you should consider getting involved with a younger but more affordable franchise system, or a mature system that has a lower cost of entry. Your brand recognition might not be as high, but you can find opportunities to grow with the system. Or you may catch a rising star. Wouldn't you like to have been one of the first McDonald's franchisees?

While you're operating your business, the franchisee will usually pay the franchisor an ongoing royalty fee. It can be based on a percentage of one's revenues, usually about 3 to 8 percent, or it can be a fixed amount based on other considerations. You'll find this information in Item 6 of the UFOC. This money can and is often invested in the company in research and development programs, training services, technology upgrades, or other updates that will ultimately benefit the entire system. To find out what the typical royalty fees are in your targeted industry, search the franchise database at www.franchise.org, which is searchable by industry category.

Be aware of how this royalty fee is calculated. If you have to pay royalties even if you aren't generating net income, there will be a drain on your resources. You will be paying for the right to do business under the franchisor's name, even if you aren't making a profit.

> **Definitions** _____
>
> If a franchisee wishes to sell his or her unit to a new owner, a **transfer fee** is paid to the franchisor.
>
> If, at the end of the term of the franchise agreement, a franchisee wishes to sign a new agreement, a **renewal fee** is paid to the franchisor.

Additional fees can also be found in Item 6 of the UFOC. You can expect to pay into an advertising fund, even if it appears you may not benefit from it. You may have to pay extra for training or other services. If you are audited by the franchisor, you may have to take care of those costs, too. *Transfer fees* and *renewal fees* are also listed here.

Another varied—but highly important—cost relates to construction of your shop, restaurant, or office. If you'll be working at home, this can, of course, be next to nothing. However, if you'll need to build a new unit in a desirable part of a hot market, expect this cost to be significant. Then add in all of the expenses related to this: the real estate agent's services, the lot, architect's fees, licenses, contractor, materials, equipment, landscaping, and so on. Even if you are remodeling an existing building and not starting from scratch, you'll still need to cover a number of these costs.

You'll find some of these costs in Item 7 of the UFOC, but this may be an unreliable number. Remember—these numbers are estimates, and your location's commercial property prices may differ drastically. Talking to franchisees currently in the system can help you verify these costs.

Franchising Eagles

Although getting started in franchising involves crunching a lot of numbers, it's also a business made up of people. And one of the most dominant personalities in franchising was Bill Rosenberg, the founder of Dunkin' Donuts. He began his business in 1950, and now the brand has more than 6,000 outlets in 30 countries, and is a leading retailer of donuts, coffee, and bagels.

Beyond Rosenberg's business success, which was considerable, Rosenberg was successful in other areas. He was the founder of the International Franchise Association, which you by now know well. (If not, refer back to Chapter 3, where I discuss this organization at length.) He owned Wilrose Farm, which became the top stable in New England, and then donated the farm to the University of New Hampshire in 1980. Fourteen years later, the university sold the farm and endowed the William Rosenberg Chair in Franchising and Entrepreneurship, the first such faculty position in the university world.

Rosenberg's philanthropy didn't end there. In addition to his many charitable contributions, in 1986, he established the William Rosenberg Chair in Medicine at Harvard Medical School through the Dana Farber Cancer Institute, and in 1999 he assisted in funding the Vector Laboratory at the Harvard Institute of Human Genetics in Boston.

Bill Rosenberg died in 2002, but he was a true Franchising Eagle.

Also, remember that this agreement will serve you for many years to come, and during this time you'll likely see many changes in your business. For example, décor will change with the times, and currently emerging technologies will become standard in business in the future. The UFOC and the franchise agreement should spell out who will be responsible for covering various costs related to upgrades. This isn't something that you can predict with much certainty now, but you should be aware of this issue as it will affect you in the future.

Be aware that in many instances you may not be buying outright the site of your business. You may be leasing it from the franchisor or other leasing agents for the duration of your agreement. Be warned that while this will save you money up front, when you're at the end of your franchise agreement, you won't own your building or site. This may be a benefit, and it may not be. When or if you do sell your franchise, your assets may not include real estate.

Other initial costs found in Item 7 of the UFOC are your additional start-up costs, and they include things that you probably overlooked—signage, labor, insurance, inventory, equipment, computers, utilities, taxes, licenses, professional fees for a lawyer and accountant, business-support expenses, supplies, and so on. These are all estimates, and should be examined closely. Add in your own living expenses while your business gets going, and you can sometimes have a hefty bill in your hand. In addition, note that it will take time to set up your business, so calculate your costs from the time you receive the UFOC to the time you celebrate your grand opening—and then keep counting.

Eagle Eyes

I have much more to say about how you can get creative with your location and maximize your investment in Chapter 11. You may be able to reduce your costs by securing a nontraditional site for your business. You will have more options than you realize.

Aviary Alert

Remember to match the information in the UFOC to the information in the franchise agreement. The terms should be the same. If there are discrepancies, have your attorney ask about the differences. In addition, take a second look at Item 9 (the franchisee's obligations) and Item 11 (the franchisor's obligations) of the UFOC for each party's responsibilities in this venture. Then check this against the franchise agreement, too.

A good CPA will be able to help you understand these expenses so that you go into franchising with your eyes wide open.

Raising Capital

If you've got sticker shock over the amount of *working capital* you'll need to begin franchising, you may get some comfort from the information I present in this section.

Definitions

The amount of money you'll need to fund your business until it begins generating income is called **working capital**. This is usually an estimated amount.

Liquid is cash on hand.

Because even though it will cost money to be admitted to the franchising community, there is available money out there for you. You just have to know where to look. A franchisor will usually ask that you have about 20 to 50 percent of your start-up costs *liquid* while you finance the rest.

You can find sources of capital in a number of places, which I cover in this section. I discuss financing later in this chapter.

However, let me back up a bit. It's important that you get your personal finances in order, not only so that you know how much money you can invest, but also how much you can afford to lose. Any lender will want to know about your credit history and finances, so make sure you have a clean credit history.

You may have to part with a significant amount of your personal savings to get involved in franchising. If you've built up a nest egg over the years, you'll probably tap into it now. However, don't tap into it so far that you risk your family's future unless you are absolutely comfortable with that kind of risk. You may want to set up separate accounts for your kids' college education so that you don't—however unintentionally—leverage their future.

Aviary Alert

When coming up with your investment, do not touch your credit cards. Don't expect to finance your business or your living expenses with plastic at high interest rates. This should be self-evident, but when times get tough it can be tempting. However, it's a terrible idea. I've observed this happen through my years in business, but it isn't okay just because you can do it.

You may also have other sources of wealth that you can use as private equity. A common strategy is to refinance your home or obtain a home equity loan to make more money available to you now. However, don't drain all of the equity from your home. If you need to take out another line of credit in the future, you should have at least 25 percent of your home's value intact.

In addition, you can sell other assets, such as stocks or bonds in your portfolio, collectibles, property, jewelry, or anything else to come up with your start-up cash. You can ask friends or family members to help you get started, but this should be done with caution. Draw up an agreement between you and your relative or friend, and make sure you stick to it.

> **Eagle Eyes**
>
> A former employer may inadvertently assist you in getting started in franchising. If you've been laid off you may have money from your severance package. In addition, some retirees can take money out of their IRAs or 401(k) plans to come up with liquid capital. Although this may not work for everyone, the Entrepreneur Rollover Stock Ownership Plan (ERSOP) may be the right option for you. Your accountant should be able to help you decide if you qualify and if this would be a good move.

Overall, consult your accountant and review all of your sources of capital before doing anything. There are tax implications and other considerations that a professional will foresee, while you may not.

Writing a Business Plan

Now that you're gathering numbers and brainstorming about how you're going to make your venture happen, it's a good time to sit down and develop a business plan. Some franchisees feel that if they're buying a franchisor's business model they're also buying the franchisor's business plan, but this isn't true. Other franchisees may feel that they can wing it without a business plan and make it up as they go along. However, this is a big mistake that many prospective franchisees make.

Business plans help you clarify your thoughts and strategy, get a handle on your finances, and set some goals. It's absolutely imperative that you have a sound business plan to take to possible investors so they can look at what they're buying into.

Fortunately, business plans aren't terribly difficult to write, and if you've gotten this far in your search for a franchise, you most likely have many of the pieces for it right now. Although many of the numbers will be estimates and you may need to revise them as you learn more about your business and industry, your plan will help you focus on the practicalities of achieving your dream.

Your plan should include the following:

- ◆ **Executive summary.** This overview describes the franchise, its services or products, market, competition, and some financial data.

◆ **Mission statement.** This presents what you and the franchisor intend to do, and why you believe that this strategy will work. This can be a more personal statement that allows investors to get to know your background and ideas a bit better.

◆ **The business structure.** This section offers background information about the franchisor, its finances, and the history of the business. It also gives information about your personal and financial history, why you believe you would be a good fit, and what your investment is.

◆ **Industry analysis.** This provides necessary information about the industry you're getting into, your competitors and their products or services, which factors contribute to success or failure, relevant legislation or trends, and anything else you feel is needed to understand this industry.

◆ **Market analysis.** This section analyzes your customers, industry trends, a bit about how your marketing strategy will attract attention, and how your product or service fills a need.

◆ **Operations plan.** You can offer information about your vendors or suppliers, your staff, business hours, and services. Show that you have a thorough knowledge of what it takes to actually run the business.

> **Eagle Eyes** _____
>
> Why reinvent the wheel when you can learn from those who came before you? Franchisors often offer business plan templates that allow you to personalize their standard information.

◆ **Marketing plan.** This encompasses both the franchisor's overall strategy and your own marketing initiatives. Include information about your grand opening and how you will continue to attract customers. Your pricing strategy can also be presented here.

◆ **Management and staffing plans.** You can insert information about your employees, training, benefits, and recruitment plans. Add what you will contribute to the franchise, as well, and if you plan on being a hands-on operator.

◆ **Financing.** You already have some money to fund the business, but this section presents how you intend to come up with the remaining amount. Include projected profit and loss and cash flow statements for a few years, and when you intend to begin turning a profit.

◆ **Strategy and timetable.** This section describes what you intend to do, how, and when.

♦ **Appendix.** You can provide supplemental information such as newspaper articles, financial statements, or other documents to help build your case.

Once again, your accountant can help you verify the information in your business plan. You can also get advice from other franchisees, entrepreneurs, or business executives before you present it to a lender.

Talking to Funders

Armed with your own investment and business plan, you're now ready to seed your business with other people's money. This may feel daunting, but there is a pool of money out there that you can access. If you have a good credit history and a sound plan, you can start investigating sources.

Franchise Facts

It's true that getting a small loan—say, under $100,000—is usually more difficult than obtaining a big loan—say, anything over $5 million. That's because, from the lender's point of view, it takes about as much work to create a small loan as it does to do the work for a big loan. The return is bigger, too. However, if you are tenacious and are willing to look into at least three types of loan sources, you are more likely to secure financing for your venture.

One source of capital is a bank. Meet with bankers in your area and develop relationships with them. Find bankers that have invested either in your franchise in particular or in the industry in which you'll operate. Your franchisor or fellow franchisees may have some recommendations for you.

In addition, your franchisor may provide financing, which is presented in Item 10 of the UFOC. Some franchisors will offer some type of financing assistance, and often at competitive rates. It's a good option to explore if it's offered to you. After all, a franchisor wants you to have enough money to invest in the franchise, and can work with you to find the financing you need.

Eagle Eyes

Many franchisors can also help you finance your equipment or property, not just your initial start-up costs. Check with your franchisor about any programs that may help you get started.

The Small Business Administration (SBA) can guarantee loans, but does not actually lend money to small business owners. The most common loan is a 7(a)loan, which is provided by lenders who choose to structure their own loans by SBA's requirements and who apply and receive a guarantee from SBA on a portion of this loan. You can find more information about the SBA at sba.gov.

The SBA also guarantees other types of loans besides the common 7(a)loan. The SBA's CDC/504 loan program is specially designed for real estate or other fixed asset loans. These loans are ideal for franchises requiring extensive investments in bricks and mortar, such as hotels or restaurants. The 504 loans cannot be used for working capital or inventory. A Certified Development Company (CDC) is certified by the SBA. A CDC is a private, nonprofit lending source for small businesses, especially those in heavy industry and machinery. If this applies to you, you should look into this source of financing.

The SBA can also be a resource for those of you who are looking for about $250,000 to $5 million of seed money. The SBA Office of Advocacy works with the Securities and Exchange Commission to offer ACE-NET (www.ace-net.org), which links accredited investors with small businesses.

> **Aviary Alert**
>
> Venture capitalists, too, are other sources of financing. Many specialize in certain industries, but they do provide money for start-ups. However, they look for high returns and quick payback. And they usually will want a significant piece of your business, too.

In addition to working with a federal program such as the SBA, you can also look at what is offered in your state. Business Investment Development Companies (BIDCOs), for example, are available in a handful of states, and offer long-term debt financing that's backed up by federal guarantees. It will require some research on your part, but if this is available to you, you may want to look into it.

Another source of capital is to find a private investor, often referred to as an angel. You may know someone who wants to buy into a business, so you can contact that person. Some private companies also provide capital to prospective franchisees. You can find them under the "supplier forum" on the IFA website at www.franchise.org. In general, franchisees have an easier time securing loans than individual entrepreneurs because banks and private lending institutions will be able to check into the track record of the franchisor.

And don't overlook angel investors, individuals, or groups that provide seed money to entrepreneurs. However, investigate how much input they want to have in the company. Will they be hands-on? Passive? Provide advice? Or just get in your way? Even angels may have strings attached.

The last source of capital can be your family and friends. If you go down this road, be forewarned: it is relationally complicated. Make sure that you discuss all details before going into it, and then get all promises and obligations in writing. Then make sure you stick to the payment plan so that you don't destroy your relationship.

Although this is a lot of information to present in a very small space, you can wade through this alphabet soup of lenders and find the financing you need. And remember—you aren't in this alone. Your franchisor wants you to secure funding for your franchise, and they can help you either by financing your business, recommending companies or institutions with which they have relationships, or by being the "brand" that adds security and value to your venture. This diminishes your risk, and your financer's risk, too.

Eagle Eyes

Veterans, you're in luck. The IFA's VetFran program provides capital to invest in a franchise. If you can come up with 10 percent of your total investment, many IFA members may be able to help you come up with the rest. It's my observation that veterans make great franchisees. You can find more information at www. franchise.org.

Projecting Income

Although you may have an inkling of your potential earnings, setting this out on paper will help you get closer to reality. Again, the numbers you'll be working with are estimates, but they are based on real numbers from the real world.

An accountant and the right software can help you develop a projected income and cash-flow statement, but you'll also have to do some legwork. You'll need to determine all of your costs for the first two years and what you'll need each month to operate your business. Take into consideration rent (or a mortgage), inventory, payroll, taxes, and so on. Get it down on paper, even if it seems excessive. It's better to overestimate your expenses here than to have to scramble to come up with cash down the road.

You'll also need to project your sales for your first few years in business. You can get estimates from the UFOC or other franchisors, franchisees, or business owners in your industry. Be realistic, and account for variations due to season (if you're in the tax prep business, for example) and other business trends that affect your market.

The Least You Need to Know

- In addition to consulting your lawyer, you should work out all financial issues in the UFOC with an experienced accountant.

- In addition to the initial franchise fee, franchisees will have to cover other start-up and ongoing charges.

- Franchisees must come up with 20 to 50 percent of start-up costs and can finance the rest.

- Writing a business plan is essential to securing a loan.

- Franchisees often have an advantage in obtaining a loan because the lender can evaluate the franchisor's track record.

10

Seeking Training and Support

In This Chapter

- ◆ Why training is important
- ◆ How to assess the training program
- ◆ Getting trained before you open your business
- ◆ Ongoing support

Part of the appeal of franchising is that you don't have to come up with a new business idea or build your own business from scratch. When you buy a franchise you buy a complete business model, and that should include everything from the products or services one offers to the marketing materials to send to clients. A franchisee buys the entire system, from soup to nuts, and it's in the franchisor's best interests to supply a well-thought-out method of operating.

The key to this success is in the training and support of new and existing franchisees. In this chapter, I show what you should look for in a training program and how to determine if you'll get the support both before you open your doors and long after you've hung out your "open for business" sign.

Training Is Important—Not an Intrusion

When you buy a franchise, you buy an entire system for operating a business, from how to provide the product or service to how to market it, purchase your supplies, and calculate your revenues and payroll. It's a huge advantage that franchisees have over individual entrepreneurs who are building a business from scratch.

Training is the lifeblood of a franchise organization. It's the vehicle that ensures continuity from store to store and center to center, and it is the ability to replicate all of the systems that make a franchise unique. What happens at one store happens at the other stores. What keeps this consistent is the training.

> **Franchise Facts**
>
> Ninety-five percent of start-up businesses fail in the first three to five years, according to the U.S. Chamber of Commerce. One could draw the conclusion that this may be due to the lack of training, support, and experience that entrepreneurs need to operate a business. On the other hand, in a franchise, business owners receive this support from their franchisors. One of the reasons why franchising has been so successful in our economy has been due to the support that franchisors give their franchisees.

However, a franchisee is also buying much more than products and procedures. The franchisee is buying into a culture or a business philosophy. Learning about that culture is just as important as learning how to fry chicken a certain way or taking out an ad in the local paper. The culture should permeate each establishment and attract loyal customers to the franchise through its high standards and brand recognition. The culture or philosophy of each particular franchise system should be conveyed through its training program.

> **Franchise Facts**
>
> In my opinion, training doesn't just pertain to new franchisees joining a franchise system. There are actually four levels or types of training: for franchisees, the franchisor, the entire organization staff, and the franchisee staff. In fact, the whole organization needs constant training and ongoing, constant support. Franchise training has to be a long-term commitment developed as a curriculum, not as an individual event that begins and ends before the grand opening ceremony.

Therefore, it's important to get the most out of the training and support provided by the franchisor. This is true for franchisees who are just starting out in a specific industry and have to learn skills and procedures from scratch. Franchisees who have never managed people or run a business will need extra help in learning bookkeeping and other business procedures.

However, even those franchisees who have the relevant technical skills and a thorough knowledge of the industry will need to be trained. This includes businesspeople who are *conversion franchisees*. Although this training may feel redundant and unnecessary, it's important to learn the franchisor's method of doing things. This helps maintain consistency and high standards throughout the entire franchise system. It's also another reason why franchisees should be ready to follow rules and not work independently, no matter how much business or technical experience they have. Incidentally, this ability to be interdependent is why I believe that veterans make great franchisors—they can take orders and know the value of working within a system.

Definitions

Training is the instruction provided to new franchisees or to all franchisees when new products or procedures are introduced.

Assistance to up-and-running franchisees to help troubleshoot and tweak procedures is called **ongoing support.**

A **conversion franchisee** is an independent business owner who joins a franchise system and adopts the franchise's name and method of operation.

However, perhaps one of the most important reasons why franchisees should make the most out of their training opportunities is that they paid for it. Sometimes the training is included as part of the initial franchise fee, while some training may have to be paid out of pocket. Regardless of when or how it's financed, training is part of the franchising package, and a franchise unit can't be developed without it. The quality of the *training* and the *ongoing support* determines the success of the franchise.

Franchisees aren't the only ones who benefit from a thorough training program—franchisors should see training and support as integral parts of their business strategy. It helps franchisees avoid making costly and preventable mistakes, and ensures that all units within the system are providing consistent, reliable, and recognizable services and products. A franchisor's training program represents the successes, failures, and collected wisdom of the entire system. In my years in franchising I've found that successful franchisors are dedicated to training their franchisees in all areas of the business—and even put an extra emphasis on the business skills and expertise a franchisee will need to operate a successful unit.

Franchising Eagles

I've been fortunate to work with Heather Rose, first at Mail Boxes Etc., The UPS Store, and now at Sona MedSpa. As chief operating officer of Sona MedSpa, Heather has overseen and helped to create a number of training programs that have helped our franchisees reach top performance. At MBE/UPS, we carried out many innovative training and support programs, such as creating multitiered curricula for everyone in our system, including our franchisees, master franchisees, managers, and others who are affiliated with the brand. We pioneered an online campus for franchisees that was completely interactive and convenient for everyone. We had a franchisee advisory council that provided mentoring support for our franchisees, and our annual conference included more than 50 workshops, many of which had top franchisees on panels. According to Heather, "The educational opportunities were the number-one reason for attendance." What's more, we were the only franchise system to have our curriculum accepted by a university (the University of Phoenix) for certified educational units (CEUs).

At Sona MedSpa, Heather and the rest of our support staff are taking training to a new level. Because we are concerned with our clients' safety, we train in detail all of our franchisees' staff members, including their nurses, salespeople, and front office coordinators. We hope to have our program certified for Continuing Medical Units, the CEUs for the medical community.

You'll hear more from Heather later in this chapter. She's a true Franchising Eagle and an expert on the training and support of franchisees.

A franchisee should never see training and ongoing support after the business has opened as an intrusion or interference from corporate headquarters. And franchisors shouldn't believe that franchisees can keep going without direction and input. In fact, it is part of what franchisees pay for. An involved, proactive franchisor will keep all of its franchisees up-to-date on procedures and new products or services, as well as shore up borderline units within the system. After all, a franchise system is only as strong as its weakest link, and training and support is the key to maintaining high standards. Further, you do not want an untrained franchisee to ruin the brand that you bought the right to use.

CAUTION

Aviary Alert _____

I've found that experienced franchisees—in addition to novices—are in need of constant training. In fact, franchisees who own and operate multiple units need to be trained on how to do this, because operating three or more outlets requires specific skills, strategy, and insights. Commonly, a franchisee can operate one unit just fine. He or she then adds another unit by duplicating this system and that will work out well, too. However, add in a third unit, and the franchisee cannot just continue on as usual without it unraveling. A different method of operating and different skills are needed to make it work. Therefore, the franchisor must train the franchisee on how to operate multiple units.

Assessing the Training Program

One of the most vital components of the franchise relationship is the training program. It should be front and center during any discussion before purchasing a franchise. And all promises or claims should be put in writing in the UFOC and franchise agreement.

Still, the reality is often different than what is assumed at the time of the purchase. Training programs, just like franchise systems, differ in kind, thoroughness, location, and price. In fact, a training program can be the deciding factor when evaluating two similar franchisors. If one sign-making franchise offers a top-to-bottom, hands-on training program, while another just supplies some manuals and a 1-800 number for questions, you'll have a good idea about how each system treats its franchisees and what it expects from them. Generally, you don't want a franchisor to skimp on training and support, no matter how much experience you have in the industry.

A franchisee should consider the following points when evaluating training programs before buying a franchise:

◆ What kind of training is provided to the franchisee?

◆ Is training covered by the initial franchise fee, or must it be paid for separately?

Eagle Eyes _____

Generally, a mature system will have a better-developed support system than a new or smaller franchise. A mature franchise will have a system that's more standardized and comprehensive, because it will have more experience with all of the problems that franchisees encounter while setting up and running the business.

- Where is the training facility located?

- What kind of hands-on training is provided?

- What kind of support system is provided?

- Which staff members are included in the training? How do new employees get trained?

- Does the franchisor use its training and support system as a selling point? How much effort has been put into training?

- What do other franchisees say about the training program?

Eagle Eyes

Heather Rose, our Franchising Eagle for training and support, has many insights about how to evaluate a franchisor's training program. When I asked her for some tips, she offered some helpful answers. First, she told me to look at the quality of the instructional design and curriculum. The franchisor should care deeply about training its franchisees. Second, look at the length of the program. "In my experience, franchisees often think that the programs seem long, and they push back, thinking that it's excessive," Heather said. "But later, they'll say that they wanted even more training." Heather also advises franchisees to look at the level of support in the system, and the qualifications of the instructors. The balance of classroom to hands-on training should be about even. Franchisees should also think about support long after they open their doors. They should have regular support sessions, even if they're online, and they should have contact with brother or sister franchisees. Lastly, Heather said that franchisors should utilize new technologies—such as webcasts and online courses—but this should never be a substitute for in-person training.

- Does the franchisor provide instruction on business operations?

- Do any franchisees "flunk out" of the training program? If so, what happens to them?

- Who will be doing the training? Will any of it be outsourced to another company?

- Are there regularly scheduled conferences, seminars, or meetings?

In addition, make sure that all of the company's claims about training and support appear in writing in the UFOC and franchise agreement. It's easy for a franchisor's representative to promise extra services, but following through on them may be a different matter.

Although these aren't the only questions a prospective franchisee should ask about a franchisor's training program, these can help you learn more about what's being offered.

Preopening Training

Some of the most important—and intense—training happens before a franchisee opens her doors for business. This is when the franchisee learns the business inside and out, including technical skills and business operations. The franchisee will learn about building up the site, marketing, staffing, and sales. She'll also learn much about the culture and mission of the company as a whole.

What You'll Learn

There's a huge learning curve before a franchise opens. New franchisees must learn the entire business and be an expert before the grand opening celebrations. The franchisor typically offers a number of training components to help bring franchisees up to speed. Franchisees should look for these components when evaluating franchisors before buying into the system.

Perhaps most important, franchisors instruct franchisees in the technical knowledge needed to run the business, whether it's how to groom a dog or sell a house. Even if the franchisee won't be doing these tasks on a day-to-day basis, he'll need to know the core skills so that he can either pitch in when necessary or supervise employees who will be doing the work. Franchisees should also learn how to operate all of the equipment and software, not only to solve problems and teach others, but to understand how the business is run.

> **Eagle Eyes**
>
> In my opinion, training is most effective when new skills can be utilized immediately and applied to a real-life situation. Therefore, the training should be held as close to the opening date as possible.

Franchisees will also learn how to operate the business, including using accounting software to keep the books, pay employees and vendors, and set up business practices that keep everything running smoothly, with the right amount and type of inventory. The franchisor should also include information about vendors or suppliers and how to keep the right amount of inventory.

Franchisees will need help in selecting the site and turning it into an operational franchise unit. Some franchisors provide more guidance than others, but most will approve the site or help franchisees construct (or renovate or redesign) a building and obtain necessary permits and licenses.

> CAUTION
>
> ### Aviary Alert _____
>
> Some franchisors require their new franchisees to meet certain criteria before opening their doors. Franchisees should see this as a good thing and not as unnecessary nitpicking. By asking franchisees to attain a certain level of proficiency, standards will be high and the company's product or service will be trusted. This means that the franchisor cares about who is representing its brand. You, as the franchisee, should care as well. You don't want an unskilled or untrained brother or sister franchisee ruining the brand.

Hiring, training, and managing employees will usually also be covered by training programs. This is an important point for many business owners, and this "training the trainer" aspect shouldn't be overlooked by the franchisor.

The training program should also cover marketing and sales techniques. The franchisor should help franchisees target their market and then provide sales materials and tips for growing one's business.

Lastly, the franchisee should learn about the franchisor, its mission, culture, and staffers. The franchisee should feel like an integral part of a larger whole, and not as an independent unit only tenuously connected to a corporate parent. The training program is a great time to start building the relationships that will make one's franchise succeed.

How You'll Learn It

Franchisors can conduct this preopening training in a number of ways. Some franchisors have set up training facilities at their headquarters. The advantage of this arrangement is that training is standardized and franchisees aren't distracted by many of the other things going on in their lives. This also ensures that the franchisor is in control of the process.

Many franchisors provide hands-on training in other franchise units. There could be simply a requirement that a new franchisee work in another unit for a week or two.

However, others make it more formal. There may be a mentoring program, which matches new franchisees to experienced ones. After new franchisees undergo two weeks of training at corporate headquarters, they may be able to spend a week at their mentor's outlet to put this information into practice. This not only provides another training opportunity, but it also helps build relationships among franchise owners.

Some franchisors assign field support staffers to spend time at the new franchisee's site, helping to launch the business, train staff, promote and market the business, and make sure that the unit is up to standards.

 Aviary Alert

Although spending time at the franchisor's headquarters sounds like a nice little vacation, think again. Franchisees may have to pay extra for travel and lodging expenses. Get the details before you sign the franchise agreement.

Franchisors often provide written materials to help franchisees get set up in business. These materials can then be referred to as the unit operates. Videos, DVDs, websites, and other sources can help support a new franchisee run the business and train new employees.

No matter what type of training program you encounter, take full advantage of it. After all, you've paid for it, and your business depends on your knowledge, skills, and reputation. The best way to get up and running is to fully participate in every educational opportunity your franchisor offers.

Support After You Open Your Doors

Any good franchisor will be around long after the grand opening ceremony by offering continuing education opportunities. And any good franchisee will seek out ongoing support the franchisor provides to established units in the system. There are a number of ways this can happen.

At the top of the list is communication and participation. Some franchisors have regularly scheduled conference calls with their units, and this is a good chance to maintain contact with other franchise members and keep well informed. I've personally participated in webcasts and I've found that this technology is effective, too. Some franchisors have quarterly, biannual, or annual regional or corporate meetings. This is a great way to get to know other franchisees in person, recognize those with outstanding contributions, and learn more about the direction of the company.

> **Eagle Eyes**
>
> Your franchisor doesn't have to be your only source of training. For example, if the skills you need are generic to the industry, trade sources also provide additional training. Trade associations often have a number of offerings. For example, management training is available though the American Management Association, franchise-specific training is available through the IFA, food service training is available through the National Restaurant Association, and suppliers often provide training on their equipment or systems.

Many franchisors have a fully developed support staff that will check in on units and provide any guidance they need. This can be done by a field representative or another contact person. Again, this may feel like a franchisor is being over involved, but it ensures that all units in the system are operating as one. And, when you need help, it will be absolutely essential that you know this person and can trust him.

Any new employees or managers will need to be trained as they're hired. Some will be required to—or opt to—go through the corporate training at headquarters. However, others will need to be trained by the franchisee (or manager), so franchisors should provide instruction on how to do this. This "training the trainer" material is vitally important to keeping the business running smoothly, despite a change in personnel.

Any time a new product, service, or procedure is launched, the franchisees and staff must be brought up-to-date. This can be done via headquarters, regional field staff, or by disseminating new materials to the franchise units. This ensures that franchisees will continually upgrade their skills and keep up with promotional campaigns, product developments, and distribution specials. Some franchisors require that their franchisees become certified in the techniques or services offered by the franchise.

> **Eagle Eyes**
>
> If you're buying an existing franchise outlet, expect to go through all of the steps of training just as you would if you were launching the franchise. In fact, the franchisor should require it. You'll need to know the entire business, from top to bottom, and not feel that you can just step in and take over and all will be well.

However, even if a franchisor doesn't provide much opportunity for learning after the business has been launched, franchisees can still gain knowledge. As I explained in Chapter 3, the International Franchise Association provides online courses in everything from how to recruit talented staff to how to run *management information systems* that support the business. Many of these programs help franchisees earn *continuing education unit* credits.

After reading through this chapter, I hope you have a new appreciation for the training and support that's involved in running a successful franchise. I appreciate it, too, because it's how a franchise system ensures that all of its franchisees are operating properly, and with a common mission. In fact, I've found that training has taken on an increasing portion of the total franchise experience, one that has the power to lessen the risk of owning a business and increase your success rate. Make the most of your opportunity to learn.

Definitions

A computer system designed to help managers plan and direct business and organizational operations is called a **management information system.**

A **continuing education unit** (CEU) is a nationally recognized method of quantifying the time spent in the classroom during professional development and training activities.

The Least You Need to Know

- Training and ongoing support are critical components of the franchising experience.

- Training in business skills and procedures is becoming increasingly important for franchisees.

- All franchisees—novices, conversion franchisees, and those who buy existing franchises—must be thoroughly trained by the franchisor.

- Training can be complemented by ongoing support tactics such as workshops, regular conference calls, meetings, Internet material, webcasts, videos, and manuals.

- Training can include instruction at corporate headquarters, at another franchisee's unit, or at one's own unit.

Chapter 11

Picking Your Location

In This Chapter:

- How to find and evaluate a good site
- Input from the franchisor
- Building a new structure
- Home-based franchises
- Considering nontraditional sites

Although location won't necessarily make or break your franchise business, a good one will give you many advantages over competitors, while a bad location may force you to work harder to reach your customers.

In this chapter, I cover the basics on choosing your location, whether you'll be working at your kitchen table or breaking ground on an empty lot. I look at what makes a good site, where you can find help, what to look for in a lease, and also a bit about building your own structure, as well as nontraditional sites you may want to consider.

What's a Good Location?

There's no one "good location" that will serve any franchise. In fact, site selection is more an art than a science. I think that there are better and worse sites for you and your business. The same site you may succeed in might be terrible for a different type of franchise, or even another unit in your franchise system that's owned by someone else. The appeal of a location depends on what you need from it and how you run your business.

Eagle Eyes

A good location may be in a currently "bad" location. This is sometimes true with a currently operating franchise that's struggling. The business may be having problems for reasons unrelated to its location. The owner may not be the best operator, perhaps, or the service may be below the franchisor's standards. Find out what the problems are before you take over that location.

Generally, a good location is safe, affordable, and serves your business. If you will be in a retail business, you'll need to be near your targeted customers, be easily "findable," and provide lots of parking. If you're opening a quick-service restaurant, you'll want to be in a high-traffic location, whether it's in a food court at a mall or near a freeway exit ramp. You'll also want to have access to a pool of prospective employees—a high school will do. If you'll be going out to your customers—in a carpet-cleaning or landscaping business, perhaps—you'll need a very different type of location, one that is convenient for you and has appropriate storage space. If you'll be working at home, you'll need to set aside enough space to provide for a robust communications system, perhaps by putting in a new phone or DSL line. Each of these locations is good in its own way.

Researching and Evaluating Sites

Your first step in securing the right location for you is to locate and analyze your *territory* and identify the site selection criteria set out by your franchisor. Although franchisors vary in how involved they'll be in the selection of your site, most will specify your territory and the requirements of your site. Most will also want to approve your site as well. Your territory will be defined in your franchise agreement, along with the conditions assigned to it. You should know if you have rights to an *exclusive territory* and if or where there are other franchise or corporate units nearby.

Definitions

The area in which you will conduct your business, usually defined geographically, is called a **territory**.

An **exclusive territory** is the area in which you, and only you, will have the right to represent your franchise brand.

In addition to determining your territory and what your franchisor requires from it, you should make a list of what you'll need from your site. Don't discount your own needs. You may want to set up shop near your home or your kids' school, or in a neighborhood you're familiar with.

Be aware that the more popular or competitive the franchise system, the less likely you will have such choices. Some franchises in great demand may dictate your location, which may be different from where you reside. In fact, it may even be clear across the country if that's where the opportunity exists, and if this new location will help build the overall brand. For example, the area in which you live may be completely saturated with your brand, but the franchisor is interested in expanding in another part of the country. If that's the case, you may be asked to relocate to open your franchise.

Now that you've defined your territory, you're ready to start researching prospective sites. Your franchisor will probably give you a site selection packet that contains its requirements. You'll need to do your research, fill out the forms in the packet, take photos or videos of the sites you're interested in, and send it back to the franchisor for approval. Get ready to do some legwork—what's often known as "kicking the dirt."

Franchising Eagles

In at least one case, location led to the development of a franchising system—to the development of an entire industry, in fact. That industry is the convenience store industry, one that's based on selling you goods wherever or whenever you need them. 7-Eleven was there first.

"7-Eleven, Inc. operates, franchises, and licenses more than 20,000 7-Eleven and other convenience stores worldwide," James W. Keyes, president and chief executive officer of 7-Eleven said in an interview. "The business began in Dallas, Texas, 73 years ago when an employee named Johnnie Green began selling ice off a dock at an icehouse. He then discovered that they could sell other things such as bread and milk, which created a much better business that had a competitive advantage over other icehouses in Dallas. That humble beginning led to what we know today as the convenience store industry, and 7-Eleven is the clear leader."

In the case of 7-Eleven, it was a clever combination of products and location that fueled its success.

You'll want to look for traffic volume, whether it's shoppers in a mall or cars driving down the street. Check it out during different times of the day or on different days of the week so that you understand the traffic pattern and how it may affect your business. Make sure you're there during the appropriate time, too. If your business is primarily a morning one, do your research during your operating hours. Easy ingress (the entrance) and egress (the exit) can be very important.

You'll also want to look into the demographics and population density of the area. Are mostly families or singles living in the neighborhood? Are there many small business owners or large chain stores? Is the neighborhood on the rise, or going through a rough patch? Whatever the case, make sure it's a good fit for you.

Look at your target market and whether you can reach your customers at this location. Hotels must be where visitors are, and do best near business parks, airports, freeways, and convention centers. Pet groomers, on the other hand, will draw from a different market and most likely would not do well in those locations.

Franchise Facts

Quick-service restaurants, a category that includes fast-food and "fast-casual" restaurants, tend to do well where there are other established quick-service restaurants. In this case, there is safety in numbers.

Take a long look at your competition, too. Although you may not be the first ice-cream shop in the neighborhood, you don't want to be too close to your competition. If you can build in an advantage, you'll do even better. Perhaps you can locate your ice-cream shop near a park or playground, while your competitor is in a strip mall with a dry cleaner and an insurance agent's office.

Zoning can be an issue. You should find out—pretty quickly—whether the municipality will allow you to do your business in the location you want. If not, you may be able to apply for a zoning variance with the hope that the local zoning board will make an exception for you. If not, move on.

Parking is key, too. Customers may avoid your site if there isn't enough parking or they have to plug the meters every half hour. In addition, adequate handicapped parking is necessary, especially if you are in the health and wellness industry.

Eagle Eyes

One of your best resources is a good real estate agent who specializes in commercial properties. He or she will know what's vacant right now and why, and also what will open up in the near future. Your agent will also have connections with landlords and be privy to inside scoop on the local market. Many franchisors also have available real estate support personnel who can assist you in your search. Find an agent who specializes in "tenant representation"—that way they will be working only for your best interests.

A very important factor is visibility and signage. The local municipality may have restrictions on what kind or size you may use, and this could impact your business.

You'll need to be seen from the street—or the freeway, if you'll be pulling customers off of the interstate.

It's also wise to look at the mix of businesses in the area you're interested in, because you can maximize your traffic if you're catering to similar clients. For example, a Pilates studio, which draws mostly women, may do well in a strip mall with a vitamin shop or pharmacy, a coffee shop or café, a dry cleaners, or a health-food store.

When doing your research, look at your business from all angles, and consider other issues that may be decisive for you, such as security or the business practices of the landlord. If there are some drawbacks, perhaps you can find a way around them. However, if the site just doesn't work for you, keep investigating other locations. Deciding on the site of your business is one of the biggest decisions you'll make— second only, perhaps, to your decision to go into franchising.

Franchisor Involvement and Assistance

Almost all franchisors will have some sort of input into your site selection. Some may offer you guidelines, while others will send a member of their support staff to work with you every step of the way. You'll find their level of involvement specified in the UFOC and in your franchise agreement.

Most franchisors will offer you criteria for evaluating prospective sites and will approve your site before you sign a lease (or buy a piece of property). You'll have to do the legwork, and fill out and submit the site-selection packet, but the franchisor will indicate what to look for.

In some cases, the franchisor will try to interest you in a site they've already selected and want to develop. The franchisor may want to sell you a company-owned unit they want to franchise—what's called *retrofranchising*—or it may want you to get into a unit it's currently building. If this is the case, do your own thorough research on the benefits and drawbacks of that location. Just because the franchisor has approved the site doesn't mean that it's right for you.

Definitions _____

Retrofranchising occurs when a franchisor sells a company-owned unit to a franchisee.

Still, remember that it is in the franchisor's best interest to locate you in the best site possible so it's more than likely that it has done its legwork, too. In fact, the franchisor may have more information than you do on the demographics of various areas because it often uses data from research companies. This is one part of site selection that is a science, not an art.

Regardless of how you find your site, the franchisor will usually have standard floor plans, décor, and signage for your unit, and it can provide assistance on turning an empty storefront into a state-of-the-art franchise outlet. Some franchisors are more flexible than others about the look and feel of each unit, but there should be some sort of recognizable, standard exterior, signage, and interior to draw in customers. However, remember the power of franchising is in brand recognition, so it's to your advantage to have identical-looking units across the country and the world. If one or two or more outlets decide to change the look and feel of their sites, it will water down the brand and confuse customers.

Avoiding Cannibalization and Encroachment

When making decisions about setting up a new franchise, you want to find a good balance between supply and demand. In general, you want to have enough franchise units in your system so that the brand is recognized and customers can find you, but you don't want so many in your area that there aren't enough customers to go around. Sometimes, it seems, if you build too many, not enough will come. Although this is a valid concern, in general, unless a franchise has become a megasystem with thousands of units, this should not be a serious concern.

One way of protecting yourself is the right to work within a protected or exclusive territory. If you have exclusive rights within a certain area, the thought is that you'll work harder to build up your client base. What's more, you'll avoid competing with brother or sister franchisees that should be helping to raise up the entire system, not bring it down. This type of competition is called cannibalization, and happens when another store opens up in your vicinity and starts to pull away your customers.

CAUTION

Aviary Alert

Although you may be worried about a brother or sister franchisee opening up near your site, you'd be even more worried if a competing franchise in your industry opened up near you. That outlet would cannibalize your customers and increase that other franchisor's market share. Wouldn't you rather build up your own brand by "competing" with your own franchise, instead of your true competition? That way, the profits stay within your system, which gives you an edge over your rivals.

However, you shouldn't be too afraid of a brother or sister franchisee cannibalizing your customers. Although the second location will tend to pull in your customers, this is usually a temporary phenomenon. With time, both stores will be serving more customers than they had before. In this case, increased supply will also increase demand. And most important, the franchisor will also be advertising and marketing the brand to make it stronger in your marketplace.

Although it's usually an advantage to have exclusive territory, because this decreases competition from other units in your franchise system, exclusive territory doesn't always guarantee success. If you must serve a large market, it may be harder for you to reach all of your customers. What's more, your place may be inconvenient for many of your clientele, and they'll shop elsewhere— they'll get their coffee or lunch near their workplace, for example, instead of trekking across town to your franchise deli. In addition, your reduced visibility may also mean that you'll have reduced brand recognition as well.

> **Franchise Facts**
>
> A large, exclusive territory isn't always an asset. It's a fact that the greater the number of units in a market, the more successful each unit is, thanks to increased visibility, access, and shared marketing resources.

On the other hand, you don't want a lot of competition from other franchisees—or even the franchisor—and you don't want your protected territory to be chipped away at, either. This happens through encroachment, which is when someone else in your system begins operating on your turf. The franchisor may open up a company-owned unit in your territory or may sell your products via the Internet or through catalogs, which takes away from your sales. It may sell some of your products in other venues. For example, pound bags of coffee from your franchisor may show up on grocery store shelves in your area, which will decrease the amount you'll sell in your café.

When this happens, the franchisor should try to do what's fair and compensate the franchisee in some way. If you're concerned about this issue, check your UFOC and franchise agreement one more time and contact your franchisor with your reservations.

Research Tools

Besides getting out there and actually looking at various sites, working with an experienced commercial real estate agent, and coordinating with your franchisor, you should do your own research, too.

You can begin by calling or checking out the websites of the IFA, the Small Business Association, and the Department of Housing and Urban Development. You may also want to look at the trade associations in your industry. You can also obtain demographic reports from private companies as well. Consultants specializing in franchising site selection are members of IFA and can be accessed through www. franchise.org.

Leases and Leasehold Improvements

After you've narrowed your search to one or two places, you're ready to take a look at leases. You'll need a lawyer experienced in real estate to help you out, but you can get started on your own. Don't be shy about your intentions—being a franchisee can be an asset in this area. Many landlords appreciate the stability and track record of franchises and will prefer to rent to you, rather than take a chance on renting to a brand-new mom-and-pop store.

Commercial leases generally contain the following clauses:

- **Use of premises.** This states what type of business you'll run, and it's in your advantage to keep it as broad as possible so that you can add new products and services in the coming years.

- **Noncompete clause.** This will allow you to be the only store in the complex that offers your product or service.

- **Signage.** Make sure that the landlord's signage requirements match your franchisor's standards, and vice versa.

- **Cross-default clause.** You should be allowed to terminate your lease without penalty in the event you lose your right to operate as a franchise, unless the franchise assumes your obligations under the lease within 30 days and finds someone else to operate your store.

- **Assignment/sublease.** Make sure that if you sell your business to a new franchisee or if the franchisor takes over your unit, the new owner can take over your lease.

- **Termination.** Like any good agreement, you'll agree on how you can get out of it without penalty.

In addition, your franchisor may have some language or terms that it'd like to see in the lease. One of these clauses may be a collateral assignment, which states that the landlord must notify the franchisor if the franchisee (the tenant) is in danger of defaulting on the lease. This allows the franchisor to assist the franchisee to get back in good terms with the landlord and avoid being evicted. Sometimes, the franchisor requires that this clause is included in every lease to prevent eviction of a struggling franchisee.

Another issue at stake is leasehold improvement, defined as an improvement of a leased asset that increases the asset's value. For example, the franchisee may be renting an empty space, with only a main storefront, a bathroom, and some storage space. If the franchisee requests that the landlord build shelves, subdivide the space, or make other permanent changes, the landlord will assume the costs at first, but then pass on the expenses to the tenant (the franchisee) as increased rent.

In addition to understanding the terms of your lease, you'll need to have a firm grip on what it will cost you. Leases usually contain the following costs:

- **Base rent.** This is usually calculated per square foot, and can be compared to other tenants in the building or in other buildings.

- **Common-area maintenance.** This is usually calculated per square foot, too, and is used for janitorial services, repairs, parking lot maintenance, and so on. This can add up, so check what various malls and shopping centers charge their tenants.

- **Rentable square feet versus usable square feet.** Leases usually quote rent as so much per rentable square foot (RSF). You will pay rent based on this amount. Usable square feet (USF) is the RSF minus the percentage of the building that is used as common area, and this is the actual amount of space you will receive. This percentage is known as the "load factor" or "loss factor."

- **Leasable versus leased space.** If stores in a mall are empty, the missing rent can be passed on to other tenants in the mall.

- **Real estate taxes.** The property taxes of the mall or shopping center are also paid by the tenants, and this is also typically proportionate to the size of your shop.

- **Percentage rent.** Some landlords base an additional rent on a percentage of sales in your unit, which, if you're doing well, can benefit the landlord, not you.

- **Cost of living increases.** Some landlords may try to increase rent when the cost of living increases as well, but this generally is a disadvantage to the tenant.

- **Merchants association.** You may be asked to contribute to the merchants' organization in your mall or shopping center.

♦ **Relocation.** Some landlords retain the right to relocate your business from one part of the mall or shopping center to another part of the mall. While this could work in your favor if you are asked to set up in a more favorable part of the building, this could in some cases confuse your customers and decrease your business. Your location creates value, and a move may have a huge impact on your business. Be aware of your landlord's right to change your location.

Overall, it's a good idea to look beyond the monthly rent as determined by square footage so that you have a clear idea about all of the extras that will add up to more expenses for you. Before you sign the lease, make sure you know how much you will have to pay for improvements. A good lawyer or commercial real estate agent will help clarify these terms and costs for you.

Building a Location

If you decide that renting is not an option—or if the franchisor doesn't offer it as an option—you'll need to build your own structure on your own site. As you can imagine, this can be an enormous undertaking but, in the end, you will own your property and will be able to sell this asset if and when you choose to sell your franchise.

When you build your structure, expect a lot of input from your franchisor, which most likely will send a staff member to help you through the process. You'll need to cover everything from locating the right site to conducting feasibility and environmental studies, obtaining permits and licenses, securing the services of an architect and contractor, paying taxes, building and landscaping the site, and much more. You might consider hiring a construction management company to help you set up your location.

All of this will have to be done within the parameters set by the local zoning board and government, as well as your franchisor. However, if your franchisor has assisted the construction of other units in your area, you should get some good guidance and, like everything else in franchising, you'll be able to learn from those who came before you.

Working from Home

One of the advantages of franchising is that the franchise community is made up of so many different types of people, businesses, and methods of operation. Franchises can be as grand as a new hotel complex or as simple as a work-at-home situation that employs only one person.

Some of you will want to run a franchise business out of your home. You may want to be closer to your kids, or you may be sick of the corporate life and want to be independent. You may see working at home as a quick, temporary, inexpensive situation that you'll transition out of when your business grows and prospers. You may want the flexible hours that working at home sometimes offers, or you may just want to work in your pajamas every day.

Whatever attracts you to working at home, you should make note of what you will need to do to make a success of it. First, you'll need to establish a location. You know that it'll be in your home, but where? Your best bet is to create a discrete, contained space that's reserved for your business, and your business only. You can work at your kitchen table and keep your files in your sock drawer, but you can't stay on top of things that way. A business space will also help prevent your family from feeling like their territory is being encroached upon.

> **Aviary Alert**
>
> Before you invest in a home-based franchise, make sure that you're allowed to run a business out of your home. Many towns don't have a problem with most home-based businesses. However, you should check just in case, especially if the telltale signs of your business—a truck, equipment, or sign—are apparent to anyone passing by.

You'll also need to have the right office equipment. Although this may vary with the type of business you're operating, you'll probably need an extra phone line, Internet access, an answering machine or voice mail, a computer and printer, filing space, storage space, and business supplies. You'll also need to store the tools of your trade, whether it's dog-grooming equipment or beauty products. If you're located near a copying or shipping office such as The UPS Store, you won't need to race all over town to get your business done.

As many people have realized during recent years, working from home is an option that's just as fulfilling—and profitable—as businesses run out of office complexes or shopping malls.

Nontraditional Sites

One of the franchising success stories of recent years is the rise of the nontraditional site. You probably come across them every day, but they are a fairly recent—and lucrative—development. Nontraditional sites can be the cellphone kiosk at the mall, or the sub sandwich outlet at the grocery store, or the convenience store on a military base, or the Mail Boxes Etc. in the airport. These sites aren't typical brick-and-mortar storefronts, but they're doing great business by being innovative.

One of the advantages of a nontraditional site is its convenience. Customers will be able to shop at your business in places that are convenient to them. This helps a franchise system reach customers who aren't able to stop off at one of their other units.

 **Franchise Facts**

Getting started in a kiosk franchise can cost as low as $5,000 to $15,000.

Nontraditional sites tend to be less expensive than traditional storefronts. Kiosks and carts, for example, generally cost far less than a typical storefront. And, what's more, they can be moved to other locations. If one doesn't work out, the owner can take it to another location and become more profitable.

Nontraditional sites also allow franchisors to extend their brand reach into areas that are underserved by their brand. For example, many downtown areas lack franchise businesses other than fast-food outlets. However, this can be a great opportunity for franchisors, as well as for residents. Franchisors will conduct business where they once had little presence, and residents will be able to shop locally instead of going to other neighborhoods for various products and services.

Overall, nontraditional sites are a great way to get creative about meeting your customers' needs. If you can go to them and provide a quality product or service, they'll return to you again and again wherever they are.

The Least You Need to Know

- Location is an important element of franchising success, but a unit's lackluster performance may not be due to its location.

- An experienced commercial real estate agent is essential to helping you find and secure the right location for you.

- Exclusive territory isn't always a benefit to the franchisee.

- A smaller territory can make your individual unit more profitable because it will be more convenient for a concentrated customer base.

- Nontraditional sites offer opportunities in locations that many retailers have overlooked.

Chapter 12

Supplying Your Store

In This Chapter

- Why you shouldn't overlook your supplies
- The advantages of being a franchisee
- Your franchisor's input
- Finding the right vendors for you
- Making sense of invoices
- Tracking inventory

In this last lesson in learning how to fly like a Franchising Eagle, you learn the importance of having the right supplies at the right time. This subject often gets overlooked in franchising, because topics like the initial franchise fee and the power of franchising are attention grabbing.

However, supplies and suppliers are your lifeblood and require your attention. They're what you work with day in and day out, and with your expertise you'll take these items and offer them to your customers as finished products, whether they're sub sandwiches or engagement rings. Oftentimes your supplies could be the tools of your trade, such as the chemicals you'll use while taking care of lawns or the forms you'll use when filling out a client's tax returns. If you don't have the right supplies—or the right amount—your business can go south very quickly and your profitability will diminish.

In this chapter, I discuss how to handle your supplies, and how your franchisor may be involved. I also discuss how to read an invoice and track your inventory—two topics that can boost your revenues.

Why Your Supplies Are So Important

In business, you're nothing without the right *supplies* from *suppliers*. Your supplies make up the food you serve, the items you sell your clients, the tools of your trade, your office supplies, and your day-to-day business necessities. Even if you only rely on printer ink and paper, you still need those supplies to turn your ideas into a business-making venture.

> **Definitions**
>
> **Supplies** are the items you'll need to run your business, including the products you'll sell and items that are part of the structure, such as shelves, computers, etc.
>
> The companies that will provide you with your supplies are **suppliers**.

In franchising, supplies go one step further—they build consistency. Like your sign in front of your shop and the logo on your business cards, your supplies help develop loyalty to your brand. They're predictable, reliable, and in demand. In some cases, changing even one of your supplies—the sausage on your pizza, for example—could cause an uproar.

> **Franchise Facts**
>
> Frequently, vendors screen their customers to make sure that they have adequate credit and sound business practices. They may not offer their newest lines of products to their smallest or newest clients. In these situations, independent entrepreneurs are at a distinct disadvantage to franchisees, whose franchisor's reputation and purchasing power will speak volumes.

As a franchisee, the consistency of your supplies is part of your power. Because all of your brother and sister franchisees will be using the same supplies, you can concentrate your resources and purchase them in bulk from the best suppliers at the best rate. This consistency will also ensure that customers return to you—and other franchisees in the system—to buy precisely what they want. Given the choice between an unknown hot fudge sundae and one that they know and like, customers will most likely go for what they know.

Your Franchisor's Involvement

Looked at it in this light, it's no wonder why franchisors are usually involved in the purchasing decisions of their franchisees. You can find out how involved your franchisor is in Item 8 of the UFOC. There, you'll discover if you must buy your stock from your franchisor, from a franchisor-approved supplier, from any supplier that sells franchisor-approved items, or from any supplier. In fact, this is something you should talk about before you invest in the franchise so you know exactly what you're getting into.

Keep in mind that this level of involvement often differs according to the industry and the maturity of the franchisor's system. In some industries, such as fast-food or quick-service restaurants, the franchisor has direct control over supplies. This helps ensure consistency and quality—no surprises for anyone diving into a frozen yogurt from a franchise business. Other industries may not require as much control over the actual supplies.

Older, larger franchises tend to have better-developed systems of purchasing and distribution and are better able to assign staffers for these functions. They're working with a larger pool of money from a larger number of franchisees, so they are able to finance this type of function. In addition, these franchisors have years of experience and have established relationships with suppliers and distributors. (You didn't think that the importance and impact of relationships would end with the franchisor/franchisee partnership, did you?) Younger or smaller franchises may rely more heavily on franchisee involvement.

Besides being involved in the supply and distribution system, your franchisor will explain how you can manage your supplies. Ordering and receiving supplies almost certainly will be covered during your training sessions before opening your franchise. Most likely, your franchisor has set up a system you can follow for ordering, tracking *inventory*, receiving deliveries, and returning damaged goods. If your training doesn't cover these topics, ask your contact at the franchisor. You may need to talk to fellow franchisees to find out how they handle their supplies and vendors.

Definitions

The goods you hold before you sell them are called your **inventory.**

Buying Directly from Your Franchisor

Some franchisors require their franchisees to purchase their supplies directly from the franchisor. Similarly, franchisors may produce items and offer them to franchisees through specific distributors.

In both cases, the franchisee has no choice about his or her sources. However, the franchisee is ensured of purchasing precisely what the franchisor wants to sell, and exactly what customers expect. This usually happens when the items are *proprietary information* and specific to that brand. These items are integral to the business and can't be created by anyone.

This direct involvement of the franchisor has gotten a bad reputation, as some may feel that the franchisee is being taken advantage of. After all, if the franchisee has no choice in purchasing decisions, then he or she must be paying exorbitant prices for supplies—and the franchisor must be turning a profit—the thinking goes.

Actually, it's been my experience that franchisors are not in business to make a profit off of supplies. In fact, franchisees usually pay less for supplies, thanks to the franchisor's purchasing power. The franchise system buys in bulk. After all, it's in the franchisor's best interest to secure low prices for its franchisees and increase profits in each unit.

Another benefit to the franchisee is the convenience of this system. The franchisor has done the legwork—it has developed the products, created methods to reproduce them, and found suppliers and distributors. These are all functions that the franchisee won't have to do. And, what's more, this is part of what the franchisee has paid the franchisor to do. This frees up the franchisee to carry out other duties, such as serving customers and marketing the brand to his or her community.

If you are concerned about whether the franchisor is profiting off of supplies, take a look at the UFOC. In

> **Eagle Eyes**
>
> Some franchisors will estimate the costs of equipping the entire unit with their preferred supplier, but then allow the franchisee to use another supplier if he or she can meet the requirements and save money. The franchisee can go ahead with the best—and least expensive—supplier, but this is usually the one chosen by the franchisor.

> **Definitions**
>
> **Proprietary information** is confidential information that was developed by the company for use by the company, and only by the company. This can include trade secrets such as recipes, financial information, product designs, client lists, computer programs, and the operating manual.

it, the franchisor will disclose information about its supply and distribution operations. If you want more information, talk to your franchisor's representative before signing the franchise agreement.

Buying from a Franchisor-Approved Supplier

In this setup, franchisees may buy their stock from a supplier approved by the franchisor. The supplier has been vetted or cleared by the franchisor and will provide high-quality, consistent products. Here, too, the power of numbers aids the franchisee. If, say, 100 franchisees are all buying their ink cartridges from a specific supplier, they'll most likely pay less than an independent business owner who buys 1 percent of what the franchisees are buying. In addition, franchisees will most likely receive better service, too. Since the franchise will be sending a lot of business to the supplier, the supplier will make sure to take good care of the franchisees' accounts.

This is another efficient setup for the franchisee. The franchisor has found and negotiated with the supplier, leaving the franchisee free to do its own business. Although it may be true that some franchisors make a percentage off of these sales, it usually covers the cost of having to develop and maintain the relationship with the supplier. In fact, the franchisor and the brand becomes an attraction for the supplier or vendor. They'll have a larger account even if their profit margin is lower.

Buying Franchisor-Approved Products from Any Supplier

In this case, the franchisor has vetted certain products that the franchisee can purchase from any supplier he or she chooses. The franchisor must set up guidelines about what franchisees must look for, whether it's the quality of a product or the brand of the item.

Franchisees can find the most convenient or least expensive supplier to do business with. There's more flexibility in this system, but also more responsibility for the franchisee.

Although this may look good on the surface, there is a catch. In this setup, franchisees begin to lose their power in numbers. If 100 franchisees can purchase from up to 100 vendors, they'll become more like independent business owners who only purchase for their business. The price and service advantages of buying in

> **Eagle Eyes**
>
> You can find suppliers who are IFA members on the IFA website at www.franchise.org under "Vendor's Forum." If a vendor is a member of the IFA, it will have to adhere to the IFA's Code of Ethics, and you can be more secure in your business dealings with the company.

bulk shrink. Plus, this is more work for franchisees that often don't have time to spend on contacting vendors, negotiating prices, and evaluating products.

Another Option: The Co-operative

Franchisees can maintain their power in numbers yet be independent of their franchisor (perhaps) by creating a co-operative (co-op) organization. These are very diverse, and fit the specific needs of the franchisees, but what they have in common is that franchisees become members and buy their purchases in bulk. The co-op finds and negotiates with vendors to receive the best-quality products at the best prices.

Creating a co-op will almost always be done with the approval of the franchisor. The arrangement, if it exists, will be listed in the UFOC. There may be some requirements about membership, so discuss it with your franchisor.

Evaluating Vendors

If your franchisor doesn't specify which vendor you must use to source your supplies, you will have to find and evaluate vendors on your own. However, like everything else in franchising, you won't be completely alone. You will have the experience of brother and sister franchisees to draw on. You can ask other franchisees about their vendors, and whether they can make any recommendations. In addition, your franchisor will most likely provide you with some guidelines for products.

You will also need to know exactly what you'll buy—the brand or description of the item, the quantity, and the timing. You'll need to know when you need it, how often, and if there are any fluctuations due to promotions or seasons.

> **Aviary Alert**
>
> The lowest quote isn't always the best bargain. A less expensive supplier may be less reliable, deliver damaged goods, or add hidden charges it's not telling you about up front. Or the vendor may slash its prices to get your business, but then will raise them when it can't sustain doing business with you. Get a reference from a supplier's other customers to discover more about its business practices.

Once you know what you'll need, you can begin calling vendors. Give them the specifics of your needs and obtain a quote from them. Find out about their terms of credit (you may be asked to pay COD at first, until the vendors know and trust you). Ask about additional charges, such as delivery and handling charges. And let them know when you will be able to receive deliveries—you don't want to schedule deliveries during your busiest time of the day, when you should be working with customers.

When you have one quote, call another vendor for another, and when you feel you have enough information you can make your decision.

Receiving Deliveries

No matter who your supplier is, you will have items delivered to your establishment. Although this depends on the type of business you're in, you'll do best if you follow some sort of system for receiving deliveries. It's most likely that your franchisor will cover this in your training sessions, but you should remember to follow these general rules:

♦ Keep a record of your orders and know when they will arrive.

♦ Assign specific employees—perhaps yourself—to receive deliveries and train them on how to do it properly.

♦ Set aside a specific place for receiving shipments, one that doesn't interfere with your ability to conduct business.

♦ Watch the deliveries as they are unloaded from the truck and are carried into your place.

♦ Keep your receipt for future reference.

♦ Watch your employees empty or put away the boxes in the appropriate places.

Although this may seem like a lot of work to do when you're a busy business owner, you'll be rewarded for keeping a close eye on your inventory and deliveries. Your vendors will not be tempted to cut corners or mix up invoices or send you inferior products. Your employees will know that they must attend to this—and not try to pick up a few pieces of your inventory for their own use.

Understanding Invoices

You can keep track of your supplies in a number of ways—manually or with software—but you won't be able to get away from the invoice. This slip of paper verifies that you received the items you ordered, that all of them arrived in good shape, and that you will pay for them according to terms you agreed upon with the vendor.

When you receive your deliveries, you should have your invoice or delivery receipt. Check the date and address so that you aren't mistakenly receiving someone else's items. Make sure that the number of boxes matches your purchase order and delivery slip. Open up a box or two to verify that the items match the packing slip and are in good condition. If there are any discrepancies or problems, call your vendor immediately, before the delivery person leaves.

When you are finished receiving the delivery, keep the delivery slip. This protects you against any future difficulties with your vendor. It goes without saying that you should pay your bills on time and maintain a good working relationship with your vendor.

Maintaining and Tracking Inventory

An often overlooked but important part of your business practices includes maintaining and tracking your inventory. There are many different ways to do this, and your franchisor will likely train you on the system that it feels works best for your business. Again, this is something that varies with the type of business you're in. If you produce or sell perishable items such as food or flowers, your franchisor no doubt will have set up a well-defined storage system for you, and federal, state, or local regulations may also provide guidelines for you. However, if your supplies are less integral to your business, you may have more discretion in how you store your supplies.

No matter what you hold in your inventory, you should make sure that it is well taken care of and stored properly. Your customers should be able to purchase items that have been refrigerated or frozen according to instructions and be confident that the end product is safe for them to eat or use. Your employees should also be assured that they are working in a safe, clean workplace.

Just as important as how you store your supplies is that you know exactly what you have in your inventory. You need to know what is selling well, what isn't, and what you need to reorder and when. You'll need to know what you should order more of because of seasonal or promotional fluctuations. After all, you wouldn't want to find out too late that you're running low on gift certificates right before the holidays, would you?

You'll also need to know precisely what you have in your inventory for your regular bookkeeping and taxes. In general, you don't want to tie up too much of your money in your inventory. You'll want to carry enough inventory to meet your needs and have enough cash to keep the business operating.

There are a few ways to calculate the value and movement of your inventory, and I won't go into them in detail here. However, you should know that you can use a first-in, first-out or a last-in, first-out system to value your inventory. You can also utilize a just-in-time system to make sure that you're only holding as much as you can afford to.

Your franchisor should be able to guide you through this important aspect of your business. If your franchisor doesn't train you on this, consult your accountant or book-keeper for advice. This may not be your favorite aspect of running your business, but it's definitely a rewarding one.

Use Technology to Your Advantage

Although some of your supply management will have to be done the old-fashioned manual way, such as watching the delivery person unload boxes in your storage space, you'll be able to use technology to your advantage.

Some franchises use scanners to check in their inventory. They scan over the barcode and know precisely what is coming into the franchise. Then, when these goods are sold, the cashier scans the barcode again. This information is recorded in a database, and, thanks to the point of sale technology, the franchisee has an accurate count of what's flowing through the system.

Franchising Eagles

Technology is powerful enough to create a new service sector, that of fulfilling orders. For example, NuMarkets, a franchise run by Russ Grove, uses its original software to post, sell, and send items on eBay. In NuMarkets' business, clients bring their items to a NuMarkets drop-off center (the franchise outlet), where a representative enters it into the system, writes a description of it, takes a digital photo, packs it, calculates the shipping cost, posts it on the website, and then sends it to the buyer—and sends a check to the seller.

Unlike many businesses, 70 percent of the operations are done centrally with the franchisor's software. "This allows the franchisee to focus on his or her business and serving customers," said Russ Grove, president and CEO of NuMarkets. "Our franchisees' relationships with the community are important. They can live with the technology, but they don't have to know it. We take care of that centrally, and that makes us more efficient."

NuMarkets' process seems to be working. According to Grove, about 92 percent of the items they post are sold within seven days—that's about 120,000 items in the past 14 to 16 months that have been shipped to 51 countries and every state in the United States.

This is sometimes linked to the franchisor's system, providing much-needed information about purchasing habits and customer preferences. Although some franchisees aren't comfortable with this link, it can help build the system. After all, better customer data will enhance the franchisor's efforts to identify markets and reach out to them with specific products or messages, and this will help all units in the system become more efficient and profitable.

The Least You Need to Know

- A franchisor may create and distribute supplies, or approve certain products or vendors that franchisees must use.

- Franchisor control of supplies helps ensure that the franchisor's outlets are all producing items of consistent quality.

- Tracking inventory is crucial to being efficient and profitable.

- Having good point-of-sale systems can help franchisees and the franchisor know what their customers are buying, which can lead to better service.

Part 4

Flying Like an Eagle

I believe that eagles are the mightiest creatures in the sky. I also believe that franchising is like an eagle, a powerful force to be reckoned with. This power comes from franchising's relationships—between the franchisor and franchisees, among franchisees, and with all of the people who are employed in a franchise system.

In this section of the book, I look at how those in the franchising community can make the most of their powerful relationships. First, I explain how franchises market their brand and the unique advertising arrangement that franchise systems use. I take an in-depth look at some of the relationships that make franchising so vital and, sometimes, terribly complicated. And I also discuss how franchisees can hire and retain the best employees for their needs.

Chapter **13**

Marketing Your Business

In This Chapter

- What marketing is and why franchisees have a head start
- Examining an effective marketing campaign
- Franchising's unique marketing methods
- The biggest marketing mistakes you should avoid
- Attracting and keeping customers
- Is marketing worth the effort?

I may not know you personally, but I do know one thing about you: you aren't going into franchising because you need another hobby. You want to be a successful business owner, and you think that franchising is the best way for you to get there.

Frankly, I agree. Becoming involved with a well-operated franchise system has many rewards—especially financial rewards. However, even the best-run franchise is nothing without its customers. Therefore, no matter how many outlets are in your system or how amazing your product is, you've got to market your products, services, and brand. If you don't define your market and deliver products to it, your competitor will, leaving you in second place.

As you'll see throughout this chapter, franchisees have a head start in marketing, and they retain many advantages over independent business owners. That advantage is the structure of the franchise itself and how the system allocates its marketing resources.

In this chapter, I explain what a marketing strategy is, how franchises typically market their brand, and how you can avoid costly mistakes. In addition, I discuss how to deliver on your advertised promises, as well as how you can evaluate the effectiveness of your campaigns.

What Is Marketing?

Marketing is a term that's tossed around a lot but many people may not know exactly what it is. It differs from *advertising* and *promotion*. A *marketing campaign* or *plan* also differs from a *sales plan*, even though many executives confuse the two. This confusion can be a costly one.

Definitions

Marketing is a company's overall strategy for building its brand.

A specific strategy meant to identify and convey a message to a targeted market segment is called a **marketing campaign** or **plan**. It looks at present activities and the competitive environment.

A **sales plan** identifies the product to be sold to the identified market, how it will be sold, and where. This plan is developed after determining one's market.

Advertising is the vehicle through which the message is conveyed—through print ads, for example, or via billboards.

Promotions are temporary sales, offers, or gimmicks that encourage customers to buy one's products.

Marketing experts often refer to the "four Ps" of marketing, which are the basic elements of any effective marketing strategy. These are ...

- Products—having the right ones to fill a need.

- Price—assigning the right one at the right time.

- Promotion—finding the right message.

- Place—being convenient for your customer.

However, one expert I spoke to goes even further when developing a marketing strategy. When I was researching this chapter, I spoke to Kurt Shusterman, who was executive vice president of marketing at MBE and is now chief marketing officer at Sona MedSpa, for insights on how franchise marketing campaigns work in practice. You'll read Kurt's advice throughout this chapter, and his comments are very valuable.

Kurt knows all about the "four Ps," but he believes in the "seven Ps," which include the four elements I listed previously, along with …

> **Franchising Eagles**
>
> I believe that Kurt Shusterman is a brand-management genius. When MBE became The UPS Store, he presided over the largest brand change in franchising. He oversaw the conversion of 4,000 locations at one time, as well as all of the marketing and public relations issues that went with that change. His insights have proven to be key to that transition's success.

- The physical environment—the look and feel of the establishment.

- The process—how clients or customers are treated.

- People—both staff members and customers.

By looking at all of these elements, Kurt is able to create comprehensive marketing campaigns that account for everything from the overall message to the customer's shopping experience.

I asked Kurt about what he thought made up a great marketing campaign. First, he said, "everyone must believe in the message" and deliver on it consistently. Second, he felt that the marketing experts should be able to do their job without undo interference that could derail the entire campaign. Third, Kurt suggested that all of the various marketing tactics should be integrated so that there's positive synergy created by the marketing mix. For example, the national TV ads should have the same message as the local ads, the in-store promotions, special events, and product. In addition, the local franchisees should take advantage of their links in their community to do demonstrations or be involved in civic events, such as parades or other special occasions. Lastly, Kurt advised that franchises should market their message in whatever way is appropriate for their product or customer. For example, sporting goods shops should reach out to weekend warriors and athletes, not to junk-food-eating couch potatoes.

The Advantages of Being a Franchisee

Franchisees have many advantages in marketing their product or service. For one, they're harnessing the national (or regional) awareness of their brand, and this speaks volumes. When you're a franchisee, more people know about your mouthwatering steaks than just those who drive past your steakhouse. Potential customers from all over the country—all over the world, perhaps—will recognize your business, thanks to your franchisor's branding efforts.

Franchisees also have more financial resources than an independent business owner. Although I discuss this in more detail later in the chapter, it is important to know that franchisees pay into advertising funds and many franchise systems require that a certain amount or percentage of revenues go toward marketing and advertising. In addition, franchisees in a specific region can and do pool their resources to buy ads, which cuts down the costs for each individual franchisee while benefiting all units.

Franchisees are also able to utilize the experience and expertise of their franchisor. Most franchisors employ a marketing department made up of professionals who use demographic data, devise marketing strategy and campaigns, and test the brand's message. Most franchisees or independent business owners can't afford to do this, nor do they have the time.

Franchisees can also make use of the marketing materials provided by the franchisor. Many franchisors develop coupons, displays, banners, ad scripts, and other materials that help convey the brand's marketing message. Oftentimes, the franchisee can personalize these materials by printing its address and operating hours on fliers and inserts or distribute promotional items provided by the franchisor's marketing department. In this way, franchisees are able to integrate their local, person-to-person efforts with their franchisor's overall message.

> **Eagle Eyes** _____
>
> According to Kurt, if an outside agency is hired to develop and carry out the campaign, they should be paid—at least in part—on the results of that campaign. Develop some markers of performance, such as increased sales on the items being promoted.

> **Aviary Alert** _____
>
> Before launching your own marketing efforts, make sure your franchisor knows about your intentions. Most franchisors require that they review and approve of any materials that make use of their logo or trademark. Remember—the franchisee has the right to use the trademark, but he or she does not own it.

The image of the brand is set by the franchisor, but delivering on that image is, at least in part, the responsibility of the franchisee. For example, your franchisor can run national ads that highlight how much people enjoy your brand's mouthwatering steaks, but you'll have to make good on that promise. If you disappoint a customer, they may never come back. However, if you—or a brother or sister franchisee—match the experience portrayed in the ad, your customers will be more likely to come back again and again.

The power of franchising is in this interdependence of the franchisor and franchisee. Think about Kurt's additional three "Ps" of any marketing strategy—physical environment, process, and people. In many cases, you'll have a huge impact on how those elements are put into practice. You'll have control over how welcoming and pleasant your establishment is. You'll make your way through the process of advising your customers and selling to them every day. And how you treat the people who work in and come to your business should always be a top priority.

How Franchises Market Their Brand

Franchises have developed a unique system for marketing the brand. It's a pyramid structure, with three tiers—national, regional, and local. Smaller or newer systems often have two levels—local and regional—depending on the reach of their franchisees.

Each of these tiers has a different message and function. At the national level, the message is: *buy my brand*. At the regional brand, the message is more urgent: *buy my brand today*. And at the local level, the message is even more urgent and specific: *buy my brand today from me*.

In the best case, these three messages will be consistent and targeted to the right customers. For example, a national TV ad may promote your brand's new flavored coffee drink. Its underlying message is: Buy my new drink. At the regional level, a TV ad playing in your local market offers a discount on this new drink for a limited time. (This adds the urgency needed in a regional campaign.) Also at this regional level, franchisees can develop a newspaper insert with a coupon for the drink and the addresses of the franchisees. At the local level, individual franchisees can post the offer on the sign in front of one's shop and display a poster of the drink behind the cash register. Franchisees can even hire people to distribute coupons or samples anyplace there's foot traffic, such as the sidewalk, mall, or a special event.

> **Eagle Eyes**
>
> Keep this sense of urgency in mind when developing regional and local marketing campaigns. It's not enough to tell your prospective customers that you've got great products. You've got to tell them that they've got to have it now—from you.

In this way, customers see a consistent message and have an incentive to act on this message. Kurt likens this to a three-legged stool in which each leg supports and reinforces the other. If one goes missing, the entire campaign is in danger of collapsing. Franchisees can opt out at the regional or local levels, but they'd just be working against their best interests.

This system seems to be pretty unique to franchise systems. For example, a chain coffee shop may not offer this type of flexibility to the managers—not owners, as in franchising—of their local units. In a national chain, all marketing decisions are made by the corporation, and they must be carried out by their outlets. In franchising, individual franchisees or groups of franchisees can develop marketing techniques that will work in their local market, which is usually defined as the area within three to five miles of the franchise or three to five minutes from it. For example, if you're in a resort town, you may place spokespeople on the boardwalk, which attracts lots of tourists. If you live in a commuter town, you can post ads in subway stations or trains.

Kurt told me, "There's nothing else like this system. And when it works, it exceeds anything a corporation can do."

Paying for the Ads

A good marketing campaign will drive business to your door, but it doesn't come for free. Franchisees generally pay for these campaigns, either directly or indirectly. This varies according to each franchise system, but the details of your franchisor's advertising fees are included in your UFOC and franchise agreement.

In general, though, if you belong to a national franchise system, the franchisees will pay into a national advertising fund that goes to the franchisor. This goes to the marketing department, which develops the strategies and campaigns used on the national level. This department usually also provides the blueprints for regional and local campaigns, such as a newspaper insert template or direct mail pieces.

Franchise Facts

There are 210 designated marketing areas in the United States, and they're determined by the signal reach of local TV and radio stations. A marketing area defines a franchise region. So when franchisees take out a TV ad, they do so at the regional level.

Franchisors will charge various amounts for this service, but the fee is usually less than 10 percent of a franchisee's sales and revenue. However, according to a recent IFA survey, the majority of franchise systems require a contribution to the advertising and marketing fund of less than 2 percent of sales.

In addition, the franchisor may require that franchisees pay into a regional advertising fund, which goes toward ads in the local media market, what's known as a designated marketing area or DME. This, again, varies according to the franchise system, but in general, building regional awareness of your brand will help you capture your customers.

Many times, individual franchisees will band together in an advertising co-operative, which aims to produce and fund ads that will run in their DME. These co-ops vary according to the members' needs and the market, but most have boards that make the decisions about ad strategy while members pay into the co-op's funds. According to Kurt, this works best when there's a spirit of cooperation and no individual member expects to benefit more than another. The co-op is meant to benefit the brand, not the individual stores.

Last, but certainly not least, are your local efforts. This is where franchisees can really make their mark. Although you may feel tapped out financially after contributing to your national and regional marketing campaigns, you'll be happy to discover that you can get the word out locally without spending a lot of cash.

At the local level, you, the franchise owner, are your best asset. You can personally get the word out, whether it's talking to friends and neighbors about your new venture, getting involved with civic groups that bring you into contact with a lot of people in your community, or contributing to charitable events. In this sense, you represent your brand every time you're out in public. If you make a good impression on people, whether it's in a one-to-one situation or when speaking to a crowd, you'll encourage people to patronize your business.

Eagle Eyes

Franchisees make a commitment to a community when they make a commitment to a franchisor. They'll locate their franchise in a specific shop, and their franchise agreement usually lasts from 10 to 15 years. That's more of a commitment than the one made by a manager of a corporate-run chain. That manager may be transferred or leave the company at any time. Since franchisees are rooted in a specific community for at least a decade, they should be an integral part of it.

However, there are many other cost-effective ways you can advertise your business locally. You can take out an ad in your community newspaper, or in programs distributed at concerts, plays, or other events. You can hold weekly business card drawings for a free meal or other promotion. You can donate items to raffle off at a local event or offer a promotion with another local business owner.

Remember, though, that your franchisor will usually offer you guidelines for your local marketing efforts. It will want to either know about or approve of anything that has its logo or trademark on it. It will want to make sure that anything you do is consistent with its national efforts to market your brand.

Marketing Mistakes You Should Avoid

When marketing campaigns succeed, everyone benefits. Brand recognition increases and traffic to individual franchises increases, too. However, even the best thought-out marketing campaigns can fail. According to Kurt, there are a few common mistakes that franchise systems can avoid making.

- **Using the wrong medium.** If your customers are teenagers, they probably won't read your ad if it's placed in the business section of the newspaper.

- **Conveying the wrong message.** Your pet food may delight dogs and cats, but if your message is that pets don't have taste buds and might as well eat your pet food, you're not creating demand.

- **Putting together the wrong offers.** For example, if you're representing a high-end brand, you don't want to cheapen it by slashing prices to be in alignment with discount stores in your area. This will only confuse the customer.

- **A lack of trust.** Many franchisees feel that the franchisor is out to turn a profit on advertising fees. However, this money funds the marketing department, which should hire the best in the business. Their strategy should be trusted by individual franchisees, since it's usually based on hard data and has been focus tested thoroughly.

- **A lack of integration and coordination.** If the franchisor takes out a national ad, franchisees would be wise to build on that message in their regional and local efforts.

- **Overpromising and underperforming.** If the ad portrays the franchise as a clean, well-run, efficient operation that serves its customers well, and individual franchises are unwelcoming and serve inferior products, the reality won't match the advertised promises, and customers won't return.

In addition, I'd like to add that franchisees should give a marketing campaign a chance. Ads must be repeated many times before the message sinks in. If you feel that your advertising money is being wasted on ads that are replayed over and over again, it isn't. The message needs to be repeated to build brand awareness.

Overall, Kurt says, marketing campaigns work best when everyone is open to new ideas and can get enthusiastic about them. If a franchisee doesn't promote new products, or doesn't know anything about them and therefore can't properly sell them to customers, the brand will weaken. However, if franchisees are willing to try something new and be well informed about the newest promotions and products, the customer will be satisfied on all levels.

Serving the Customer

Think about those last three "Ps" that go into a marketing campaign—physical environment, process, and people. These three elements are all service oriented and directly affect the customer. If these three elements are disregarded, believe me, your customers won't return even if you have the cleverest ads that run during the Super Bowl half-time show. Fortunately, the franchisee has a lot of control over these three service-related elements.

Let's start with the physical environment. Most likely your franchisor will have developed a floor plan and décor scheme that all franchise units will utilize. However, if your store, hotel rooms, or delivery van is in terrible shape, that speaks volumes about how you conduct your business. It can look like you have very little business and can't afford to maintain your place, or it may look as if you don't care.

Regarding the process, you and your employees should know all about your products and services and be able to discuss them with your customers. You should develop ways to greet those who walk into your establishment and then take care of them the entire time they're there. You should even find ways to stay in touch after they've gone, either by having a mailing list or calling those who have registered a complaint.

Last, don't forget the people who staff your franchise and make up your customer base. The personal touch always works wonders, even with strangers. Remember your regular customers, and do everything you can to make your place inviting to those who aren't quite ready to purchase from you. Remember—the customer is king or queen, and you are there to serve them.

And it goes without saying that you should treat your employees with respect, a topic I discuss at length in Chapter 15. If you can motivate them, their positive attitude will be conveyed to your customers, who will have a good experience and come back again. Haven't we all been waited on by someone with a bad attitude who hated his or her job? And did that make you want to return for even more of that bad attitude? I highly doubt it.

At the end of the day, you are nothing if you don't have customers. If you aren't generating business, then your franchise will become a very expensive hobby—not your livelihood.

Assessing the Effectiveness of Your Marketing Campaign

You're putting out your message for a reason—you want results. You want more people to recognize your brand and patronize your business. You want to sell; you want to be profitable. You need to know if your marketing campaign is generating the results you want.

There are a few different ways you can assess this. First, you can look at overall sales and the sales of the specific items you promoted. If they aren't going up, you may want to investigate why. Did you convey a clear message to the right people? Is there something wrong with the product? Did your employees know how to sell it properly?

You can also look at brand awareness, which can be measured in many ways, but is usually done by the marketing department of the franchisor, or the agency that handles marketing for the franchisor.

You can also look at shopping patterns. Through customer data you can collect via credit cards or surveys, you can figure out who's buying what and why. You can also observe your customers, too, and pick up on details that can't be gauged by computers.

Lastly, you can look at customer satisfaction. If you have feedback forms, you can look at the comments to figure out what you're doing right and what you're doing wrong. You can also talk to customers, who usually appreciate your personal attention.

The Least You Need to Know

◆ Franchisees have an edge over their independent or corporate-run rivals, thanks to the marketing strategies developed by their franchisor.

◆ Franchises market at the national, regional, and local levels.

◆ Franchisees pay into an advertising fund at the local level and also at the regional level, which may be pooled together into a co-operative fund.

◆ A big mistake franchisees make is to neglect or go against the franchisor's branding efforts made at the national level.

◆ To avoid making common marketing mistakes, know your targeted audience, put together an attractive offer, and convey your message via the right medium.

Chapter 14

Making Friends in Franchising

In This Chapter

- ◆ Trust—the master value in franchising
- ◆ Building a healthy franchisor-franchisee relationship
- ◆ Making the most of franchisee advisory councils
- ◆ Working with brother and sister franchisees
- ◆ Seeking out networking opportunities
- ◆ Solving conflicts

If I've emphasized one idea in this book, it's this one: franchising is a system based on relationships. This is its strength, but it's also the source of many of its conflicts.

In this chapter, I take a look at some of the most critical relationships in franchising—the one between the franchisor and franchisee, and the relationship between fellow franchisees. I also discuss how each individual can make the most of these partnerships, as well as how conflicts can be solved to the benefit of everyone involved.

Your Franchise Is Like a Family

A franchise system is in many ways like a family. The parent (the franchisor) has its offspring, which are the brother and sister franchisees. Like any family, there are rules that must be followed. When this gets off track, the entire system can become dysfunctional, just like so many families. And although the brother and sister franchisees often get along, some may struggle with sibling rivalry. This can also turn the system into a dysfunctional one.

What makes a franchise system different from a family is that the offspring—the franchisee—gets to choose its parents. This happens during the due diligence phase, the time before the franchise agreement is signed when the prospective franchisee checks out anything and everything about the franchisor. If it seems to be a good fit, then the two entities enter into their partnership.

Many times, problems start when this due diligence hasn't been done thoroughly. Perhaps the prospective franchisee doesn't ask enough questions, or doesn't ask the right ones, or ignores answers that don't seem quite right. Or the franchisor may not be too picky about who joins its system and overlooks many warning flags about the prospective franchisee.

Whether you've asked all of the right questions or not, after the franchise agreement has been signed, there's no going back. Therefore, it's vital to the health of the entire franchise system—the family—that all members understand how to make their relationships work.

These relationships are the source of franchising's strength. For a franchise system to work in the long term, the franchisor and its franchisees must be able to communicate. That includes talking, of course, but also listening. In my view, listening is the most deficient skill in the workplace today. Ultimately, effective communication will lead to the growth of the entire system.

Interdependence in the Family

Just like a family, a franchise system is made up of interdependent individuals. The franchisees depend on the franchisor for the business system and support along the way. The franchisor depends on the franchisees to follow that system and grow.

Each franchisor establishes a system that, if devised properly and followed properly, creates a healthy, profitable franchise system. However, if the system hasn't been developed properly, or if one side or both sides don't adhere to it, the system will collapse.

Recognizing this interdependence is essential to creating and maintaining a healthy franchise system. I know it's easy to feel, if you're a franchisee, that you achieved your success on your own, without the help of the franchisor. You may feel that your customer service, your sales expertise, and your tenacity have combined to create your singular growth. However, no matter how much sweat equity you've put into your franchise, you got there through the assistance of the franchisor.

I've found that most franchisors know that successful franchisees may feel this way. Therefore, they must show that they've earned the respect of their franchisees. The franchisor must keep up its end of the bargain by supplying ongoing support, providing excellent leadership, recognizing outstanding performers, and giving back to the community. In this way, franchisees will be proud to represent the brand and will be motivated to achieve even more than they have in the past.

There is a flip side to this as well. Just like successful franchisees may feel that they've gotten there on their own, underperforming franchisees may feel that the franchisor is entirely to blame. And it may be true that the franchisor isn't providing the kind of support that its franchisees require. However, the franchisee must ask him- or herself: Am I following the program? If not, where am I deviating? And can I get it back on track? If it turns out that the franchisee can turn things around by more closely adhering to the system, then great. However, if there's a problem with the franchisor, then you'll have to do a little more to get back on track—a topic I cover later in this chapter.

Franchising Eagles

At its inception, the International Franchise Association admitted only franchisors. Although its founder, William Rosenberg, wanted to include franchisees into the new organization, most franchisors believed that franchisees and franchisors would always be in competition, and that the group couldn't include both parties. However, in 1992, this conventional wisdom shifted when Stephen Lynn, CEO of Sonic Restaurants, served as chair of the IFA. Lynn, who I believe is a Franchising Eagle, argued that franchisees should be admitted into the IFA so that the entire franchise community would be included in and represented by the organization. In this way, the perception of the franchisor-franchisee relationship began to shift. Instead of seeing this relationship as a conflicting one, those in the franchising community began recognizing that all members are interdependent.

The Importance of Trust

At the heart of the interdependence of the franchisor and franchisee relationship is trust, what I think of as the master value of franchising. Sure, both sides sign a legally binding franchise agreement, but this only formalizes their relationship. Trust is what seals it and fuels it. As I've said before, if you have to refer to your franchise agreement every time you communicate with your franchisor (or franchisee), the relationship is dead. Trust, on the other hand, keeps its spirit alive.

Trust, in franchising, is a two-way street. The franchisor must trust the franchisee to represent its brand according to its specifications. The franchisor will—and should—check in regularly to oversee its operating franchises, but the franchisor won't be there everyday to make sure that everyone is operating according to plan. It simply can't—and shouldn't—check over each franchisee's shoulder during business hours.

The franchisee must trust the franchisor, too. It must trust that the franchisor has its best interests at heart when developing the system and its new products and services. Franchisees must trust that the franchisor wants each unit to become profitable and has created strategies that will meet this goal. Even if a franchisee is baffled by the latest marketing strategy, he or she should trust that the franchisor has thoroughly tested this message and believes that it will produce results. This may be hard to do at times, but a quality franchisor will make good on its promises again and again.

Following the Rules

Related to all of this is the requirement that all franchisees follow the rules set up by the franchisor. As I said, the franchisor can't be on the franchisee's premises every day, so it must trust that the franchisee is following the rules.

There are many reasons why this should be the case. First, the power of franchising is in its uniformity and consistency of each and every brand. The customer should never be surprised by the products or services offered by a franchise. A tune-up in San Diego should be the same as a tune-up in Philadelphia. The cosmetics you can buy in Atlanta should be the same as the cosmetics you buy in Seattle. Consumers recognize the brand, rely on it, and return to it.

The franchisor has spent countless hours and much energy creating the products or services offered by their brand. They became franchisors because they offer something special—but also something that can be replicated at any outlet.

The catch, though, is that a specific system must be followed to do so. And that's the system that franchisees buy. Deviating from it weakens the brand. When this happens often enough, consumers will be confused. If their tune-up is botched at one establishment, dissatisfied customers will likely take a chance on a new brand, and that company will capitalize on the mistakes that had been made at the first shop.

Therefore, too much independence can weaken your brand. If you feel you must go your own way, you're better off outside of a franchise system than constantly bucking the one you're in.

Eagle Eyes

One way you can tell if you're adhering to the system is by visiting brother or sister franchisees who are doing well. Does your unit look like theirs? Are your employees as knowledgeable as theirs? Are your customers as satisfied? If not, why? In addition, it doesn't hurt to return to your operating manual to see if you've forgotten anything you learned in training.

The Franchisor-Franchisee Relationship

As franchising continues to evolve as a way for companies to distribute and market their services, the demand for qualified franchisees increases. I believe the ability of a system to maintain a competitive edge depends on the quality of its franchisees. This means that franchisors should have a well-developed franchisee recruitment and selection process.

Many of the problems that are experienced in some franchise systems begin with how franchisees are recruited, selected, and brought into the system. Franchisors can't just focus on closing the deal and increasing their number of operating units. They must find the right family members. With the wrong family members, some systems will never realize their true potential.

Aviary Alert

If you're a prospective franchisee and the franchisor you're interested in is not interested in you—beyond your ability to come up with the initial franchise fee—you should see this as a red flag. Franchisors should be very selective about who they allow into their systems.

This means that the purpose of recruitment should be seen in a different light. In this view, recruiting is meant to create the future of the franchise system. This goes beyond a numbers game and turns into a consultation process between the franchisor and franchisee. Rather than convince someone to buy a franchise, franchisors should grant a franchise to the right candidates, and franchisees should make an informed business decision. The candidate should fit in with what the franchise system needs and should be able to contribute to the overall goals of the organization. Each franchisee should be valued for what he or she brings to the organization.

Franchise Facts

Remember—technically, franchises are granted, not sold. Franchisors grant franchisees the right to use their brand and operating system for the term of their agreement. Instead of being a purely commercial transaction, this is an agreement intended to fulfill the purpose of the business: to attract and keep customers.

Eagle Eyes

The franchisor's field representatives should circulate among the franchisees to make sure that the system is being followed and that problems are solved quickly. Franchisees shouldn't see this as an intrusion. It merely shows that the franchisor is concerned about how their outlets are running and take franchisee contact seriously.

Each partner in this relationship needs different things to build a trusting, mutually beneficial relationship.

The franchisor needs franchisees who …

◆ Follow the system.

◆ Become profitable and grow.

◆ Adhere to their payment schedule.

◆ Maintain high standards.

◆ Participate in marketing campaigns.

◆ Can communicate with the support staff.

◆ Are enthusiastic about the brand.

◆ Offer excellent customer service.

◆ Get involved in their community.

When the franchisor is guaranteed to get this from their franchisees, they're more likely to lead the system into a new realm of success. Instead of becoming too involved in franchisees' affairs, they'll be able to allocate their resources to other ventures.

Franchisees need franchisors to live up to their end of the agreement, too. Franchisees need franchisors that …

◆ Have a clear system and a superior product or service.

◆ Offer thorough preopening training and ongoing support.

◆ Can anticipate problems and find areas to innovate.

◆ Listen to their franchisees.

◆ Have a strong support staff.

- ◆ Recognize star performers.

- ◆ Reinvest in the brand.

- ◆ Have a long-term vision.

- ◆ Treat their franchisees fairly.

If all of these elements are in place, the franchisor-franchisee relationship can be one full of trust and with little conflict.

Franchisee Advisory Councils

To help ensure that franchisors are attending to their many franchisees, many have set up support structures that allow franchisees to have input into the franchise system's operations. Some franchisors create *franchisee advisory councils*, or FACs, which take care of franchisees' concerns and provide a forum for discussion.

FACs grew out of the recognition that franchisors and franchisees should have clear channels of communication. FACs rarely have the power to set policy, but they collaborate in policy making by providing advice and consent. They can help identify problems and opportunities presented in franchise outlets. After all, the franchisees are on the front lines of the business and experience the effects of decisions made by the franchisor. There is wisdom in listening to those who interact with the customer daily.

Definitions

A **franchisee advisory council (FAC)** is an advisory committee made up of franchisees within a franchisor's organization.

To be effective, a FAC should be fairly independent; it shouldn't uniformly agree—or disagree—with the franchisor's wishes. Those in the franchisor's organization should listen to the franchisees' ideas and criticisms, and the franchisor must follow through on the promises that are made and respond to every issue raised. Both the members of the FAC and the franchisor's staff should see this forum as a way to problem solve, not just register complaints. Personally, I like to involve the FAC in my corporate strategic planning; in this way, they are well informed of the programs that the company will initiate.

FACs can be set up in a number of ways, and they usually evolve according to the needs of each franchise system. Franchisees tend to be skeptical about the effectiveness of a FAC, so members should be patient with their progress. I've found that it takes about two to three years before everything gels. Members can be selected in a number of ways, but I think that they should be elected from the field at large. Terms should be staggered so that there's continuity, although there should be some sort of term limits so that there's always new blood in the system. The meetings should be scheduled regularly and should be accessible to all members.

In addition, franchisors should show that they're willing to contribute to the success of the FAC. They should allocate resources for it, such as funds, staff, and administration. The franchisor should also pay the traveling expenses for the members, some of whom may have to come a long way to attend the meetings.

The Franchisee-Franchisee Relationship

Whereas the franchisor-franchisee relationship may be like a parent-child relationship, the franchisee-franchisee relationship has a different dynamic. This one is more like a sibling relationship. Brother and sister franchisees are on a more equal footing. They can be distant or close, rivals or friends. In the best case, they know how to work together to build a strong brand. Like the franchisor and its franchisees, sibling franchisees are interdependent, and their relationship must be built on trust.

This relationship, in some cases, can be quite competitive. The brother and sister franchisees may develop a sort of sibling rivalry. One franchisee may feel that another is getting preferential treatment from the franchisor, such as better territory or more support.

Franchisees should note that the success of one unit will enhance the image of all units. Even if brother and sister franchisees are in close proximity, they shouldn't feel threatened. As I explain in Chapter 11, a large exclusive territory doesn't always equal success, and a high number of sibling franchisees clustered in one area doesn't mean that there won't be enough customers to go around. Although this is often confused with cannibalization, it isn't. In many cases, this strong presence in one area will help build the brand and will actually increase the franchise's customer base. So, even if a franchisee's exclusive territory is small, it shouldn't be threatened by the nearness of a sibling franchisee.

In fact, I believe that franchisees should see their successful sibling franchisees as a source of support. For example, when just starting out, a new franchisee could claim one as a mentor who can provide guidance.

In fact, many franchisors have set up formal mentoring programs as part of their training package. Even if done informally, franchisees should always offer their support to others in their system.

Another reason why franchisees should be grateful to have successful sibling franchisees is that their success will enhance the image of the brand and reflect on fellow franchisees. After all, if a customer knows that she will get superior service at the nail salon near her home, in a pinch she'll check out the sibling hair salon near her office.

> **Aviary Alert**
>
> Many customers don't understand the nature of franchising and don't realize that individual owners operate their own outlets. Many may think that all units are run from a corporate headquarters. Therefore, if they receive poor service at one outlet, they may believe that all units in the system are run just as poorly. And, not surprisingly, they'll shop elsewhere.

Financially, franchisees will also benefit from the success of their siblings. All franchisees have the same task—to establish the brand name as the dominant one in the market. More sales mean that more money is sent back to the franchisor, which can be spent on developing the entire system. In addition, more money will be sent back to the franchisor for national advertising, too. And the regional advertising pool will also swell from the contributions made by successful franchisees. You'd be smart to recognize this advantage.

> **Eagle Eyes**
>
> Successful or older franchisees can and should speak up if they see that a sibling franchisee isn't doing well—especially if that unit is dragging down the brand in the local market. Many times this is due to not adhering to the established system set out by the franchisor. The franchisee can speak directly to the other owner, or he or she may discuss it with the franchisor's field representatives. Being critiqued may be painful, but ultimately it can lead to a more successful operation.

Therefore, brother and sister franchisees should get to know each other and band together. They can set up regular networking meetings to discuss the local climate and how they can increase their customer base. They may want to do additional promotions above and beyond their usual marketing efforts, such as sponsoring charitable events or hiring a local public figure to endorse their brand.

Networking Opportunities

Given that the health of a franchisor's relationships contributes to the health of the overall system, all franchisees should take part in as many networking opportunities as they can.

The franchise system may provide many of these opportunities. For example, it may have regular workshops, seminars, and meetings for its franchisees. A good franchisor will understand the importance of these gatherings and will encourage participation. Franchisees will be able to learn from each other and get to know others who are also walking in their shoes.

Eagle Eyes

Franchisees can take the initiative and network among themselves, too. In the UFOC all, or at least the nearby franchisees, are listed along with their phone numbers. If they want to get together, another franchisee is just a phone call away.

Franchisees can also find networking opportunities through the International Franchise Association. As I explain in Chapter 3, franchisees can participate in the Franchise Business Network, which was initiated by Fred DeLuca, the founder of Subway. Franchisees can communicate via the IFA's electronic forums on its website. There seems to be a forum for every concern, ranging from women in franchising to newcomers to franchising. Also, the IFA has established a Franchisee Forum in addition to their Franchisor and Supplier forums. All three forums provide opportunities for each segment of franchising to provide guidance and counsel to IFA's governance.

Dealing With Change and Conflict

The relationships that make up a franchise system are inherently full of conflict. Franchisees may feel that they're in competition with one another or that the franchisor isn't earning its franchise fee or royalty payments.

Although I don't advocate becoming overly critical or vocal about many matters that might be insignificant, I do recommend that franchisees speak up if they feel that something is going wrong. They can speak to the field representative in the area to see if they can resolve the matter without much fuss. Incidentally, this is yet another reason why franchisees should get to know the staff of their franchisor—when things become difficult, these personal relationships can help a franchisee find resolution to challenges.

Many franchisors have an ombudsman who addresses complaints from franchisees. The IFA has also developed an ombudsman position for conflict resolution. The ombudsman is a neutral party whose job is to help find solutions for problems to the satisfaction of all parties. Franchisees can look to this as an extra arena in which their voices can be heard.

In addition, although it hopefully will not get to this level, the UFOC spells out how conflicts can be sorted out at a more formal level—either through mediation or via the courts in a specific state.

Many times, conflict is generated when the franchise goes through a big change, and franchisees are expected to go along for the ride. For example, a franchise may decide to upgrade its entire software network, and the franchisees will be forced to undergo rigorous training and be inconvenienced during installation. They may even have to bear some or all of the cost. This software will, incidentally, allow the franchisor to have access to more customer data, which the franchisees aren't so crazy about.

However, in this case, franchisees should understand that a change such as this one will benefit them in the long term. Despite the short-term inconvenience or expense, this software will give them a competitive edge over their rivals. In addition, the data will help the franchisor develop more targeted strategies to reach the right customers. It isn't excessive prying or snooping—it's being involved with technology that can grow the business for all.

Whatever the change is, franchisors should communicate their strategy and rationale clearly, and franchisees should listen—as well as find an appropriate way to voice their concerns. Again, this goes back to trust. Franchisors must trust that franchisees are operating their units according to the system, and franchisees must trust that the franchisor is making decisions that will benefit the entire system.

The Least You Need to Know

- Relationships are franchising's source of strength, but also a source of conflict, if they aren't managed properly.

- Many conflicts can be avoided if the right franchisees are recruited into the system, instead of focusing on signing as many franchisees as possible.

- Although some of the franchisor's decisions can seem perplexing, franchisees should trust that the company's leaders are making the right decisions for the entire system. Only the franchisor has a broad, overarching view of the entire organization and its strategy.

- Although a franchisor's rules may seem limiting, they ensure that each franchise unit within the system operates as one. This will help build customer loyalty.

- Franchisee advisory councils can provide franchisees with a voice within the franchisor's organization, although most are not able to set policy.

- Franchisees shouldn't view sibling franchisees as competition, but as teammates who are interdependent and a source of support.

- Franchisees should seek out opportunities for networking, since the new relationships and information can help them build their business and find support during times of need.

Chapter **15**

Hiring and Managing Staff

In This Chapter

- ◆ Attracting and hiring great employees
- ◆ Your role as a leader
- ◆ Providing thorough training for employees
- ◆ Creating a supportive workplace culture
- ◆ Terminating employees
- ◆ Labor regulations you must know

Unless you're truly flying solo in your franchise venture, you will need to assemble a great staff you can trust and grow with. This isn't going to happen by magic, and depending on the labor pool in your area, this may be difficult. Depending on your needs, you may start small with an office manager or assistant. You may need to hire experienced professionals, such as a team of techies for your computer consulting business. Or you may have to bring together a variety of staffers, such as nurses, salespeople, office staff, and finance pros.

Whatever your needs, your franchisor will no doubt have staffing and training guidelines for your specific franchise. To get you started though, in this chapter I cover the basics of hiring great employees and making your franchise a supportive working environment. I also discuss your role in the business, whether you're a hands-on manager or an absentee owner. In addition, I look at how you can terminate a bad employee and make sense of labor regulations.

Hiring a Great Staff

Opening a new franchise means piecing together a number of important items. You've got to look at everything from coming up with the initial franchise fee to determining your operating hours. One factor that's critical to your success is your team. Your team includes your franchisor and its support staff, but it also includes all of your professional advisers, such as your attorney and accountant, as well as all of your regular staff, whether they're cat sitters or car salespeople.

Just like most other aspects of franchising, your franchisor will most likely have developed employment guidelines for you. These are just suggestions, of course—your employees are yours, and not your franchisor's. You will be responsible for them, their safety and training, their paychecks and their schedules. Your franchisor can help you determine your staffing needs and how you can employ them legally and effectively.

Finding and Screening Candidates

The hiring process begins with developing job descriptions and circulating them. Your franchisor may have samples you can use in your ads and it may have sample applications, too. This can help you evaluate job seekers so that you're hiring the right people for the job. You should also have a good idea of your proposed schedule, benefits or other perks, and wages so that you can discuss them during your interviews.

Eagle Eyes _____

You can be effective and save money by narrowing your advertising focus. If your community has a weekly newspaper in addition to a larger city daily, you may want to start with that smaller paper first and then move your ad to the daily paper if you're not getting the results you need. Many cities have local websites for job seekers that are often cheaper than national employment sites. If you do a little research, you can find the right applicants—they may be closer than you think.

Then you've got to advertise these job openings. You may put an ad in the local paper, hang a "Hiring Now" banner outside of your shop (still under construction, perhaps), talk to your friends in the industry, hang an ad on a job board at the local college or high school, or post an ad online. Whatever you do, make sure that your ad will reach the right applicants. If your employees will be trained professionals, place your ad in the profession's trade magazines.

After you've started advertising, you will need to sift through the applications and resumes you've received. If job seekers must apply in person, you might be able to form an impression of them—whether they're well spoken or professional, enthusiastic or lethargic.

You'll need to identify the people who best meet your needs based on your job descriptions. Start contacting the best on your list quickly, especially if your franchise is located in a hot job market or if your doors will be opening quickly. You don't want the best ones to slip away. You may want to quickly contact those who can fill the most difficult jobs, such as those who will work the night shift or in highly technical positions.

Aviary Alert

If you'll need to fill many entry-level positions, your job applicants may not have much recent work experience. Some may still be in school or others may be returning to work after spending time raising children or after being laid off. This shouldn't deter you from hiring them. You'll have to look at other qualifications besides job experience. Has the applicant volunteered? Is he or she responsible or enthusiastic about getting to work? Some of these personal characteristics are more important than knowing the various skills he or she will need to work for you.

You'll be able to get some information from applicants when you call them to set up the interview. Look for someone who is happy to talk to you, is willing to meet you even if it's inconvenient, and is eager to hear about your business. If the applicant can't even remember sending you his or her resumé, that's usually a bad sign.

Interviewing Candidates

The interview process can be grueling or enlightening—it all depends on your attitude. Make sure you've read the applications or resumés thoroughly before you meet the job candidates. Haven't you been on job interviews with a manager who had no idea about your qualifications and employment history? And didn't that make you feel unimportant?

Your interviews should be conducted in a quiet, fairly private space. If your business is already up and running, you should schedule your interviews during an off-peak time, such as the middle of the afternoon if you're in the food business or in the morning if your business gets busy in the afternoon.

Aviary Alert _____

If your site is still under construction, you'll have to conduct your interviews elsewhere. Perhaps you can meet at a sibling franchisee's location or you can find a quiet restaurant or café near your site. Just make sure that the job candidate knows exactly where your business will be located—you don't want to confuse him or her right off the bat.

Aviary Alert _____

Always ask for references, and if you're serious about the candidate, definitely call the people on the list. Some applicants may be too good to be true—literally. Occasionally, a job seeker will get creative with his or her credentials and be a complete phony. If the references don't pan out, stay away from that candidate.

A whole genre of literature has been written on how to conduct a successful interview, and I suggest that you dip into it, as well as any information your franchisor may have passed onto you. Generally, though, you want to follow these guidelines:

- Have the candidate's application or resumé with you during the interview.

- Know the qualifications, schedule, wages, and duties of the position you want to fill.

- Give the applicant enough time to respond to your questions—don't dominate the interview.

- Avoid discussing more personal matters, such as marital status, age, possible disabilities, ethnicity, and other matters. These matters shouldn't be discussed at all, a topic I cover later in this chapter.

- Be candid about the drawbacks of the job. If the person must stay late or have to do heavy physical labor, the candidate must know in advance instead of being surprised after he or she is hired.

- Explain why your business would be a good place to work. Perhaps you offer flexible schedules, dole out bonuses or rewards to excellent employees, or can teach people the skills that will be in demand in the future.

Lastly, remember to ask open-ended questions such as "Is there anything else I should know about you that we haven't already discussed?" This will give the candidate a chance to tell you about his or her scholarship, personal interests that are relevant to the job, or knowledge about your business.

Training Your Staff

Even if your new hires have a lot of professional experience, they'll still need to be trained on how to conduct business according to your franchise's system and standards. In some cases, you may need to start from scratch. In others you'll be able to walk a new employee through the process and they'll be able to catch on quickly.

Most franchisors provide some sort of training assistance, a topic I cover at length in Chapter 10. You, the franchisee, will have undergone some sort of preopening training, whether it's at the franchisor's headquarters or at another franchisee's site. In addition, your manager or other employees may be allowed to—or required to—be trained at headquarters as well.

During your training, the franchisor most likely will cover how you can hire, train, and manage your staff. This "training the trainer" material is essential to running a smooth venture. Your employees must be thoroughly knowledgeable about your products and services, how the business is run, and what the culture is all about. The franchisor may provide you with training materials you can cover with your new employees, whether they're written, on the web, or recorded on a video or DVD. You'll still need to personally walk employees through their tasks to reinforce these lessons, but the franchisor-developed materials can give you a head start.

Eagle Eyes

Your franchisor may send a representative to your site before you open your doors, and you can begin training your employees with his or her help. You can do dry runs of various tasks and get feedback on performance. This involvement can be critical in helping your franchise get off to a good start and live up to the franchisor's standards.

An important part of training is knowing how to correct your employees' mistakes in a constructive manner. I recommend doing so in a relatively private way; I wouldn't criticize an employee in front of another one, unless all of the employees are making the same mistake. After you explain the employee's error you should do the task yourself, the right way, then walk through it with the employee as he or she does the task. Ask your employee if he or she has any questions, then try it again. If this doesn't work, try to figure out why—perhaps the directions weren't clear or the employee simply isn't good at that task. If the employee continues to have difficulty, try to reassign him or her to a more appropriate task.

Definitions

Cross-training is training employees in a number of tasks, including those outside of their job description.

You should also consider *cross-training* your employees so that they are at least aware of the duties of your other staffers. For example, your hostess should know a little bit about how the kitchen is run and the cooks should know a little bit about how reservations are taken. Although they may not switch positions, this information can help them feel more like a team or enable them to answer customers' questions.

Being the Leader—Whether You're There or Not

During the early days of your business, your employees will be looking to you to lead them. Now, you may feel as confused or overwhelmed as any of them might—more so, in some cases—but being a franchisee requires you to be a leader.

Some of you may want to be a hands-on owner and manager. You will be there to open the doors in the morning, read the mail, greet customers, make sales calls, and close up at night. You'll work arm-in-arm with your staffers, and you'll know how to do their jobs if you need to pitch in in a pinch.

However, some of you will be absentee owners. You won't be there everyday; you'll have a manager who operates the business and reports back to you. You may have set up this arrangement because you own another business or because this franchise is an investment for you. Whatever your reasons, your franchisor must be in the loop about your intentions. Some franchisors may require that you are on-site all of the time, whereas others may require that you are there for a certain number of hours each day or each week.

Franchise Facts

You can find the franchisor's requirements about your level of involvement in Item 15 of the UFOC—the section on the franchisee's obligations. Make sure you and the franchisor are in alignment before you sign the franchise agreement.

Whatever your arrangement, you will still be called to lead your staff. Leadership is an art as much as a skill, although some people seem to be naturals at it. (You may want to return to Chapter 7 for my discussion about attitude and leadership.) Keep in mind that leaders are able to do the difficult thing, whether it's to work long hours or to have challenging but honest conversations with your staff. If you set a good example for your employees they will know what they will have to do, too. And they'll know that you're working just as hard to make the franchise a success as they are. This is especially important for those of you who will be absentee owners. If your employees rarely see you, or see you as someone who is profiting off of their hard work, they will resent you. Let them know that you appreciate them and are doing the behind-the-scenes things to keep the business running. Keep the dream in front of them so that they know what they're working toward.

Franchising Eagles

Charles Kemmons Wilson—Kemmons to everyone who knew him—didn't come into life with any advantages. He was born an only child in Osceola, Arkansas, and his father died when Kemmons was nine months old. He and his mother moved to Memphis, where his mom worked as a dental assistance. During the Great Depression, she lost her job and Wilson quit high school to work. With a $50 loan from a friend, he bought a popcorn machine and set it up in a movie theater lobby. By 1933, he had made $1,700 from the popcorn business and bought a house for himself and his mother. He then mortgaged the house to buy the local Wurlitzer jukebox franchise, and, thanks to his various businesses and real estate deals, he became a millionaire by 1951.

Kemmons didn't stop there. During a vacation to Washington with his wife and kids, he realized that there were no safe, clean, and affordable hotels that catered to families. He wanted a chain of motels where children could stay free. "I didn't take many vacations, but as I took this one, I realized how many families there were taking vacations and how they needed a nice place they could stay," he once told an interviewer.

Holiday Inn was launched and Kemmons Wilson became the father of the modern hotel. Kemmons started with four hotels in the Memphis area, and at its peak, a new Holiday Inn was opening somewhere in the world every $2^1/_2$ days. Today, there are more than 1,000 Holiday Inns across the United States, and more in other countries.

Besides being an innovative businessman and franchisor, Kemmons was known for giving great quotes that could inspire anyone. Some of them are:

- "Mental attitude plays a far more important role in a person's success or failure than mental capacity."

- "There are two ways to get to the top of an oak tree. One way is to sit on an acorn and wait; the other way is to climb it."

- "Eliminate from your vocabulary the words, 'I don't think I can' and substitute, 'I know I can.' "

- "A person has to take risks to achieve."

- "Only work half a day. It doesn't matter which half you work—the first 12 hours or the second 12 hours."

You can find out more about Kemmons Wilson from the man himself. *His book Half Luck and Half Brains: The Kemmons Wilson, Holiday Inn Story* is a must-read for anyone in business.

Developing a Healthy Workplace Culture

As the leader of your franchise, you'll be responsible for setting the tone of the workplace. Your professionalism, caring, concern for safety and security, and ability to meet standards of performance will set a good example for your staffers. They'll know what to strive for if you've set a good example.

However, your example isn't the only factor affecting the tone of your workplace culture. Your franchisor has a corporate culture, too, one that you should have checked thoroughly before you joined it. You should have also learned more about it during your preopening training.

Corporate cultures vary, but they're important to the health of your franchise system. If your franchisor is ultracompetitive and will ignore cut corners and irregular deals as long as you're profitable, that message will be conveyed to everyone in the system. However, if the culture is more people-focused and penalizes those who behave unethically, those values will be filtered throughout the system.

You'll need to convey this message, too. It doesn't have to be in the form of lectures or heavy-handed tactics. You can recognize and reward those who are excellent performers. You can set incentives so that employees will meet their goals. You can work around their obligations if that's what it takes to keep them happy. You can make the workplace a fun one by being enthusiastic about the business.

In addition, you'll have to make the workplace a safe and comfortable one for all employees. This means that you cannot tolerate any kind of discrimination, sexist or racist comments or behavior, religious insensitivity, or a general lack of respect for anyone on your staff. Pregnant women should be accommodated and single moms should receive the same benefits as the married moms on your staff. You'll want to adhere to safety regulations so that your workers won't be hurt on the job. You'll need to ensure that employees who work alone, those who open up or close down the business, or those who work with a lot of cash or other valuables are protected from thieves. Remember—your employees are your responsibility, and their health and happiness is in your hands.

Terminating a Bad Employee

Despite your best efforts to screen, hire, train, and support your employees, almost inevitably you will have to terminate one. This is unfortunate for everyone involved, and it's never easy. Your franchisor may provide you with guidelines for this, but labor laws in your area may affect you as well.

Eagle Eyes _____

I've found that few employees are fired for being incompetent. The vast majority of them are fired for problems with their relationships. They may tick off a fellow employee, or a manager, or even you, or not communicate well about problems they're having or matters pertaining to their job. This is yet another reason why you should emphasize the building of good relationships and healthy communication.

Before you terminate your employee, you should be sure to give him or her warnings about the substandard behavior. For example, if an employee is chronically late, you'll need to talk to him or her about the problem. You may have a standard for acceptable behavior, such as three strikes and you're out. Whatever it is, make sure you discuss the problem and give the employee a chance to correct his or her behavior. Then document your discussion.

When you do have this conversation with your employee, make sure it's in private. Discuss the employee's exit strategy and how outstanding pay and other issues will be resolved. You may want to send them to an outplacement firm or to a counselor.

In addition, don't forget about the rest of your employees. They will certainly react to your decision to terminate one of their colleagues. They may feel a sense of relief to be rid of a problematic worker, or they may resent your action. Whatever the case, talk to your other staffers and let them know why you did it, and that it's for the benefit of everyone. Assure them that they aren't in danger of being fired—if they aren't—and then begin moving forward. If you don't address the issue in a straightforward manner, your employees may fear for their own jobs or think that you're being unfair or cruel.

Adhering to Labor Laws and Regulations

Although you are part of a franchising system, you are responsible for what happens in your own business. Your franchisor may have developed an operating system for you, but you'll need to make sure that you are following national, state, and local regulations.

Regarding employment, you'll need to follow the federal statutes enforced by the U.S. Equal Employment Opportunity Commission (EEOC). You'll need to understand this in detail, but the major items are as follows:

◆ A prohibition on employment discrimination on the basis of race, color, religion, gender, pregnancy, medical conditions, or national origin. Harassment based on these elements is forbidden as well. This applies to any business that employs more than 15 workers, including part-time and temporary ones.

◆ A prohibition on employment discrimination based on age; this applies to businesses with 20 or more employees including part-time and temporary ones, and also employment agencies.

◆ A prohibition on employment discrimination based on disability; this applies to businesses with 15 or more workers, including part-time and temporary ones.

◆ A requirement to offer equal pay for equal work, regardless of gender.

◆ A prohibition on employing those who are not legally authorized to work in the United States. It's the employer's responsibility to verify the eligibility of all prospective employees.

You should find more information at www.eeoc.gov or any of the agency's 50 field offices throughout the United States. In addition, become familiar with any state or local regulations that affect employment. You especially must be familiar with and comply with federal and state minimum wage laws. Your franchisor should be able to help you out.

The Least You Need to Know

◆ Hiring and training your employees is critical to your success as a franchisee.

◆ Besides teaching your employees the skills they'll need, it's important to teach them the franchisor's culture and to motivate them to do well.

◆ You cannot ask certain questions on job interviews, nor can you discriminate against people who are protected by EEOC guidelines.

◆ Terminating employees should be done tactfully, because your remaining employees will know what happened and the firing will reflect on your abilities as a leader.

Part 5

Soaring to New Heights

If you do everything correctly and thoughtfully, you should be able to launch a successful career in franchising. You can soar to new heights and grow your business to whatever size suits your ambitions.

In this section, I explore how you can reach your potential by acquiring a new franchise unit or perhaps by becoming an area franchisee who is charged with developing an entire territory for a franchise brand. You can also acquire another franchise brand if you aren't able to grow within your original franchise system. You can also take on partners, raise money from private investors, or even take your business public. In some cases, you may become a franchisor yourself, if you've got a great idea for a business and the elements that every great franchisor needs.

In addition to all of these options, you can also keep it simple: you can renew your relationship with your existing franchisor.

Chapter 16

Planning for Growth

In This Chapter

- ◆ Looking at growth alternatives
- ◆ Advantages and disadvantages of expanding your business
- ◆ Building another location from the ground up
- ◆ Buying another location that's already operating
- ◆ Can you become an area franchisee?
- ◆ Doing the math

After you've launched your first franchise unit and find that you enjoy it, you may wonder where you can go next. Perhaps you have your eye on a sibling franchisee's location, or think that a kiosk in the mall would complement your full-service site. When you're having these thoughts, you're thinking about expanding.

In this chapter, I look at the pros and cons of taking on another site, whether you want to build from scratch, buy a sibling franchisee's unit, acquire a unit from the franchisor, or take over a competitor's unit. I explain what a master franchisee is and discuss whether expansion makes sense for you.

Exploring Your Growth Alternatives

For some of you, taking on another site will make a lot of sense. You may thrive on the challenge of setting up a new business, and you believe so much in your brand that you'll do what it takes to build it up yourself.

Aviary Alert _____

Some franchisors may outright deny their franchisees the right to open another location. They may have good reason for doing so. They've probably found that in the past, two or more locations are too much to handle. These franchisors want a hands-on owner in each and every one of their franchise outlets.

Eagle Eyes _____

Many franchisors offer additional training for those who are acquiring additional franchise units. These franchisors have found that operating multiple units requires a different skill set, one that can be taught during training sessions. Check with your franchisor for the support they offer to franchisees who are interested in expanding.

However, before you start looking at sites, take a look at your franchise agreement. Your franchisor may have put restrictions on your ability to take on another location. Your franchisor may require you to operate your first unit for a designated amount of time or until it reaches certain benchmarks of performance.

Besides your franchisor's permission, you will need to consider other factors, too. First, you must have a full knowledge of the business. It's not enough to just understand how your unit operates; you need to understand the industry, its potential for growth, and how the franchisor is positioned to take advantage of these factors. With a second or third franchise, you will become more involved in this industry, and you want to make sure that you're investing in a winner.

Second, you should look at the financial issues involved in acquiring another franchise. Although I discuss this in detail later in this chapter, be warned that taking on another franchise is taking on another financial obligation, one that will cost you money before it begins generating revenue. However, you do have at least one advantage: many franchisors lower the initial franchise fee on the second (or third or more) unit that's acquired by a franchisee. This is because the franchisee already knows the system, doesn't need to be trained again, and is a more certain bet the second time around.

However, this doesn't mean that setting up a second shop is cheap. If you're starting from scratch, you'll have to find the right location, build or renovate a site, hire new employees, and advertise the business. You'll probably need to allocate resources from your existing business, so you should have enough cash on hand to do this.

Your time isn't cheap, either. You'll need to split your time between your current site and your new one. You'll also need a strong manager to handle the daily affairs of your first franchise so that you can focus on your expansion.

You will need a strong relationship with your franchisor and its field staff. With a second location, you'll become more involved in the system, and you'll also need a different kind of support from it. Instead of needing help with operating a business, you'll need more support in learning how to juggle your two businesses and make them profitable. This may mean that you'll consolidate resources, such as purchasing supplies and processing paychecks, but it also means that you'll need to market both locations, whether they're in the same media market or not.

Advantages of Opening Another Location

The benefits of owning two or more franchise outlets are many. For one, you already know how to run this particular franchise, and you can transfer this knowledge to another location and generate business there. You fully believe in the brand, and you're sure that you can make a second location profitable.

Another benefit of having two or more locations is that you will have more power and be more efficient. When you order supplies from vendors you will be ordering more; this often leads to lower costs for you. You've already developed business procedures for paying bills, cutting paychecks, and scheduling your staff; you can use these same procedures for your second site with little extra cost to you.

If your sites are in the same media market, you'll get more out of your local advertising dollars. The extra site's resources will give you more money for the collective ad pool and both locations will benefit from it. If you send out flyers, the addresses of both locations can be listed on them. The cost of sending them out is the same, but it benefits two sites, not one.

A big advantage is that, if your sites will be located near each other, you can develop a bigger client base. As I discuss in Chapter 11 on location, many times an individual franchisee

Eagle Eyes

Your second site doesn't have to be a carbon copy of your first franchise. If your second site is an "express" or limited service site, it can complement your original site and utilize its resources. You may need only one kitchen to support both of your cafés, or only one lab to support the extra photo-processing outlet.

will feel threatened by the addition of a sibling franchisee near their unit. They may feel that their customers are being cannibalized. However, this fear is usually unfounded; after a temporary dip in business, the second site will actually generate more customers for both stores. If you own both of those sites, you—not a brother or sister franchisee or even your competitor—will benefit from this phenomenon. As I've said before, it's better for you to build out your territory than to allow your competitor to beat you to it.

The Disadvantages of Owning Another Site

Just as there are many advantages to owning another site, there's also a downside.

One disadvantage of owning a second site is that you'll be stretched personally. You'll need to pay attention to your existing site while spending energy getting your additional location up and running—and if you've ever set up a business, you know how much work that is. Even if you're purchasing a turnkey franchise that's doing great business, you'll still need to spend a lot of time there, getting to know your employees and developing connections in that community.

Another drawback may be that your various sites are not near each other, and this distance is difficult for you, personally, and for your operations. It may become difficult for you to see each of your outlets with ease, and they may be so far apart that you can't take advantage of the efficiencies you'd hoped for. For example, your sites may be in different media markets, which dilutes your advertising dollars. Or you may not be able to distribute your products and supplies as easily and inexpensively as you'd hoped. If you do open other sites, make sure that it makes good business sense for you and helps you achieve your goals.

Eagle Eyes

Before you begin the process of buying a second site, you should start transitioning the staff at your initial location. You'll need a good manager to run the operations while you're gone, so make sure you're grooming someone in the ranks. You'll depend on him or her to take care of business while you're distracted by the second business, so trust is essential. You can't risk your current business for the benefit of your future business.

Another disadvantage is that you may not be able to duplicate the knowledge you gained and the procedures you developed while running your first business. For example, your second location may be in a very different neighborhood with a very different customer base, and you may not know how to serve them. Your first coffee shop franchise may be on a campus, and you know precisely how to sell coffee to college students. However, your second outlet may be out in the suburbs, and you have no idea how to reach these customers. They aren't responding to your funky graphics and sense of humor—and you weren't prepared to find a more sophisticated message.

And as I've mentioned previously, opening up a second location usually doesn't throw a franchisee off track. However, when a franchisee opens a third site, something changes. The operations become more complex, and this multi-unit mini-system should be run in a different way. Therefore, these franchisees need to develop a new skill set to handle their new responsibilities. If you're thinking about opening more than two locations, check with your franchisor about the support and training you can receive.

Above all, remember that the franchise agreement for your second site will almost certainly be different than the one for your original site. Although the franchise fee may be lower for your second location, other costs may be higher. For example, if your franchisor has upgraded the tech system or the décor, you may have to pay for those extra costs, costs that weren't an issue when you first opened your doors.

Building a Second Location from the Ground Up

If the disadvantages of operating more than one location haven't deterred you, you'll be interested in how you can acquire your second—or third, or more—franchise.

The most common way is the traditional way—building another location, either by constructing one from scratch or renting another property and renovating it to suit your needs.

This strategy will fairly closely match how one goes about building the first site—although the franchisor doesn't need to be investigated at this point. However, those who wish to develop a second location have to do just as much research and legwork to identify the right location. You need to conduct demographic studies, traffic studies, feasibility studies, and so on, because the second site has to be vetted just as closely as the first one.

Eagle Eyes _____

Return to Chapter 11 for my discussion of how to locate a site for your franchise. You'll need to work through those steps again to locate a site for your second franchise. You can't take any shortcuts even if your instincts are right.

You may want to look for nontraditional sites that can complement the business you do in your original location. You can open an "express" or limited service operation that harnesses the resources of your first franchise. You may want to open a kiosk at the local mall, airport, stadium, or theater to provide convenience for your customers. You may want to locate your new franchise in an underserved neighborhood in your community to build brand awareness where very little exists. Placing your new franchise in one of these locations will enhance your brand, not create more competition.

Buying a Location That Is Already in Place

If you aren't interested in launching a franchise outlet from scratch, you should consider buying one that's already up and running.

Buying from Another Franchisee

The most obvious source would be another franchisee who wants to get out of the business. It may be that this franchisee is ready to retire or to set out in a new career direction. This franchisee may own multiple units and wants to scale back. Perhaps this franchisee just isn't having any luck with this site, and wants to get out before things get worse.

If you take over an existing franchise location, you'll have to do due diligence. Find out precisely why the franchisee is selling. Open the books and take a look at how profitable the business is—and hopefully it is profitable—and how the money is being allocated. Do your own traffic studies and demographic studies and so on and consider how you could build the customer base. Identify the ways in which the current owner is not serving the business and how you could do it differently. If there are problems, make sure that it has nothing to do with the location. If the location is a problem, take a look at your other options.

Eagle Eyes

You can find these turnkey locations through your personal connections or by contacting your franchisor's field representatives, who usually know which franchisees are looking to sell. You can also find these outlets listed online. Brokers can be a source of information, too, but make sure that you research the site thoroughly instead of accepting their sales pitch without question.

When you buy an existing franchise, the deal may be done in a variety of ways. You may want to take over the franchisee's original franchise agreement if there are enough years remaining on it to make it worth your while. For example, you probably wouldn't want to take over an agreement that only had three years left before it is terminated. In some cases, you would sign a new franchise agreement with the franchisor because it has changed the terms of its agreement and wants you, the new franchisee, to be in alignment with the rest of their recent franchisees.

> **Aviary Alert** _____
>
> Even though you may be looking at a sibling franchisee's site, you may not be able to take it over cheaply. If the business is a healthy one, you may have to pay a high price to take it over. If the site hasn't been renovated or upgraded in awhile, you may have to spend a lot to bring it up to the standards of the franchisor's system. Look at the outstanding debts of the franchisee, too. You'll be responsible for them as well. The bottom line is that your accountant and attorney should be as involved in this purchase as they were in your purchase of your original franchise.

However, keep in mind that whatever you do sign, you will have to pay money for the right to do business as a franchisee. You will need to pay the current owner for the right to do business in that location. (Remember—franchisees don't buy franchises, they buy the right to do business as a franchisee.) You will also need to pay the initial franchise fee to the franchisor. Additionally, you will be responsible for paying the transfer fee to the franchisor. You may be able to negotiate this with the franchisee you're buying from, but one of you will be responsible for paying this fee to the franchisor.

> **Aviary Alert** _____
>
> Even though you are buying an existing franchise from its current proprietor, you will still have to operate within the franchisor's system. Therefore, the franchisor usually retains the right to refuse an individual as a franchisee, even if the seller agrees to the deal. The franchisor is rightly concerned with the backgrounds of their franchisees, and you may not fit the profile the franchisor is looking for. Besides getting the franchisor's approval, you may also need to undergo training, too.

Where you do save money is in construction. You don't have to locate the site, set up the site, or obtain any permits. The original owner has done all of that for you. He or she has also established relationships with customers and clients, relationships that you will benefit from.

> ### Franchising Eagles
>
> Chick-fil-A, the quick-serve chicken restaurant franchise founded by S. Truett Cathy, has an interesting arrangement with its franchisees. According to the company, franchisees can sublease a Chick-fil-A chain restaurant for only $5,000. All operators sign the same agreement, which requires that each month, the operator pays Chick-fil-A, Inc. 15 percent of gross sales and 50 percent of net profits as a franchise fee. Operators are assured a minimum income of $30,000 annually. Operators do not build equity in the business, and their contractual agreement is not transferable.
>
> Chick-fil-A's operators have more options, though. The company runs a variety of outlets: free-standing restaurants; drive-through only outlets; Chick-fil-A Dwarf Houses (full-service restaurants); Truett's Grill (a retro-style restaurant); licensed nontraditional outlets that are found in hospitals, airports, and college campuses; and satellite "lunch counter" outlets that are located in office buildings and other high-traffic areas. These nontraditional outlets can provide additional income for Chick-fil-A's franchisees. In this arrangement, the operator of a nearby Chick-fil-A restaurant acts as the "business consultant" to the licensee of the Chick-fil-A-branded operation (such as one located in an office building or on a campus) and receives a percentage of the Chick-fil-A licensing fee for their consulting services. They also ensure that Chick-fil-A product quality and service standards are met and maintained.
>
> This system must work well—Chick-fil-A is a leader in franchising, and Truett Cathy is a respected restaurateur and philanthropist. Chick-fil-A is one of the largest privately held restaurant chains with more than 1,125 restaurants and, based on annual sales, it's the second-largest quick-service chicken restaurant chain in the United States. The company offers $1,000 college scholarships to its employees, which, over the years, have added up to more than $18 million in scholarships. Cathy founded the WinShape Centre Foundation, which encompasses WinShape Homes, the WinShape Centre Scholarship Program at Berry College, Camp WinShape, and the WinShape Retreat. The company sponsors the Ladies Professional Golf Association tournament called the Chick-fil-A Charity Championship, which is hosted by Nancy Lopez. It also sponsors the Chick-fil-A Peach Bowl in Atlanta's Georgia Dome. The 2004 game contributed more than $400,000 to charitable organizations and provided a record $2.2 million to the two participating universities.

Taking Over from a Franchisor

Besides franchisees, your franchisor can be another source of existing franchises. In some cases, a franchisor may have already selected a site and is looking for someone to take it over. It may be that they found a great location and had to jump on it before they could find a franchisee to take over the site. If this is the case, you'll still need to do your own research to figure out if this is right for you.

Your franchisor may offer you one of its company-owned units so that you can take it over as a franchise, what's known as retrofranchising. This may happen for a number of reasons. Your franchisor may not be interested in running their company-owned outlets and may be pursuing the strategy of selling them to franchisees, or it may need the cash from the sale.

> **Aviary Alert**
>
> When buying a turnkey operation from either a sibling franchisee or your franchisor, consider the staff you'll be working with. Will they work for you—and will they work well? There's bound to be some turnover whenever a new owner takes over a business, but you should hope to keep at least the most vital people on the staff as long as they're willing to be as loyal to you as they were to the original owner.

However, if the franchisor is trying to unload properties that just aren't working as well as hoped, you should go into the deal with eyes wide open. The location may be the source of the problem, and you won't be able to do any better than your franchisor did with it. Or the franchisor may be *churning* a property, a tactic that isn't all that common but one that franchisees should be aware of.

> **Definitions**
>
> When a property is turned over repeatedly so that the franchisor can make money off the sales, it is called **churning** a property.

If you buy your site from your franchisor, you'll be given a new franchise agreement. Again, the terms may not be the same as your original agreement, so you should have your attorney and accountant look it over before you sign it.

Buying a Competitor's Site

To acquire your new outlet you may have to go outside of your franchise system—to your competitor. In this case, you would buy your competitor's location and renovate the site and convert the products and services to your own franchisor's standards and systems. This will cost money, but for some franchisees it may be worth the expense.

There's one obvious advantage to this strategy: you'll put your competitor out of business, at least at this unit. Instead of seeing customers get their oil changed at your rival's tune-up shop down the road, everyone in your community will have their oil changed at your two shops. If you're smart, you can corner the market and capture a larger market share.

However, this isn't always worth the risk. First, you may confuse your customers. Some may not notice that you've taken over and that your brand's products and services are now featured in the shop. They may expect to be able to redeem coupons from the previous owner, which you may or may not honor. Or they may expect to get the same service options they've had for years, and you may not offer it. For example, if you buy a rival's hair salon that offers hair cuts as well as skin care services, whereas your brand only offers haircuts, established clients may not be satisfied with your brand's services. Make sure that you can accommodate the previous owner's regular customers while building recognition of your own brand's products and services.

Another risk is a financial one. It may cost a bundle to convert the rival's location into one that looks like your brand's site. Remember, the power of franchising is in its consistency, and if your outlet just doesn't look like the others, customers will be confused and you'll have to work harder to earn their loyalty. It may become so costly for you to buy the business and to renovate this site that you'd be better off with launching a new franchise outlet from the ground up.

> **Aviary Alert**
>
> Just as in every purchase, you'll have to find out if you can legally acquire a rival's unit. It may have a restrictive franchise agreement that prohibits sale to a competitor. Or your own franchisor may place restrictions on the sale, or you may find yourself in a brother or sister franchisee's territory. Consult your franchisor and attorney before you make any serious moves.

> **Aviary Alert**
>
> As in any sale, find out what, exactly, you are buying. You want to buy the former owner's customer database as well as its physical assets.

Becoming an Area Franchisee

If you've really got grand plans for your future, you may not be satisfied with owning two or three franchise units. You may want to own a larger number of them and build out an entire territory. This option does exist, but generally only with up-and-coming franchises that haven't established themselves in certain areas of the country. A mature megasystem won't have this sort of room for growth, at least not in the United States. (For more on expanding internationally, see Chapter 21.)

If this interests you, you should consider becoming an *area franchisee*. As an area franchisee, you'll have area development rights and be responsible for developing a specific territory and building the units according to a schedule set up by you and the franchisor. In some cases, the area franchisee will develop the units himself according to the schedule.

In other cases, the area franchisee will sell the units to individual franchisees, who become *subfranchisees*. This is known as being a *master franchisee*, which is more common overseas than it is in the United States. The master franchisee is almost like a minifranchisor. It is responsible for setting up and training new franchisees and providing all of the support that a regular franchisor does. It also earns a portion of the initial franchise fee and the ongoing royalty payments. In this way, it earns revenue from its subfranchisees.

Instead of hiring cooks and cleaners and cashiers, an area franchisee needs a business support staff that has real estate experts, accountants, lawyers, human resource personnel, and marketing pros on staff. An area franchisee also needs some political savvy, because it will be developing a number of locations, some of which will need special consideration by various zoning boards and developers.

> **Definitions**
>
> A franchisee that has exclusive rights to build multiple units in a specific territory is an **area franchisee**.
>
> A **subfranchisee** is a franchisee that buys a unit from a master franchisee, not the franchisor.
>
> A **master franchisee** is a franchisee that has exclusive rights to build multiple units in a specific territory but does so by selling units to individual subfranchisees.

This is an enormous undertaking, and many area franchisees are investor groups that aren't necessarily interested in getting into the tanning bed business or frozen yogurt business. They're interested in making the best return on their investment, and if developing a tanning bed minifranchise is the way to do it, then that's what they'll do.

The advantages of becoming an area franchisee or master franchisee are that you truly do corner the market in your territory. If you're interested in building multiple sites, you won't have to do so one at a time and risk losing hot properties to your sibling franchisees. You'll be able to put units throughout your territory, as long as they're approved by your franchisor and are developed according to your schedule.

Of course there are downsides, too. As an area franchisee, you are betting a lot that you will get a return on this large investment in one brand. If for some reason this brand begins to go south—due to poor leadership or a devastating change in technology—you lose your investment not only in one site, but in multiple sites. For some who believe in an emerging brand, this risk may be worth it. However, others may feel that one, two, or three units in a brand is a big enough—and risky enough—gamble.

Eagle Eyes

Many franchisors offer additional training specifically for area or master franchisees. Being one requires business skills that aren't covered by regular training courses, and the franchisor is obviously very concerned with your ability to deliver on your agreement. Make sure that your franchisor will do all that it can to make sure you're prepared for your venture.

Another risk is that you'll be promising to adhere to the rollout schedule you consented to in your franchise agreement. Your franchisor will no doubt help you as much as it can in this endeavor. However, if you fall behind in one unit, that may push back your launch of another unit, and it can snowball from there. The consequences can be serious—not only for you and your franchisor, but for your financial backers as well.

Becoming an area franchisee or master franchisee is a serious undertaking, one that you should consider from all angles. You'll want to identify how many units you want to develop and which specific territory you want. You'll definitely want to call in an experienced franchise attorney and accountant to help you develop your business strategy.

Does It All Add Up?

If you want to develop additional franchise units, you'll need to take a close look at the financial benefits of the situation. Sure, you'll have more purchasing power because you'll be bigger, but will this really pay off for you? Is developing a second or third franchise unit the best way to invest your money?

A good place to start is to examine your original unit. Is it profitable? Does it have positive cash flow? What outstanding debts do you have, and will you be able to cover them while allocating resources to your new business? Does your projected budget match your real numbers, and will it allow you to expand? Can you cover the second unit's expenses until it becomes profitable? Can you afford to pay for all of the support services you'll need from experts such as an attorney, real estate agent, and others who are integral to your success? Remember—just because you know and can trust your franchisor doesn't mean you can skimp on professional services the second time around.

You should also take a look at the timing of this venture. Just because you may feel ready on a personal level to take on another unit doesn't mean that the larger economy is ready. Your area may be in a recession, and customers may not have enough discretionary income to spend on your product or service, especially if it's seen to be a luxury. Bank rates may not support your goals, either. You may be wise to wait until the market turns in your favor. And you may be able to find a more lucrative investment elsewhere, despite your ambitions.

The Least You Need to Know

- ◆ Buying another franchise within your system can help you grow your business efficiently.

- ◆ You're limited by the territorial rights granted to your sibling franchisees, but you can buy turnkey units from them.

- ◆ When you buy an already operating unit from a sibling franchisee, you will still need to pay the franchisor the initial franchise fee.

- ◆ You can buy a competitor's unit and convert it to your franchise's system.

- ◆ Area franchisees are responsible for developing a set number of units within an area according to a specific schedule determined by the franchisor.

Acquiring a New Franchise Brand

In This Chapter

- ◆ Buying a different brand
- ◆ Legal or not?
- ◆ Sizing up the new franchisor
- ◆ Can you mix and match the brands?
- ◆ Co-branding for fun and profit

Maybe you're the restless type, and just one franchise may not satisfy you. In addition to owning an outlet or two under one franchisor's brand, you want to add another outlet, one that isn't your current franchisor's brand. Perhaps there is simply no more room for you to expand within your current system.

In this chapter, I explore how and why you can acquire another brand, and what you need to be careful to avoid. I also discuss co-branding, which has proved to be an effective way to add synergy to franchises that mix well.

Why You May Want to Buy Another Brand

Many franchisees are happy with—and have become financially well off from— running one franchise outlet. They worked hard and grew their business and are willing to grow that business even further.

However, other franchisees have a larger dream. They want to expand, but growing their one outlet isn't enough for them. They may inquire about adding another unit in their current franchise system, but for whatever reason that doesn't work out. Perhaps there are no available units in the territory they want, or they may feel that they want to diversify their investments. (For more about adding another unit of your franchisor's brand, go back to Chapter 16.)

These franchisees often look into opening up a different type of franchise outlet. Their original outlet may be a gym, but they're interested in doing something else that's related to health and fitness, such as owning an athletic shoe store or a smoothie beverage business. They can't open up a smoothie stand or sell shoes inside their gym through their current franchise system, so they'll have to look elsewhere to do this.

The second franchise brand doesn't have to be related to the first one. A gym owner may open a travel agency or hotel, if that's what he has his heart set on. The benefits of owning a second brand are many, if it's done in the right way. One benefit is that the franchisee won't have to wait until her current franchise agreement ends before taking off in a new direction. This franchisee can capitalize on emerging trends by entering into another franchise system now, before it matures and her desired territory is taken.

For example, a new computer service may open up, and the franchisee thinks that the new franchisor has the application that will lead the industry. Getting into the franchise system now could be very lucrative; if she waits until she's free and clear of her current franchisor, it may be too late. She'll still have to operate her original franchise, of course. If she's nearing the end of her current franchise agreement, she may feel an extra sense of urgency about her future.

Another benefit may be synergy, if the two brands are related and can build on each other. For example, the gym owner who wants to open the shoe shop can create synergy. The customer base will be similar—fitness buffs—and the marketing strategies can reinforce each other. For example, the franchisee can tell his current gym members about his shop, and vice versa. He can advertise both businesses, if the two franchisors allow it.

Aviary Alert _____

Remember, franchisees do not own the franchisor's logo or trademark. The franchisor owns it, and grants the franchisee the right to use it. The franchisor has restrictions on how the logo or trademark can be used, and may not want its brand to be advertised with or linked to another brand. Your franchisor may not allow you to use both brands on an advertisement. Make sure that you get your franchisor's approval of your use of its logo or trademark.

A franchisee with two brands can also benefit from efficiency, especially if some tasks can be combined—payroll or bookkeeping, for example. For greater efficiency, the franchisee should really own units of the same franchisor, but in some cases, having two brands can be a smart business move in this sense.

Another benefit is diversification. Just like a good portfolio should contain some slow and steady stocks, a few high fliers, and some real estate or bonds, a franchisee can diversify his business holdings. If the market for one of his franchises takes a dip—hopefully just a temporary one—he won't be sunk for good if he's invested wisely. His other business may carry him through the tough times. It's a way to hedge one's bets, in a sense. Unlike owning multiple units of one franchise system, where all of one's eggs are in one basket, owning a variety of businesses can be a less risky venture.

Location could be a plus, too. For example, a space may open up in an up-and-coming neighborhood that you want to invest in, but your sibling franchisee has locked up the territory. However, you can put in a unit belonging to a different franchisor. You may even find that a space opens up in the strip mall or shopping center where you're currently located, and you can open up another brand in that space. You wouldn't be able to open up another unit of your original franchisor, of course—then you'd be in competition with yourself.

Looking at the Legal Issues

Your ability to own a franchising empire may be restricted by either franchisor. The franchisors may not allow their franchisees to open units outside of their franchise system. In fact, a franchisor can refuse to allow a franchisee to own a business outside of her franchise unit. These franchisors may require that she spend all of her workday at the franchise, because they have probably found that a hands-on owner, and not an absentee owner, is the key to success in their particular system. This shouldn't deter you from owning this type of franchise, though. You should just be aware of the time commitment that's required of franchisees.

You'll find out if you can acquire another brand in the noncompete clause in the UFOC. This clause states whether you can own other businesses during the term of your franchise agreement. The restrictiveness of this clause varies, so know exactly what it means before you sign it. For example, a gym owner most likely would not be able to open up another gym brand, or a quick-service taco franchisor most likely could not open up another franchise's taco joint, and so on. However, the gym owner may be able to open up that athletic shoe store, as long as the gym doesn't sell shoes and has no intention to in the future. The taco restaurateur would most likely be able to open up a pizza place, because these two businesses aren't in direct competition.

Franchise Facts _____

You'll find the noncompete clause in Item 9 (the franchisee's obligations section) of the UFOC of your original franchisor. Make sure you and your attorney understand what it defines as competition before you sign your franchise agreement. Then be sure to check the noncompete clause in the franchise agreement for your second brand. Both franchisors must allow you to own two brands, including the brands that interest you. You should also check out Item 16, which defines what products or services you may sell at your franchise. This may be relevant to your new business.

Other restrictions may be placed on this new venture. Franchisors may specify that the businesses have no connection at all; they can't share back office support or employees or advertising space. These franchisors want a complete separation of the two brands, most likely to preserve the integrity of their brand. They may want to protect their trade secrets or not confuse customers.

Before you get too carried away with your dreams of developing a franchising empire, make sure that you and your attorney have verified that you can acquire the new brand without breaking your franchise agreement. Then make sure that your second franchisor allows it, too.

Investigating the New Franchisor

Just because you've been able to build up one franchise doesn't mean that every franchise system is worth buying into. You'll need to investigate the new franchisor just as closely as you investigated your original franchisor. There simply are no short cuts in this part of the process. You cannot take a chance on a franchisor you haven't inspected from top to bottom, inside and out.

You'll have to start at the beginning and look at what's out there and which franchisors offer what you're looking for. You may have your heart set on one market segment—say, the athletic shoe segment—so you may have a head start. However, you may have a few franchisors to choose from. Ask about whether they allow their franchisees to own a second brand, because this will be a deal breaker for you.

Eagle Eyes

For an extensive discussion about laying the groundwork for multiple-unit ownership, return to Chapter 16. You'll need to be ready on a personal level, but also a financial one. Your current franchise should be running smoothly, too, because you will be spending a lot of time and resources on your newest acquisition.

You'll also have to consider your territory. If your two outlets are not near each other, they will stretch you to the maximum. You'll spend precious time traveling between them, time you could be spending with your employees or customers. Your new venture will have to fit into your new franchisor's plans, too. You will have to locate your place in the territory they decide is right for you.

Aviary Alert

Although some franchisors lower the cost of entry for franchisees who want to add another unit of their current brand, you most likely will not receive the same discounted franchise fee when you acquire a new brand from a different franchisor. So when you consider the costs, remember that you'll have to come up with the initial franchise fee, the other start-up costs, and money to cover your first few months—or more—of the business until it begins generating revenue. Your accountant should be able to help you crunch the numbers.

Another important point to think about is your new franchisor's operating system and culture. You may have gotten so used to working within one franchise system that you think that all systems are the same. However, believe me, no two franchisors are alike. Each franchisor has a specific way of doing things, and this operating system is what makes the business tick.

When you get involved with a new franchisor, you'll have to learn their rules, do things their way, and you must leave your current methods at the front door. You'll have to undergo training, even though you have some experience owning a franchise.

(This can also take you away from your business for a certain amount of time, which can stress out your employees.)

The culture can be very different, too. Even if you believe in the product or service, the culture of the organization may be less than optimal. You should consider very carefully whether you will fit in and can respect those you will work with. The culture may be a great one, but very different than the culture of your current franchisor. Again, you'll have to fit in, despite your previous experiences.

Besides these big issues, you should investigate your new franchisor as thoroughly as you can. Even if it delays your deal, it's better to go into an agreement with eyes wide open, rather than be surprised—or disappointed—after you've made your commitment. Remember, after you sign the agreement you cannot go back. Most initial franchise fees are nonrefundable, so it pays to ask questions up-front.

Mixing and Matching Brands

An important aspect of your decision to take on another brand is whether you can mix and match the brands to your benefit. After all, you're taking on another business to make more money, not to have another expensive hobby. Your second brand should be part of your strategy for growth.

If your franchisor allows it, you can find a brand that complements the product or service of your original franchise concept—an athletic shoe store for the gym owner or a home-repair service for the owner of a carpet-cleaning service. When this happens you can make your clients aware of your new venture, so your second brand will have an existing client base right off the bat, and that's a great advantage. You'll also be pretty familiar with this industry, and that knowledge will help you run the business efficiently.

> **Eagle Eyes** _____
>
> Sometimes, you may not have to go to another franchisor to find your second brand. Some franchisors operate more than one brand. For example, The Service Master Company owns AmeriSpec, Furniture Medic, Merry Maids, Rescue Rooter, ServiceMaster, Terminix, TruGreen, and other brands. Although each brand has its own niche and culture, if you're happy with your brand you may not be happy with one of your franchisor's other brands. However, don't think that you won't have to investigate the second brand—you will. And you won't automatically be accepted by the franchisor, either, nor will you automatically be profitable.

Your brands can complement each other in a different way, too. They can have complementary timing, whether it's the time of the day or time of the year. You can build a morning-oriented business such as a coffee kiosk in an office building with an afternoon- or evening-based business such as an ice-cream shop in a strip mall. You may combine two seasonal businesses—tax prep with a back-to-school business—so that you're busy all year.

> **Aviary Alert** _____
>
> Although you may get a little bored during the downtime provided by your existing venture, when you think about it, you're probably not totally idle. You may attend to paperwork, training, networking, repairs, or inventory tasks during that time. If your new franchise will keep you busy during those hours, you'll be busy around the clock. That may be precisely what you want, but it may be too much for many franchisees.

In some cases, you may be able to allow your employees to work in both franchises. Again, this is up to the approval of the franchisors, but by owning two businesses you can offer your employees more hours, which may help you find and keep better workers. You can keep them busy all year round, too, if you combine two seasonal businesses.

Your businesses can also have complementary workloads and personal investment, too. For example, your first franchise may be an employee-intensive business, such as a fast-food restaurant. However, your second business may be a florist's cart in a mall that only employs one or two people. Your investment will be lower, and your responsibilities won't be as great as running a quick-service restaurant.

As long as you work within the restrictions set out by your franchisor, the combinations are almost endless. Make sure, though, that you don't overextend yourself when taking on your second franchise. It's easy to get caught up in the excitement of becoming involved with a new brand, but this is a long-term commitment that will affect all aspects of your life—including your original franchise and its employees.

Can You Co-Brand?

You can take this mix-and-match approach one step further by *co-branding* your franchises. Again, some franchisors may specifically prohibit this sort of mingling of franchise brands, but some are more flexible—and encouraging—than others.

> **Definitions** _____
>
> **Co-branding**, sometimes known as piggyback franchising, is offering two or more franchise brands under the same roof.

You're probably already familiar with many of these co-branding ventures. You may have wondered why you always see the same combination of franchises across the country. For example, you've probably bought lunch from Taco Bell and KFC's communal units. These are co-branded businesses owned by the same parent company, Yum! Brands, Inc.; it's found that these brands work well together without confusing the customers.

Franchising Eagles

In an effort to make life more convenient for its customers—and make the business more profitable for their franchisees—Yum! Brands, Inc., offers five brand concepts in its organization. These brands are familiar to anyone around the world: KFC, Taco Bell, A&W All-American Food Restaurants, Long John Silvers, and Pizza Hut. Although these brands have thousands of outlets, according to the company about 367 of its units are "2n1s"—units that share two brands, such as KFC and Taco Bell or KFC and Pizza Hut. In this way, friends or family members don't have to agree on what's for dinner tonight.

If your franchisor allows you to co-brand, you'll need to find the right brand to partner with. You'll want to complement each other, not compete for customers. You won't want to confuse them, either. Although co-branding may make sense for some franchisees, it can sometimes lead to diluting the brand, and that would negate all of your hard work.

Eagle Eyes

You don't need to go into co-branding alone. You can partner with someone who owns the second brand, and then find a communal space that works for both of you. Then you can split the shared expenses, such as maintenance, some supplies, and rent. Just make sure that you check out this partner thoroughly, so you won't be stuck with the bills or have their business reflect poorly on your own.

You'll need to think carefully about where you locate your co-branded businesses. You may find that your real estate costs are lowered—instead of building two units, you'll only need one. This can be a significant savings, especially when you consider how much it costs to pay for a real estate agent, do feasibility studies, pay taxes, cover maintenance services, and so on. You may be able to afford a site in a more desirable neighborhood, one that you may be shut out of on your own.

You'll need to consider how you present these two brands to the public. Both brands' signs will need to be visible and not confuse the public. Both businesses will need to present themselves carefully within the space, too. Customers must be able to recognize each brand; the individual spaces should have the same look and feel as individual units of that franchisor. If a customer comes in to buy a bagel and coffee and isn't sure that she's in the right place because it looks like a taco joint, you've got a problem.

Your franchisor may be able to help you devise a floor plan that works best. It almost surely will want to approve how you present the two brands under its collective roof. Remember—the franchisor worked hard to develop its brand awareness and it doesn't want to confuse customers who have come to depend on the products and services provided by that brand.

Whether you co-brand or keep your businesses completely separate, make sure that your decision makes good sense for you and your business. Unlike your first foray into franchising, your decision will affect more people—your original franchisor and employees, for starters. If your first franchise suffers from your lack of attention, financial backing, or leadership, your second venture will struggle, too. You can't be in two places at once, so think long and hard before you sign that second franchise agreement.

The Least You Need to Know

- ◆ Your franchisor may allow you to purchase an outlet outside of your franchise system—but many franchisors prohibit it.

- ◆ Both franchisors should allow you to own the two businesses; they may be related, but they can't be in direct competition with each other.

- ◆ Some franchisors own more than one brand concept and allow their franchisees to own two or more brands.

- ◆ Co-branding allows you to offer two or more franchise brands under one roof.

Chapter 18

Going Public

In This Chapter

- Understanding business types
- Why companies go public
- Advantages and disadvantages of going public
- Going public
- Finding money from other private investors

Going into franchising may seem very simple: a prospective franchisee signs a franchise agreement and gets to work. However, business isn't always this simple. Franchisees—and franchisors—can form a business entity that can shield the individuals from personal liability or help the individual raise capital for the business venture. Further, with the mindset of beginning with the end in mind—meaning that you don't get into something without having an exit strategy—you may want to consider cashing out or a liquidity event at some point in the future. These activities can boost your profitability and turn your franchise experience into a source of wealth.

In this chapter, I explain what the most common business types are but I also discuss a couple of ways of raising capital for the business or cashing out. (I cover cashing out in depth in Chapter 20.) I also cover how a franchisee or franchisor can raise capital for the business. One method would be the initial public offering or IPO. Another would be to seek private investors. The road to the initial public offering is a long and complicated one, which I'll also discuss as well. Although IPOs in recent years have made some investors wary, thanks to the dot-com IPO boom and bust, when done correctly a public offering can benefit everyone involved.

Types of Businesses

As a franchisee or a franchisor, you're in business. However, you have a choice about what kind of business entity you are. This will depend on how much you have invested, how much protection you want from liability, and whether you're in business with a partner or other investors. The main business types are: the *sole proprietorship*, the *partnership*, the *limited liability company*, and the *corporation*.

Definitions

A **sole proprietorship** is when one person funds and runs the business and assumes all responsibility and liability.

An entity that has two or more people who conduct business for mutual benefit is called a **partnership**.

A **limited liability company** is a business entity in which the officers or members are not personally liable for debts and other liabilities—the company is.

In a **corporation** the owners have limited liability, shares of stock are issued, and the entity exists separate from its owners.

Going Solo

A sole proprietorship is a business where one person furnishes all the capital and assumes all the responsibility and liability. This simple setup works for people who have the skills and capital necessary to operate a business. The proprietor funds the business, has complete control over it, and is responsible for everything that happens. All profits go to the owner, and the owner may receive some tax advantages, too.

The sole proprietorship has the greatest regulatory freedom; it doesn't have to register with the state or develop a written declaration of its scope. One disadvantage is that if the venture goes into debt, the creditors may take personal assets from the proprietor. The proprietor isn't personally protected from lawsuits, either.

Eagle Eyes _____

At some point in the future you may want to sell your business—cash out—or somehow restructure your business to achieve a liquidity event. These events are primarily the result of one of three transactions: an IPO, a financial restructuring of the business by taking on a partner or another investor, or outright sale of the business.

Forming a Partnership

In contrast to the sole proprietorship, a partnership has two or more people who conduct business for mutual benefit. It is unincorporated; the partnership doesn't pay income taxes but all partners have to report their profits or losses on their individual tax returns. The partnership depends upon the people involved in it. It lasts as long as the partners agree to work together; it ends when one or more partner withdraws or dies.

Not all partners are equal. General partners manage the business and are equally liable for the debts and responsibilities; each general partner could lose—or make—an unlimited amount of money. Limited partners are not directly involved in the business and are only liable to the extent of their investment. This means that a limited partner cannot lose more money than what he or she invested in the partnership.

Eagle Eyes _____

You can consider forming a partnership if you need to raise capital. You can take on a partner, who becomes a co-owner of your business, to ensure that you have enough money to finance your business. Remember—undercapitalization is one of the greatest threats to a growing business. A partner with deep pockets may help.

Aviary Alert _____

No matter how pure your intentions at the beginning, I think it's wise to put down in writing the goals, promises, responsibilities, and the structure of the partnership. This will help you keep your relationship in check and, hopefully, force you to discuss tough issues before the partnership is established. This agreement shouldn't drive the relationship, but it may help you define what, exactly, your partnership is all about.

Partners should be chosen carefully because they are personally and professionally bound to each other. In the best case, they will complement each other. For example, one partner may be a sales genius whereas the other is happiest managing the business or has all of the technical know-how. Each partner should check out the other partners thoroughly to reduce their risk in their business venture.

The Limited Liability Company

In a limited liability company (LLC), the officers or members are not personally liable for debts and other liabilities; the company is. This adds a layer of protection for those conducting business.

These companies must register with the state in which they're established. Typically an LLC will be governed by an operating agreement or other written agreement, which includes details relating to membership, including relative rights, powers, and duties. It may also provide that the LLC is headed by a manager and may even provide for classes or groups of members in the manner established in the operating agreement.

The Corporation

The corporation is the most common form of business organizations, and one that is chartered by a state and given many legal rights as an entity separate from its owners. This form of business is characterized by the limited liability of its owners, the issuance of shares of easily transferable stock, and its existence. In a corporation, the liability of the owners is limited to the amount they pay for their shares of stock. A corporation is a legal entity, and its continuity is unaffected by death or the transfer of shares of stock by any or all owners.

The process of becoming a corporation, called incorporation, gives the company separate legal standing from its owners and protects those owners from being personally liable in the event that the company is sued (a condition known as limited liability). Incorporation also provides companies with a more flexible way to manage their ownership structure.

There are different tax implications for corporations. One disadvantage of most corporations is double taxation; income tax is levied upon corporate profits and, in addition, upon dividends after they are paid to the stockholders.

However, there are other disadvantages as well. Corporations are closely regulated, so all accounting and record keeping must be thorough and standardized. It's also more difficult to organize a corporation; instead of two or more partners coming together to conduct business, an entire structure must be built and then registered with a state. It's also more difficult to terminate a corporation; with the structure comes complexity and more assets and debts in the name of the corporation.

Franchise Facts

There are several types of corporations, and they are not all equal. The C corporation designation merely refers to a standard, general-for-profit, state-formed corporation. All corporations are C corporations unless they opt to become S corporations. To be formed, an incorporator must file articles of incorporation and pay the requisite state fees and prepaid taxes with the appropriate state agency. In contrast, there's the S corporation, which has fewer than 75 shareholders and allows profits to pass through to the individual stockholders, much the same way as in a partnership. Generally, an S corporation is exempt from federal income tax other than tax on certain capital gains and passive income. On their tax returns, the S corporation's shareholders include their share of the corporation's separately stated items of income, deduction, loss, and credit, and their share of nonseparately stated income or loss. To make sense of this alphabet soup of corporation types, talk to your accountant or attorney.

The advantages of incorporation are many. Owners have limited liability for the business and ownership is transferable via stock options. The corporation exists independent of its owners, so if one leaves the company or passes away, unlike the sole proprietorship or partnership, the business entity will still exist. It's easier to raise capital as well, and the corporation's board of directors serves to create the overall strategy and goals of the business.

If you feel that your business is growing to the extent that you need to take on a partner or incorporate, discuss these matters with your accountant and attorney. If you are a franchisee, you should also discuss it with your franchisor, too, to make sure that it will do business with a franchisee who is operating as a limited liability company or corporation.

Going Public or Staying Private

If your business is growing beyond what can be handled by you, your partners, and your investors, you may want to consider going public through an initial public offering or IPO. As a public company, you will have to abide by specific state and federal regulations and be accountable to your shareholders. Getting to this point can be a long and complex undertaking, but going public allows you to raise more capital to invest in the firm.

Franchising Eagles

One of the most dynamic people in franchising is Russ Umphenour, CEO of the RTM Restaurant Group, a public company that's built on franchises. Umphenour's start in franchising is a common one: In 1967 he landed a part-time job at Arby's for $1.50 an hour to supplement his earnings as a special education teacher in Flint, Michigan. From this rather average beginning, Umphenour has achieved great success. He was promoted at Arby's and made a career of it. In 1973, he formed his own company, RTM (Results Through Motivation) and acquired 11 Arby's units in Georgia and Alabama. From this launch pad, RTM has grown to become a publicly traded company that is Arby's largest franchisee and also owns other quick-service restaurants. In 1999, RTM formed a partnership with BankBoston Development Company, a division of Fleet Bank, and the executive management team of Winners International, the franchisor of Mrs. Winner's Chicken & Biscuits and Lee's Famous Recipe. Umphenour was named the Entrepreneur of the Year by the IFA in 2003. He's also active in the RTM Foundation, which is devoted to philanthropy.

RTM's website explains a bit about its philosophy: "In order to expand our list of successes, each member of our team must be motivated to push past our old limits. We believe this motivation comes from within each of us; no one can provide it for us. Likewise, we can't motivate anyone, but it is our responsibility to provide the environment where people motivate themselves to achieve mutually beneficial goals, and to grow and develop leadership skills as rapidly as possible."

When you're at the point when you are considering going public, you must have many criteria in place. The most basic is that you have an existing business, a platform from which you want to grow and thrive. You must also have a plan for your growth, one that includes a targeted market, the anticipation of demands for your products and services, and the establishment of corporate structures that will enable you to get where you want to go. You've got the ideas, the plan, and the people in place; now you just need the cash. An IPO can help you raise it.

The Advantages of Going Public

I just mentioned the biggest advantage of going public: capital. This money can help you fund the ideas for emerging products and services that up until now have only been in development. It can also allow you to expand your business geographically and build up an infrastructure that allows you to conduct business and grow it efficiently.

Going public will also provide for a degree of independence from liability. In most cases, owners will not be personally liable to the debts incurred by the company. Further, although you may be named in a lawsuit there are generally provisions in place to insulate you from personal liability.

Going public can also generate excitement about your company, and this can contribute to your growth. When you go public, a process I explain later in this chapter, you must sell your story to your investors. It isn't always about hard facts and figures; your story is a personal one, too, one that many people may want to be a part of. Maybe you've been tinkering with your killer software since you were in high school and now you can achieve your dream of helping others communicate with lightning speed. Perhaps you've got a plan to create a hotel empire, the likes of which the public has never seen before. Whatever your story is, it should articulate your dream, and how your shareholders can be part of that dream, too.

Disadvantages of Going Public

Although an IPO can generate the cash and excitement you'll need to achieve your dreams, there are many disadvantages to going public, too.

A big one is public disclosure. Although some entrepreneurs may not feel that this is a burden, many CEOs may not like to open their books and show how they've made their money and how they're spending it. If investors don't like what they see, they will put their money in another company. Your competitors may also gain useful knowledge about your operations, information that can be used against you.

Related to this is meeting expectations. A public company must meet—or beat—expectations every quarter. Especially these days, shareholders will punish a company that's off a bit, even if expectations for earnings were unrealistic to begin with. This can lead the company to make decisions that are geared toward appeasing shareholders—and these decisions may not be the healthiest ones for the company. They may be short-term fixes for long-term problems, and these inevitably are more trouble than they're worth. Remember, if the bottom line for you is profitability, you are bound to make bad decisions somewhere along the way. That's why a healthy corporate culture is so integral to success in business.

Aviary Alert _____

In response to the corporate meltdowns in recent years, more regulations have been placed on companies going public. Although this increases the integrity of companies offering their IPOs, it also boosts the costs and burden of going public.

Public companies are also subject to strict regulation, both during the IPO phase and while they're in business. Now, this can be an advantage for investors and consumers, because watchdog entities such as the Securities and Exchange Commission will oversee the general operation or the financial reports of these businesses. However, for entrepreneurs who prefer little oversight, regulations can be a burden.

For many entrepreneurs, going public is worth all of the effort that's spent on offering an IPO. Becoming a publicly traded company may be an important part of the company's growth strategy—a process to be embraced, not avoided.

How to Go Public

You've probably seen TV reports of entrepreneurs ringing the opening bell at the Stock Exchange and dreamed of doing the same when you offer your company to the public. If you've got your heart set on this, be warned: You've got a lot of work ahead of you, work that the public rarely sees. Many criteria must be in place before you can ask others to invest in your company. Not only do you need a great product or service, but you've got to have your business affairs in place, too.

You've got to have an operating company that has a plan for the future. You've got to have timing on your side, even if you can't control market conditions. However, above all, you have to have a dream. If investors don't see your passion and dedication to your dream, they won't be overly enthusiastic, either.

To create an initial public offering, the following elements must be in place:

♦ The right market conditions. Although you can't control this, you will have to operate within a window that opens and shuts, and you'll have to do your best within it.

♦ Sales growth. Your growth should exceed 15 percent or more, and you should have a plan for sustaining or improving on this growth. You should develop increasing profit margins, meaning that you know how to become more efficient as time goes on.

◆ New ideas. You must have products or services in the pipeline that are being developed by your research and development staff. You'll also need a plan that articulates them and targets growth.

◆ Consistency. Investors hate surprises. They love consistency, even when it seems boring and safe. When you're in the franchising community, some of your consistency comes from the regular royalty payments from your franchisees, which can be an advantage.

◆ A clear strategy and the proven ability to deliver and execute your plans. This may seem obvious, but many companies lack a sound strategy. A key component of this is having a strong team, and not just a maverick CEO. You've got to have depth in all areas of the company with enough strong players who will work as a team.

Eagle Eyes

You can have the best and brightest ideas, but if you don't have the right people on your side you'll never succeed. Make sure that you have managers who can provide constructive criticism and work as a team. Do all that you can to make sure that they stick around as long as possible. And your board of directors should add value to your company. They should be experienced, tough, and hold the other executives accountable for their decisions. This toughness and experience will be comforting to your investors.

◆ A strong balance sheet. You'll most likely have debt, but it should be prudent and not a burden on the company. You'll need the optimal cash structure with your investment bank. Your cash flow is vitally important—free cash flow matters to your financial health.

◆ The ability to communicate your company's financial performance. This goes beyond investor relations. Your leaders must spend time on the business and keep the dream front and center at all times, both internally and when he or she speaks to the public. The company's story should be sold—what the company is all about and how it's going to get to where it needs to be.

If all of these elements are in place, you most likely will have a successful public offering. Developing these factors will take time and a lot of effort, but if you're set on going public, then you should start putting these pieces into place now.

Raising Money from Private Investors

Going public isn't the only way to raise capital. You can also find private investors (sometimes known as angel investors) who will invest in your business—but then they will also own a piece of it. In fact, you might do both as a matter of timing. You can find angel investors on your road to your IPO, if that's part of your overall strategy for growth.

Although generating money from angels isn't as complicated as going public, you should still be prepared to do some homework. You'll need to investigate your investors as closely as you should be checking out your other partners. And your investors should be doing their due diligence, too. After all, your angel—whether it's a private individual, an investment bank, another company, or a group of individuals—will be your partner. Your angel will purchase a piece of your company in exchange for its investment. Your angel can help you with advice and expertise; he or she can hinder you with undo interference and poor strategy. After you partner up with an angel investor, you have made a commitment. Therefore, you need to ask a lot of questions up-front, before you do the deal.

When you're evaluating your angel, you should consider the following issues.

- What is the angel's investment strategy?

- What other companies has the angel invested in? Did the companies achieve their growth objectives? What is the angel's exit strategy?

- How has the angel affected other companies it has invested in? Has the management structure changed?

- Who has invested in the angel?

- How are deals structured? What are the debt tiers? What percentage of ownership does the angel require?

- How will management be affected? What is the management's stock ownership strategy? Are there any restrictions placed on employment, or the ability to network with other companies connected to the angel?

- What's the structure of the board of directors? How often will it meet, and where? What is the format of the meetings?

- What is the budget process?

These are only some of the many questions that should be answered when investigating an angel investor. However, in addition to seeking out these answers, the other companies that have raised capital via these investors should be contacted. If they had been in trouble, find out if the angel helped them out. If they had trouble with the angel itself, find out what happened and why.

The Least You Need to Know

- There are various types of business structures, some of which can help you raise capital for your venture.

- Partners, angel investors, and other private investors can provide a business with capital while becoming co-owners of the business.

- Franchisors and franchisees can go public, provided their business is a sound one and has a well-developed strategy for the future.

- Angels and other private investors must be scrutinized fully before you sign any agreement.

Becoming a Franchisor

In This Chapter

- ◆ Can you franchise your business?
- ◆ The make-up of a good franchisor
- ◆ Clearing the legal hurdles
- ◆ Finding and selecting excellent franchisees
- ◆ Working with professional advisers
- ◆ Growing the system and building your dream

You've got a great business idea and there's nothing else like it in the market. Why not whip up a business plan and start a franchise system built around this concept?

Franchising is big business and employs millions of people; you might as well jump in before someone beats you to it. However, before you start working toward your dream, you should consider if your business would work best as a franchise. Not every business concept would make a good franchise system. Plus, setting up a franchise is a long-term endeavor, one that involves a lot of people, as well as their hard-earned cash. You want to be a responsible franchisor, not just a franchisor.

In this chapter, I discuss a little bit about how a business idea can be transformed into a franchise system. I say a "little bit" because a thorough discussion of this topic could—and does—fill entire books. If you're serious about becoming a franchisor, study up so that you will be well informed. If you aren't interested in becoming a franchisor, reading through this chapter will, I believe, give you a new appreciation for what a franchisor does to build an operating system.

Why Franchise Your Business?

Life is all about pursuing one's dreams in a manner that has integrity. I say that because I've always believed that success is the progressive realization of a worthwhile dream. Some of that dream may involve building a business. You can do this as an employee, as an independent entrepreneur, as a franchisee, or as a franchisor.

Franchisors find that the relationships that connect a franchise community will work best for its particular business type. The franchisor's responsibility in the relationship is to offer a sound business concept and operating system, capital to grow the business, a marketing framework and strategy to grow the brand, complete training and support in running the business, a plan to anticipate and increase growth within the targeted market, and a culture that franchisees can respect. The franchisee's responsibility is to operate the business according to the franchisor's standards, find and work with customers, and supply capital to the franchisor in the form of initial franchise fees and ongoing royalty payments. When this relationship works, it's unbeatable. When it sours, it can adversely affect a lot of people.

Eagle Eyes

Some franchises are regional in scope and appeal, not national, yet they're very successful. If your business concept would appeal to a large market within one or more regions of the country, you may want to consider starting a franchise system built around it.

However, this arrangement doesn't necessarily have to apply to all businesses. All businesses would not make suitable franchises. If a business is built around the owner's personality and not a product or service that's easily replicated, it probably should not be a franchise. If it doesn't have broad geographical appeal and is more suited to fit local clients' needs, it probably should not be a franchise. If the product or service doesn't reach a growing market, then it also should probably not be franchised.

However, for some businesses, franchising can be a ticket to smart growth—growth that is necessary to building the business. Franchising will allow those who buy into the system—the franchisees—to build out the business, making the franchise more efficient and profitable, which allows franchisees to become wealthier. These businesses will use the initial franchise fees to build the system's units and infrastructure, which gives it an advantage over other companies that rely on private investors for their capital.

What Every Good Franchisor Needs

If you're determined to become a franchisor, you'd better do it right. There are three basic features that distinguish franchises:

- The franchisee sells goods or services that meet the franchisor's quality standards, in cases where the franchisee operates under the franchisor's trademark, service mark, trade name, advertising, or other commercial symbol designating the franchisor that are identified by the franchisor's mark.

- The franchisor provides significant guidance in the franchisee's method of operation.

- The franchisee is required to make a payment of $500 or more to the franchisor or a person affiliated with the franchisor at any time before to within six months after the business opens.

However, beyond these basic ingredients, a franchisor will need much more. Most fundamentally, a franchisor needs an original business concept with a support system that builds the business. The franchisor sells agreements to people to develop the brand, and these franchisees use this system to acquire and keep customers.

Eagle Eyes

To see if your business can fit the definition of a franchise, test it by opening up additional locations of your business to develop the support system that's so integral to franchising. You'll need to build a new unit, develop an operating manual, work out agreements with suppliers and vendors, and so on. This will help you understand a bit about what it means to be a franchisor. If your business just can't support another unit, it shouldn't be turned into a franchise system.

This seems rather simple until you consider all that goes into the franchising way of doing business. All of these elements should be in place when a franchisor grants its first franchisee the right to do business within its franchise system.

In a sense, when a business owner becomes a franchisor, she needs to shift her focus from running the business—whether it's making donuts or operating a hotel—and must now teach other people how to run the business. Instead of being behind the counter or working with clients, the franchisor must train others how to do it just the way she wants it.

Every good franchisor needs …

- **An original business concept that can be duplicated in other units.** The product or service must be done in a specific manner to create results that are standard across all franchise units. To put it simply, a tune-up at your franchise unit in Boston must be the same as a tune-up in another franchise in your system located in Dallas.

- **Broad geographical appeal.** If the product or service can be used only by a limited number of people near your business establishment, it probably wouldn't make a good franchise.

- **Broad market appeal.** Sure, your muffins are beloved by a certain type of person, but will it appeal to anyone else? If not, find out what the problem is—it may be your advertising campaign or the décor of your interior. If it's the muffin itself, you may want to tinker with your recipe.

- **A business plan.** Every business—franchise or not—should have a business plan, not only to take to investors, but to set down on paper what your goals are. Writing a business plan helps you think about the health of your business from all angles. You can go back to Chapter 9 for more about how to write a business plan.

- **Legal documents and registration.** You'd better have an experienced franchise attorney on your side. You'll have to register and trademark your logo and other proprietary information so that others cannot unlawfully duplicate your brand's look or methods. You'll also need to register as a franchise in certain states. Plus, you'll need a host of legal documents such as your franchise agreements, the UFOC, and others.

- **A franchisee recruitment and screening process.** You need to know how you can find the right people to help you build your business at the franchise unit level. Who would make a good franchisee? What skills do they need? How can you find them? And how can you evaluate them?

- **A growing market.** Build on a trend, not a fad. You want your product or service to appeal to a growing market segment—but this growth should last longer than your average fad. Identifying your market is key; then develop a sales plan to reach these individuals.

◆ **Disproportionate market share.** You want to anticipate the need for your product and service; when people are ready for it, you'll be there. You'll also want to outmaneuver your competition in site selection and location. You should lead, never follow.

◆ **Plenty of capital.** One of the biggest problems new businesses face is a lack of funding. You'll need enough to develop your business infrastructure and then carry the business until it begins generating revenue.

Franchise Facts

Andrew J. Sherman, author of *Franchising and Leasing: Two Ways to Build Your Business*, offers 40 reasons why franchisors fail. I won't list all of them here, but some of them include: lack of adequate control, choice of the wrong consultants, failure to provide adequate support, lack of franchise communications systems, complex and inadequate operations manuals, inability to compete against larger franchisors, disregard for franchise registration and disclosure laws, not joining the International Franchise Association (IFA), lack of quality control, and breakaway franchisees.

◆ **A training program.** A franchise system is nothing without a highly developed training and support program. This program should be more than a few workshops; it should be a continual process. Highly trained and educated franchisees will make your system a success. Be sure to have enough staff to support this program as well.

◆ **Research and development.** To remain competitive—or to become the market leader—you must constantly fund your research and development department. You need to add new products and services that anticipate your clients' needs.

◆ **A concern for unit economics.** The health of your system depends on the profitability of each unit. You'll need to assign appropriate franchise fees, royalty fees, and other payments—enough to cover your expenses but not so high that your franchisees can't stay in business.

◆ **Management structure.** You'll need the right people in place to help you develop your strategy and see it through. Plus, a strong management team will inspire your franchisees and satisfy your investors.

◆ **Suitable territory.** You'll need to identify which markets should be built out and when, and how you can assign the territory of each franchise unit.

◆ **Relationships with suppliers and vendors.** You'll need to make suggestions for your franchisees, but you'll also need to create standards for your products, and your suppliers and vendors will be key.

◆ **Equipment.** Each franchise unit should have the same equipment, so you'll need to select what equipment they'll need. You may have to lease this equipment to them, so you'll have to develop this support system, too.

◆ **Field support staff.** These people will be the franchisor's eyes and ears, and they can identify and defuse problems with franchisees. An executive-level employee should also be dedicated to working with franchisees.

◆ **Proper accounting and record keeping.** You can stay out of the headlines if you record and report all of your revenues and follow proper accounting procedures.

◆ **Effective communications.** You must be able to communicate internally with your franchisees, but you must also be able to communicate with the public via advertising and promotional campaigns.

◆ **An ethical culture.** You can make a mint if you cut corners and make under-handed deals, but you won't be respected and you won't be in business for long. Ethical decisions should start at the top and permeate the entire culture.

Take a look at this list one more time: I haven't covered all of the elements a franchisor must have in place to be successful, just some of the most important ingredients that go into building a successful franchise system. If you're thinking about becoming a franchisor, you'll need to take a long-term approach to building your business so that you add all of these elements wisely. If you're a franchisee—or a prospective franchisee—this will help you understand why your franchisor charges you an initial franchise fee and royalty payment. A good franchisor will earn it.

Meeting the Legal Requirements

To begin building a sound foundation for your franchise, you'll need to set up the legal structures that will enable it to operate. In addition, you'll need to decide on which type of business will work best for you; go back to Chapter 18 for my discussion of the most common forms of business entities.

Franchises must adhere to federal regulations set out by the Federal Trade Commission (FTC), the primary agency that oversees franchise systems. According to the FTC, franchisors must disclose a minimum amount of information about its business when offering a franchise agreement to a prospective franchisee. Fourteen states require even more disclosure; these states are called *registration states*. To meet these demands, franchisees craft a disclosure document called the Uniform Franchise Offering Circular or UFOC, a document I explore in detail in Chapter 6. Later in this book, I include the Federal Trade Commission's guide to buying a franchise.

Definitions _____

The 14 states that have their own rules and regulations for the offer and sale of franchises within their borders are called **registration states**.

As a franchisor, you will need to develop your own UFOC. The information in it should be accurate and based on the franchisor's most recent fiscal year. If any of the information within it changes substantially, the document must be reworked and resubmitted. You must also offer a franchise agreement to prospective franchisees; this is the document that they will sign, and its terms should be the same as the terms outlined in the UFOC.

Aviary Alert _____

Prospective franchisees are allowed to have a cooling-off period before signing the franchise agreement. They must have the UFOC for no less than 10 business days (14 calendar days under proposed changes), and have the franchise agreement for no less than 5 days before they sign it. This allows the franchisee to make his or her decision based on facts, not emotion. However, the 5 days can be inclusive of the 10 days. For example, the franchisee can receive the UFOC on the 1st business day of the month and the franchise agreement on the 5th business day of the month and sign the agreement on the 10th business day.

Besides the UFOC, the franchisor should have other legal papers in place. The logo should be trademarked, and copyrights should be registered on all proprietary information, including the operating manual. This way you're ensuring that your ideas will not be unlawfully duplicated by others.

You should also consider whether you need to clear other legal hurdles. If you're working in the health-care industry, you should know which regulations cover you both at the federal and state level. If you're in the food-service industry, you'll need to make sure that all of your items meet standards, and that the food-handling processes you've developed are satisfactory. In addition, you'll have to look into workers' safety issues so that the employees of your franchisees—or the franchisees themselves—aren't placed at risk.

An experienced lawyer will help you through this maze of rules and regulations. Remember, you are only as good as your professional advice, so don't skimp on using a qualified attorney. You can find a listing of franchise attorneys through the International Franchise Association. Because of the IFA's code of ethics, you'll always prefer seeking counsel from an IFA member.

Finding and Selecting Great Franchisees

At the heart of the franchise system is the relationship between the franchisor and franchisee. You want to attract the best franchisees to your system. After all, they will represent you to the public and do the hard work of growing your business day in and day out. They will also be in your system for a very long time; a franchise agreement typically lasts for 10 years.

Developing a franchisee profile will help you locate and identify franchisees who would be a great fit for your system. Since each franchise requires a different type of person with different skills and expertise, there is no ideal franchisee profile. Rather, you'll have to develop a profile based on your industry and specific business.

You may have a head start if you already have more than one location up and running; you can consider who does well in that business. However, running a franchise is different than managing a corporate-owned unit. A franchisee must not only have the technical skills needed to create the product or service, but he or she must also have the business acumen to keep the business running.

Developing your own franchisee profile will help you evaluate prospective franchisees. Know the professional qualities you want; perhaps you think that salespeople will work out best, or you need computer programmers or nurses. Know the personal qualities that will help franchisees become successful, such as extroversion or attention to detail. Think about the financial resources they'll need—how much cash they'll need to finance their franchise unit.

Aviary Alert

Consider also, whether you will require your franchisees to be hands-on managers who work a full week, or if they can be less involved—perhaps just involved in the business operations or sales aspect of the business.

You can provide guidelines for your representatives so that they will ask your prospective franchisees the relevant questions. You can prepare questionnaires for the franchisees as well. However you want to handle it, make sure that you have a screening process and don't accept anyone just because they can pay the initial franchise fee.

Identifying Your Market

Even if you have the most amazing product or service, you will need to market your product. You'll need to identify who will most likely purchase your goods or services and for how much money. You'll need to know how you can build on this core market so that you can have even more customers who demand your brand.

Some of this market identification is an art, and some of it is a science. Trained marketers will understand how to test your brand's appeal and message and can identify who most likely will be your customers. The key is to appeal to a market that's growing—baby boomers, for example, or people who are interested in convenience. If you're appealing to a shrinking market then you should rethink your product or service.

Even if your product or service appeals to a niche market, you can develop this market even further. Gourmet coffee is a good example. Initially, gourmet coffee only appealed to a small market segment—people who were discriminating about their coffee and were able to afford to pay a bit more for quality. However, from this base more gourmet-coffee lovers were added. More coffee house chains and franchises opened up, making a good cup of coffee more accessible to more people. The price decreased as well, making it more affordable to more people.

Franchising Eagles

A good entrepreneur will be ahead of the curve and can anticipate what people will want in the future. Take JoAnne Shaw, co-founder, president, and chief executive of The Coffee Beanery. When JoAnne and her husband, Julius, started their gourmet coffee outlet in Dearborn, Michigan, in the mid-1970s, few people were accustomed to drinking strong coffee or espresso. However, the Shaws knew that if customers were given a superior cup of coffee, they would be hooked. As JoAnne put it in an interview, "The marketplace has grown up to meet the sophistication of our beverages." Now, with more than 200 stores in 28 states and seven countries including China and Dubai, the Shaws' dream of building The Coffee Beanery has been realized. The company plans on expanding in the United States and around the globe. In addition to her success as a franchisor, in 2000 JoAnne was the first woman to chair the International Franchise Association—a true Franchising Eagle.

As you consider your market, remember that dominance is key. If you can identify and own a particular market, you will dominate your competition and in addition you will become attractive to other companies. As an example, I sold Mail Boxes Etc. to UPS specifically because of our market dominance. If you are merely following in your rival's wake, you will eventually lose more business. And of course today, we are seeking the same market domination at Sona MedSpa. If you are late in responding to clients' needs—and not anticipating them—your customers will jump brands and patronize another company that can offer them what they didn't even know they needed.

Finding Professional Help

Some essential relationships for a new franchisor are the ones created with the franchise's professional advisers. You want to find the best advisers you can, because they will be guiding you through the world of franchising. In many ways, your franchise will reflect the quality of your advice.

- **Legal advice.** You will need an experienced franchise attorney on your side. You will also need the advice of a corporate lawyer who can help you set up your business structure. You can find these lawyers either through personal recommendations, the IFA, or the American Bar Association.

- **Accounting.** You definitely need strong accountants on your side or you could burn through all of your capital long before you should be spending it. You will also need to set up financial reporting structures that are accurate and ethical. Again, IFA's membership includes accounting firms familiar with franchising. You can also inquire of other franchisors about their accounting firms.

- **Advisers.** You can also assemble a team of advisers that will work for you permanently or as consultants. This team can include marketing pros, experienced franchisors, experts in your field, human resources personnel, salespeople, computer programmers, and more. You can find some of them at the IFA's website under "Suppliers."

> **Eagle Eyes**
>
> Your advisers may not be located where you are, so you can widen your search beyond your local bar association or Yellow Pages. That shouldn't be a problem, as long as they can meet you when it's necessary and they know the laws or regulations in your state.

Asking for help isn't a sign of weakness—it's a sign of strength. Check your advisers out carefully and be willing to learn from them, but also stay out of the way from those who know what they're doing and are applying their expertise to your business. Most professionals will provide a client list and you should speak with several of these references before making your decisions.

Growing the System

The purpose of a franchise is growth. Growth enables the franchise to be more efficient. More franchisees means higher brand recognition, which, if this association is positive, will mean more sales. This will allow the franchisor to offer more locations for development, which will lead to more franchisees in the system. More franchisees in the system also means that supplies can be purchased less expensively, which leads to more profits. And, not to be overlooked, more franchisees means market dominance.

A franchise system can be grown in a number of ways. The strategy developed by a franchise system should be appropriate to that system's product or service, goals, and overall business philosophy.

One component is the number of franchisees. Generally, an increasing number of franchisees in the system means that it's healthy. However, growing too quickly, without adequate capital or support system, will cause serious damage to the brand.

The franchisor will need to identify how many franchisees should be let into the system, and when the new locations should be rolled out. It should also determine where these franchisees should be located. Markets should be built out with care and a clear plan for the future.

Another component of growth is capital. As I explain in Chapter 18, a company can restructure itself to be able to acquire more capital. It can take on a partner, find an angel or other private investors, receive loans from a bank or another institution, or go public and issue shares. However it is done, the financial resources should be allocated wisely and should be able to carry the franchise through the initial phase of its development.

> **Eagle Eyes**
>
> Franchise systems have an advantage over other types of businesses in generating revenue. Thanks to ongoing royalty payments from franchisees, franchisors are able to receive regular infusions of cash, which it can then reinvest in the company.

A critical component of growth is brand awareness. A franchisor's brand is vital to its health, which is why so much emphasis is placed on uniformity of products, services, and appearance. The brand awareness is generated via advertising and also through placement throughout communities. As more people recognize a franchisor's outlet, they will accept it and begin to rely on it for their needs.

Don't overlook the people in your growing system, either. As you grow, you will attract more interest from prospective franchisees wanting to get into your system. As this happens, you can select the best franchisees for you. They may be better educated, more motivated, and have more business experience. This will also add to your growth. You will also be able to hire quality people for your headquarters organization, which will also fuel growth.

The Least You Need to Know

- A franchisor needs a strong business infrastructure—as well as a clear concept—before signing a franchise agreement with its first franchisee.

- While an original business concept may be the most visible aspect of a franchise system, a franchisor needs many more elements—such as training materials and appropriate legal documents—to achieve success.

- A franchisor must take a strategic approach to building its territory and adding franchisees to its system.

- Developing a franchisee profile will help franchisors screen applicants and only sign with those who are right for the system.

- Dominating a specific market is the goal of any franchisor.

- Instead of thinking that seeking advice is a sign of weakness, see it as a sign of growth and maturity. Expert advice can help you build your business if you approach it wisely.

Chapter 20

Staying or Going?

In This Chapter

- ◆ Renewing your franchise agreement
- ◆ Negotiating a new agreement
- ◆ Making changes to your agreement the second time around
- ◆ Leaving your franchise system
- ◆ Can your franchise be inherited?
- ◆ What's your business worth?
- ◆ Selling the business and alternative exit strategies

All good things—even franchise agreements—will come to an end. Of course, for happy, profitable franchisors, the end of the term of the franchise agreement isn't final. It's merely the time to sign another agreement. However, other franchisees will want to get out of the system at some point, whether it's at the end of the agreement or before.

In this chapter, I look at the termination and renewal of the franchise agreement, whether it happens due to time, the desire to sell the business, the dream of leaving it to a family member, or another reason. I point out what you need to look for, and how your franchisor may be involved.

Should You Renew Your Franchise Agreement?

Your decision to renew your franchise agreement is entirely your own—well, perhaps your family will have some input—but it isn't a decision that should surprise you. In fact, if you're wise, you will have thought about your exit strategy before you even signed your original franchise agreement.

Eagle Eyes

Before you decide to sell, think about this: how many times have you struggled with no reward, only to turn a corner and find a new level of success? Franchising is no different. Many franchisees must put in a few years of very hard work before they see any return. If you're thinking about getting out because you aren't seeing the results you want, perhaps you should hang in there if working at the franchise is in alignment with your core beliefs and your dream. If your franchising venture is no longer in alignment with your beliefs, then let go. After all, hanging on too long can often create more problems than letting go of them. Whatever you do, think about your decision long and hard before you take any action.

In my opinion, in most endeavors you should begin with the end in mind. Before you set out in franchising, you should have a dream. Through franchising, you hope to achieve that dream, whether it's to own your own business, earn enough money to put your kids through college, work with people who share your interests, or work at home so you can be closer to your family. Whatever your dream is, you should have a good idea of what your goal is. If you're on your way to achieving your dream, and find that there's room for even more growth in your territory, then you'll probably want to consider signing another franchise agreement with your franchisor.

Eagle Eyes

I've found that if you have done everything right before you sign the franchise agreement, you generally won't consider getting out of the system. That's because before you signed the agreement and you did all of your homework. You asked questions, did due diligence, talked to franchisees, and made sure that the franchise was a good fit for you. You worked hard, took part in every training opportunity presented to you, and turned a profit. Unless some unforeseen event happens, such as a spouse being transferred to another part of the country, you're in it for a very long time.

Your dream may be as unique as you, but I can bet that I know what your dream is not—and that's to struggle, be in debt, and have relationships that are full of conflict. If this nightmare describes your life, and you can't find a way to turn it around, then you should consider selling your franchise, and I explore your options throughout this chapter.

On the other hand, perhaps you've fulfilled your dream. Owning a franchise business helped to get you to where you wanted to go. Now you're ready to do something else—perhaps move across the country or work in a different industry. You may want to put your knowledge to use as a consultant and have more flexible hours. Or you may be ready to retire and reflect with pride on all of your hard work. In this case, you're ready to sell your franchise, too.

Eagle Eyes

Return to Chapter 18 for more information about partnerships, incorporation, or going public. You may have more options than just exiting your business.

Whatever the case, you should know your exit strategy before you sign the franchise agreement. You should know what limitations the franchisor will place on you, and what you must do to renew your agreement. You should know if you can sell your business to another person, or if you can sell it back to the franchisor. I walk you through all of these scenarios, but you should know how you can get out of your franchise agreement before you even sign it.

Keep Your Eye on These Red Flags

Renewing a franchise agreement isn't as simple as copying your current agreement and signing it. There are many items you'll need to be aware of long before you want to renew.

Franchise agreements are meant to last a finite amount of time, usually between 10 and 20 years. When the time is up, a franchisee can usually "renew" the agreement. However, let's be clear—the franchisee won't sign a carbon copy of the first agreement. One—or perhaps two—decades will have passed and the franchisor, the market, and the product or service will have changed. What may have been a new, emerging franchisor 10 years ago may now be the market leader, and it will have established a host of support services and operating technologies that have added value to the brand.

The second time around, the franchisee in many ways is buying into a very different system. In this case, it's easy to understand why the franchisor has changed the agreement, has perhaps increased the royalty fee, and now requires the franchisee to upgrade the site and finally install that new software program or drive-through window. The franchise system has evolved, and the terms of the agreement have, too.

You'll find the terms of the renewal in Item 17 of the UFOC. In it, you'll find if there are conditions under which the franchisor will offer you another agreement. It may state that you'll have to live up to certain criteria, such as being current on your royalty payments and running a unit that's up to operating standards. Bankruptcy, fraud, and anything else that damages the brand can be grounds for denying you the right to renew your agreement. Make sure that you're in good standing with your franchisor when you're ready to renew your agreement.

Franchisees should be aware of these conditions for renewal, and they should be grateful that they're spelled out by the franchisor. In this way, the franchisor can be rid of problematic franchisees that make the whole system look bad. It lets good franchisees know that the franchisor cares about who is representing the brand. It also prevents franchisors from not renewing the agreements of good franchisees. That would be a terrible business practice, of course, but it's always helpful to have these guarantees in place in the written agreement.

Negotiating a New Agreement

Notice the title of this section. When you come to the end of your franchise agreement, you won't renew your agreement, you'll negotiate a new one. And even though you'll likely pay a renewal fee meant to cover the costs of creating a new document, you won't be renewing your original agreement.

Eagle Eyes

If you want to renew your relationship with your franchisor, you should make your intentions known. You should notify your franchisor 6 to 12 months before your current agreement ends so that you can have your new agreement in place on time.

You will most likely sign a new agreement that's the current one used with all new franchisees now entering your franchise system. Some terms will change. The royalty fee may change, based on what the franchisor now accepts from its new franchisees. This may reflect increased services that the franchisor provides that weren't offered when you first signed on.

Your territory may change, too. If you've been sitting on a big territory that was in the middle of nowhere 10 years ago but is now hot property, your franchisor may want to add more units near you. This will limit your territory, but it will also increase brand awareness in your area and your revenues will increase. Listen to your franchisor's reasoning before jumping to conclusions about how this will affect your business.

You may also need to upgrade your unit. If you haven't had to change your decor or the exterior of your unit in a while, you'll most likely have to bring it up to current standards. For example, if all of the new units in your coffee shop franchise have drive-through windows but yours doesn't, you'll have to add one. If you're running an old operating system on your computer, you may have to upgrade to a more current system.

Whatever changes your franchisor makes, note that they're trying to achieve uniformity across their units. They don't want to have a variety of franchisee agreements in effect at one time. If you think you can negotiate a so-called better deal with your franchisor because you've proved your worth over the years, think again. You will be treated like other franchisees entering the system and will be held to the same standards.

As I've explained, consistency is key to a franchisor's success. If a franchisor makes exceptions in a new franchise agreement, that information will become known, and other franchisees will want preferential treatment. However, successful franchisees can gain benefits that aren't included in the franchise agreement. They're qualified to sit on any number of the franchisee committees, such as the franchisee advisory council. As a result, they may have access to new products and services first, which gives them a competitive edge. Or they may have more input in the franchisor's organization, which in turn will create a stronger relationship. One thing I know for sure, every franchisor will listen attentively to any franchisee that is a successful operator and is contributing to the brand value of the system.

> **CAUTION**
>
> **Aviary Alert**
>
> Note, too, that the length of your second franchise agreement may not be the same as the length of your first one. You may sign a new agreement for 5 years as opposed to your original 10-year agreement. Take a look at the termination and renewal clauses in your second agreement, too. They're just as important the second time around.

Exiting the Agreement

If you don't want to renew your agreement, you have options. You can just shut your doors, settle your debts, and move on with your life. However, you can sell your business, too. Technically, you will be facilitating the transfer of your right to represent your franchisee's brand in a particular location to another person's right to do the same. You will be selling your assets and the value of doing business as a franchisee. You've helped to build the value of your business—those long hours at work, those connections you built up in your community, the staff you assembled to develop and serve your customers—and that's what you're selling.

This may seem like a technicality, but remember, in franchising, you do not own the brand or the operating system or even your territory. You are granted the right to represent a brand (the franchisor) in a particular manner (the franchisor's operating system) in a particular place (your territory). Therefore, you will be transferring this right, not selling it. You're selling the fixed assets you own—the real estate, for example, if you own it—and the good will you built up.

When you transfer this right, your franchisor will most likely place some conditions on who you can select as the new franchisee. Your franchisor will most likely have to approve your buyer, whether it's your son or daughter, another franchisee in the system, or a big investment group. The franchisor will have to do business with this franchisee long after the transfer is made, so it will check out your buyer closely.

> **Aviary Alert**
>
> Of course, you don't have to renew your agreement if you don't want to continue being a franchisee. You can just shut your doors and put an end to this phase of your life. If you do just shut your doors, you'll have to pay off all of your debts, whether they're with your franchisor or with vendors or other creditors.

> **Eagle Eyes**
>
> If you are serious about terminating your agreement, you should notify your franchisor as soon as you make up your mind. The franchisor may be able to help find a new franchisee or buy the unit itself, making the outgoing franchisee's exit that much easier.

Your buyer will have to pay the initial franchise fee as well as the amount it pays to you for the business. The new franchisee will have to undergo training, too, and be obligated to fulfill all of the terms the two of you agreed upon.

Of course, you don't have to wait until the end of your agreement to end it. You can get out whenever you want. You may put your business on the market if you have to move or if a personal situation arises which prohibits your ability to own and operate your franchise. However, simply closing your business without your franchisor's approval may obligate you to pay future royalties or other penalties. Your franchise agreement will spell out those penalties.

Aviary Alert _____

Consider, too, how much time you have left under your current franchise agreement before selling. If you have many years left, you will have more leverage with buyers. If you only have a year or two, then your buyer won't have as much security with your franchisor. This may also determine whether your buyer takes over your existing franchise agreement or whether he or she signs a totally new one.

You may want to get out if there's no more room for growth either in your market (you're selling black-and-white TVs when color TVs are introduced) or in your territory (the biggest businesses in town just went under and many of your customers are now jobless). Problems with the franchisor or with potential regulations may compel you to leave. You may not get much for your business if there are warning flags of this type, but you can try to get something for your effort. However, do be honest in your dealings with your potential buyers. Although a sucker may be born every day, it isn't good practice to pull a fast one on someone else.

Eagle Eyes _____

You don't always have to be in the mood to sell when you sell your franchise. A buyer may come to you with a great offer. Sometimes it's a sibling franchisee who wants to add your location to his or her holdings. An employee may want to buy you out. Or perhaps someone just wants your business and will pay you for it. In fact, the buyer may be your franchisor if it wants to run more company-owned stores or if it wants to develop your territory more aggressively. If it's a good offer, you may want to consider it.

On the other hand, you may want to cash out while the market is hot, thinking that you can make more in the sale of your business than you could if you stayed in. For example, if your formerly struggling neighborhood is now a hip gentrified neighborhood, you may want to sell while people are clamoring to get in. (Of course, this development may make you want to stay, too.) If your product or service is now highly in demand thanks to a new trend or fad, you can capitalize on this, too, by selling your unit.

If you are interested in exiting your franchise agreement before it expires, you should make sure that your business is running properly. It should be profitable (hopefully), with good employees and a reasonable amount of debt. It should have a healthy cash flow and you should be in good standing with your franchisor. You should have a regular, growing client base. Again, if these things are not in place, that doesn't mean that you can't sell your business; you just won't get a great price for it. Remember, any buyer will want to look at your books, and if you're in the red, your buyer will either walk away or give you a lower offer.

> **Aviary Alert**
>
> You may want to get out because of problems with your franchisor. Perhaps you aren't receiving the kind of support you'd been promised or you are seriously disappointed with how the franchise executives are running the company. You have some options. You can try to work out the problems with your field representative or others in the organization who are dedicated to franchisee relations. Larger franchise systems may have a more formal process or ombudsman for dispute resolution. You can also try IFA's ombudsman, mediation, arbitration, or, as a last resort, bring a lawsuit against the franchisor. (Your UFOC will spell out how you can resolve conflicts.) Some franchisors include a buyout clause in their franchise agreements. Although it isn't exercised often, this clause allows franchisees to buy out the rest of their franchise agreement.

Leaving the Business to Family

Many franchisees get into franchising because they want to support their family, and they think that franchising is the best way to do so. Therefore, it isn't unusual for a franchisee to want to pass on the business to a son or daughter—many of whom have worked in the business, at least part time or in an emergency.

This is a nice scenario, one that many dream of. However, it can become a complicated venture. First, if you have more than one child, you'll have to decide who gets the business or how it will be split. Of course, perhaps only one of your children will want it, but you don't want to create any resentment if your decision seems to be unfair.

In addition, you'll have to look at the tax implications of your sale (or gift). You'll have to do it at the right time for you so that you aren't unduly penalized. Since there are so many variables involved, consult your attorney, accountant, and financial planner before you do anything.

However, remember that you can't bequeath what you don't own, and a franchisee does not own the logo, operating system, or services of the franchisor. A franchisee can will the assets of the business, but not the provisions set out in the franchise agreement. An experienced franchise attorney can help you explore your options.

CAUTION

Aviary Alert _____

If you go into franchising with the intention of passing on your business to your children, make sure you explore this option with your franchisor before you sign the franchise agreement. Some franchisors may prohibit this, so do your due diligence. You may be able to add your son or daughter as a co-owner of the business so that he or she has the same rights as the primary franchisee, but this option should be checked out with your lawyer and franchisor.

Valuing Your Business

As I mentioned, when you're selling your franchise you're selling your assets and your equity, but you're allowing the rights to do business as a franchisee to be transferred to someone else. The new buyer will pay you for your assets, but he or she will also pay the initial franchise fee to the franchisor, as well as any other fees—for training, for example, if that's not included in the initial fee.

So, what's the value of your business? If it's profitable, it'll be worth more than a failing business. If it's part of a growing industry, is in a great neighborhood, is connected to a dominant brand, has a robust customer base, offers an in-demand product or service, and is an integral part of the community, you'll get more for your business. Timing matters, too. Some of this is intangible, but some of this is based on hard evidence—those numbers you are constantly crunching.

Eagle Eyes _____

Even if you aren't required to upgrade your decor or exterior, you may want to before you put your business up for sale. It's simply one less thing your buyer will have to do to bring your unit up to the uniform standards of your franchisor. It also adds value to your business. Plus, your new look will probably enhance your business, so you will personally profit from it, as well.

Since so many variables go into valuing a business, it's difficult to provide any hard-and-fast rules about how much a business is worth. You'll want to consult a professional, either a business broker or an experienced accountant or lawyer. You can talk to your franchisor to find out what other franchises have sold for, but, again, the selling price will be different for each unit, based on property and other variables.

Selling the Business

If you're determined to sell your business, you'll want to do it right. First, you'll need to get your business in good shape. Make sure your accounts are in order, your debt is manageable, and you have a good relationship with your suppliers, the franchisor, your employees, and your customers.

If an offer hasn't been made to you, you'll have to find a buyer. One good resource is your franchisor. Franchisors often run company-owned stores, so it may be interested in taking over your unit. In addition, franchisors often have lists of people who want to become franchisees, so you can work with your franchisor's representatives to find your buyer.

> **Eagle Eyes** _____
>
> If you don't own your site, you'll need to consider your debts before you sell. If your lease is still in effect or you have outstanding debts, you'll have to clear up these issues before you sell.

You may also want to talk to your sibling franchisees, some of whom will want to acquire another unit. And if the franchisees you've talked to aren't interested, they may know someone who is. Again, your relationships can benefit you in ways that will sometimes surprise you.

You may also want to list your business with a business broker, a professional who facilitates the sales of businesses. This is different from a franchise broker, who is paid—usually by the franchisor—to find buyers for the franchise. A business broker is more neutral and is concerned with finding the right buyer for you, and the right opportunity for the buyer.

However you find your buyer, you should note that your franchisor will often retain the *right of first refusal.* This allows your franchisor to buy your outlet before anyone else. This can be done in a number of ways. Some franchisors match the first written offer you receive. Others will offer the franchisee what the franchisor thinks the outlet is worth based on your revenues or customer list. These numbers can be quite different, so it's good to know beforehand how your franchisor will exercise this right. You should also know how long your franchisor will take to evaluate the offer; if it drags its heels, that could affect your ability to sell your unit.

> **Definitions** _____
>
> The **right of first refusal** is the right the franchisor has to match an existing offer and also to approve or reject a potential buyer as a franchisee within the system.

Franchising Eagles

When offering your franchise to a new owner, it helps if you can assist them in financing the purchase of your franchise outlet. For example, Express Personnel Services offers the Bridge-to-Ownership (BTO) program. This allows prospective franchisees who have staffing industry experiences to become part of the Express system even if they don't have enough capital to cover the initial franchise fee. Thanks to the BTO program, these franchisees can pay half of the initial franchise fee up front, and then become a salaried employee while building their unit. When the business reaches a level of success, the franchise can be purchased from Express upon payment of the remaining franchise fee.

Robert A. Funk, the co-founder and CEO of Express Personnel Services, is a true Franchising Eagle. Not only has he created a network of 400 franchises, but Express is often listed as one of the top companies in the staffing industry. Funk has also contributed to the well-being of the franchising community. He has served on the board of the International Franchising Association, and was honored with IFA's Entrepreneur of the Year Award in 2000. He was also a member of the Board of Trustees for the IFA's Educational Foundation through 2003.

When you do sell, you'll have to negotiate a number of terms beyond the selling price. If you have debt, you'll need to resolve who assumes what portion of it. If you have to pay a transfer fee to the franchisor—and almost all of them require this payment—you can negotiate that, too. You can also discuss personnel issues, and whether you can stay on to help your buyer through the transition and make introductions to your suppliers and customers. If you have a partner in the business, you'll have to work out their relationship and payment as well. You may also need to negotiate the payment itself. It may be in a lump sum, but you can stagger the payment or accept noncash assets, too.

Whatever you do, make sure that your franchisor is aware of your intentions, will allow you to go ahead with your plans, and will make sure that your unit thrives after you're gone. You should also discuss this very carefully with your attorney, accountant, and business advisors. Selling a franchise is a big deal—literally—and you want to go out cleanly and with class.

Alternative Exit Strategies for Multiple-Unit Owners

Simply shutting your doors or finding a buyer aren't the only options you can explore when you want to exit your business or limit your responsibilities. Whereas franchisees who own one unit of a franchise can look at these alternative exit strategies, owners of multiple franchise units will want to take a close look at them.

- **Sell to another multiple-unit owner.** This is becoming more common as franchisees seek to expand and consolidate their holdings. It's easier to absorb a collection of units under one roof, and it means lower overhead, too.

- **Sell to one's franchisor.** If your franchisor has a larger strategy to buy back its franchises, it may be interested in buying your group. However, you shouldn't count on it—franchisors don't want to be their franchisees' preferred exit strategy.

- **The management buys out the owner.** In this scenario, one of the managers of the franchise buys out the owner (otherwise known as an MBO), a scenario that's becoming more common. The upside is that the franchisee will often get a good price for the business because the manager knows the value of the system and is also familiar with it. The downside is that the franchisee often has to finance the purchase by accepting a down payment and then subsequent payments.

- **Take the annuity approach.** In this option, the franchisee hires a professional manager and retains the assets of the business, such as the real estate. In this way, the franchisee will still generate cash flow from his or her business.

- **Find private equity funds.** This option is becoming more popular, especially with the increased number of multiple unit franchise owners. In this case, the franchisee sells to a private equity group, and the new owners will need to find managers or operators for the units. However, this is a viable option—for example, I partnered with Carousel Capital to buy Sona MedSpa. Again, if you're seeking source for private equity, I would suggest partnering with members of the IFA.

> **Eagle Eyes**
>
> When looking at partners, make sure that they are members of the International Franchise Association. Membership means that they adhere to the IFA Code of Ethics and have a vested interest in making a franchise venture work. You can find them listed under "Suppliers" at www.franchise.org.

- **Go public.** As I explained in Chapter 18, going public is an option for large operators, such as Russ Umphenour of RTM. It's now more difficult to make a public offering, thanks to the boom and bust of the dot-com sector, but for some businesses, it may be the right thing to do.

The Least You Need to Know

- ◆ Renewing a franchise agreement doesn't mean that the franchisee will sign on at his or her original terms; the franchisee will sign the franchise agreement that is then current.

- ◆ You should be a franchisee in good standing when signing a new agreement with your franchisor.

- ◆ Your franchisor may have the right of first refusal regarding your prospective buyers.

- ◆ If you intend to leave your business to your children, have your lawyer discuss your options with your franchisor.

- ◆ Multiple-unit owners can explore alternative exit strategies, such as selling to another multiple-unit owner, finding a professional manager to handle the day-to-day business, or going public.

Part 6

Using Your Eagle Vision for the Future

Eagles have amazing vision, which gives them an advantage over other creatures. The eagle can see a dime in 6 inches of grass from a height of 600 feet. The person with eagle vision can see the goal far off in the distance—and I want to help you develop your personal eagle vision.

In this section, I explore what's on the horizon for franchising as a whole. Part of that is the move toward globalization. Franchising has become a powerful economic engine all over the world, one that unites diverse individuals who are pursuing their dream of owning their own business. I also discuss more trends, such as which industries are on the rise and which types of people are becoming more involved in franchising. Last, but definitely not least, you get to hear from some of the people who make up part of the franchising community.

Chapter 21

Going Global

In This Chapter

- ◆ Deciding when to go international
- ◆ Launching a new franchises in another country
- ◆ Finding the right partners and markets
- ◆ Negotiating international agreements
- ◆ Understanding cultural issues
- ◆ Bringing a foreign franchise to the United States

At different times in my career I've focused on international development of franchise systems. Twice, I've put in more than 1,000 units outside of the United States while representing two different franchising concepts. In fact, for one three-year period I spent about eight months of each year outside of the States, often visiting as many as a dozen or more countries in two weeks. I say that because we are moving ever closer to a global marketplace and a global economy. In many ways, it's no longer enough to develop business models solely for the domestic market; businesses, even small to midsize businesses, must have a strategic plan that incorporates international opportunities. Because whether you choose to or not, you will be competing with these markets and these brands.

Many companies, including even those that do not franchise within the United States, are turning to franchising to fuel their global growth, because franchising is a "translatable" concept that enables any business to adapt to different cultures and business regulations around the world.

In this chapter, I explore why franchises are finding new markets in foreign countries and how they're doing it. I also discuss some of the elements a franchise system needs to expand internationally—including the right business model and partners, strong agreements, and cultural sensitivity. I also take a look at what foreign franchises can do to bring their concept to the United States.

Deciding to Expand Overseas

Being a company with an international reach has many benefits. For example, in the shipping business, being able to move packages overseas is a critical one, one that will draw in customers and, in time, will generate significant revenue. It'll have a significant advantage over shipping companies that only serve the American market, since those who wish to send a package across the globe will turn to the internationally focused company.

The decision to expand internationally is a big one for any company, franchise or not. Some franchises make the decision to expand overseas early in their history; for these businesses, a global reach is essential and part of their business plan from the start.

Although some companies formulate the plan to go global early, they may not do so until their American system is mature enough to handle the expansion.

However, other companies decide to move into new markets later, after they've saturated the American market. They simply have no more room to expand within the United States. To grow, they need to cross borders, where they can open up new territories and find new customers.

Franchise Facts

Today, approximately 400 of an estimated 1,500 domestic franchised companies have international operations, and their numbers are growing.

Timing of the market also factors into whether a company can go overseas. The host country's market should be just about ready for the franchisor's product or services. Currency factors have an impact as well as local laws and regulations that can either help or hinder the franchisor's international designs. Each country must be treated as a separate case; just because the business climate is welcoming in Brazil doesn't mean that a franchisor will have an easy time in other South American countries.

Whether the decision to go overseas is made right off the bat or later in the game, franchise businesses have an edge over other business types. Franchising is a particularly attractive vehicle for international expansion because it requires substantially less capital than ownership or the other forms of expansion, including joint ventures. Instead of paying for all expenses incurred while setting up a company-owned outlet overseas, a franchisor can sell the rights to set up the same outlet. The franchisee pays the franchisor an initial franchise fee and then raises the capital needed to establish the outlet. It also will send ongoing royalty payments back to the franchisor on a regular basis.

In addition to financial reasons, the franchising way of doing business is an asset. Franchising is a "translatable" concept that enables any business to adapt to different cultures and business regulations around the world. Franchises are designed to be duplicated in new territories under new ownership. Although standards must be maintained to develop brand recognition, some flexibility is built into the franchise system.

Franchise Facts

A study by one of the world's leading accounting firms indicates U.S. franchisors are pleased with the results they're seeing from their international operations. Based on responses from nearly 400 franchisors, the study revealed that 98 percent would make the decision to go international again. Equally significant is that 95 percent indicated they're planning to expand their number of international units.

While many elements will need to be modified for the franchise to work in a foreign market, the franchise system concept and relationships are essentially the same. The franchisor …

- Grants a franchisee the right to do business under the franchisor's brand.

- Provides training and support.

The franchisee …

- Sets up the business according to the franchisor's instructions.

- Uses this system and the brand recognition to find customers.

- Pays an initial franchise fee and ongoing royalty payments.

- Has a thorough knowledge of the local market.

- Has ties to a community that enhance his or her own business pursuits.

How to Launch New Franchises in Another Country

Franchising for franchising's sake won't work in foreign markets. It must be done properly. A franchisor has a number of decisions to make before establishing a toehold in another country. To be successful, the franchisor will need to determine which franchise model it will follow, who it will partner with, and how it will modify its materials and concept to appeal to another culture. The franchisor must also develop the support system that will keep everything humming, along with the legal documents that will ensure that the business is run properly.

At the top of the franchisor's list is determining which type of franchise model will work best in developing a franchise system in another country. After all, signing individual franchise agreements to individual franchisees in another country can be terribly inefficient. Each franchisee will have to be screened and selected by the franchisor. He or she will then have to come to corporate headquarters for training; the franchisor will have to help identify and set up individual locations in another country; and the team at each site must be trained. As you can see, this is terribly difficult to do and will strain the franchisor's support system.

This isn't the only option for franchising overseas. Actually, I believe the master franchisee or master development franchise agreement works best in international expansion. In this set up, the franchisor sells the rights to develop a territory that will encompass many franchise outlets to one master franchisee. The master franchisee is like a minifranchisor that sells franchise agreements to subfranchisees, who will establish individual franchise outlets. These subfranchisees pay the initial franchise fee and ongoing royalty payments to the franchisor, but the master franchisee will have earned a portion of it, thanks to its support, training, and site development, and other activities. The master franchisee also helps the franchisor and franchisees clear regulatory and legal hurdles that will govern the business.

In short, I believe the master franchisee or master developer is the most appropriate method of market penetration for the following reasons:

- Its efficiency in establishing a global network and family of franchisees.

- The master franchisee is required to provide the financial resources to establish and exploit the business development system. Whatever these resources are, they must be found by the master franchisee.

- The master franchisee is responsible for staff recruitment for the pilot as well as his or her own business organization. This blends the franchisor's business development system into local conditions through the master franchisee's local knowledge.

In addition to the people, a global franchise system must have the organization to launch a foreign venture. It needs to have a mature domestic infrastructure in place. Without a strong base from which it can build, the entire system will be strained—and could even collapse. Think about it: If a franchisor based in Tampa can't work well with its franchisees in Portland, how will it connect with its franchisees in Tokyo? If its franchisees in Austin have a hard time understanding its operating manuals, how will the franchisees in Berlin feel?

Eagle Eyes

For those of you who prefer to look outside of franchising, joint ventures are another possibility for expanding internationally. In this arrangement, the partner will invest money in the business and share the revenue. While it does infuse the business with capital, one downside of the joint venture is that it is much more difficult to disengage from because it isn't defined as well as the contractual nature of franchising.

The franchisor must adapt its domestic products and services to a foreign market. This requires some cultural sensitivity, because the business will have to appeal to another culture. (This is another way a master franchisee can help.) You don't want to change the business so much that it isn't recognizable to anyone familiar with your brand, but you don't want to be so pure or inflexible that your products or services don't appeal to customers outside of the United States.

Franchising Eagles

McDonald's golden arches may be the alternative symbol of the United States abroad. After all, it manages more than 22,000 franchise outlets all over the world. It opened its first outlet in the United Kingdom in 1974 and on January 31, 1990, it opened an outlet in Moscow. But even an institution such as McDonald's adapts its menu items for local tastes. In India, for example, many Hindus do not eat beef, so the Big Mac (known as the Maharaja Mac) is made of mutton or lamb, and vegetarian dishes also are served. In Muslim countries, bacon isn't served; in Japan, more rice dishes are served. There's a kosher McDonald's in Jerusalem. In Italy, an upscale McDonald's features indoor water fountains and marble walls and floors.

This is an area where, early on in international development, the waters were littered with franchisors' bad decisions. Domestically, one of the strengths of franchising is the operating plan in which some things are inviolate. The franchisor won't change anything—fees, products, or services. Because franchisors were committed to what works, they tried to do the same things internationally. But they needed to be more flexible. For example, I opened 13 stores in Taiwan for I Can't Believe It's Not Yogurt, and we allowed menu changes that wouldn't happen in the United States in order to accommodate local preferences. Even with Mail Boxes Etc., we found that some countries favored the document photocopying aspect of the business, not shipping, as in the States. Franchisors are learning that being flexible internationally is an asset, not a liability.

Language is another important factor. Marketing materials, advertising, training materials, and operating manuals must be translated. This has to be done well to ensure that the message you intend to send actually gets across. If potential customers don't get your slogan, or if the employees don't understand the operating manuals, they may as well be written in English.

All legal documents should be in place, too. I'll cover this topic in depth later in this chapter. This not only applies to the agreement your master franchisee signs, but also to the subfranchisee agreements, the documents that cover your trademark and your right to conduct business in the countries you choose, and any papers you need to make your U.S. business work internationally. Each country—or economic unit, such as the European Union—has its own requirements for operating a franchise within its borders, so you'll need to know what they are and then conduct your business according to their regulations.

Finding the Right Partners and Markets

Although franchising in another country presents a wide range of business, legal, and even political issues, just as in domestic franchising, the human factor cannot be overlooked. Finding the right people for the right jobs is essential. However, it should be pointed out that if finding the right franchisee is crucial domestically, it is even more crucial internationally. They represent you in that market. Their image is your brand's image. Because of this interconnectedness, the relationship has to be right. If the venture disintegrates and you have to extricate yourself from that relationship, it may be 5 to 10 years before you can re-enter that market and try to rehabilitate your image.

Just as in a domestic venture, the franchisor-international master franchisee relationship is critical to the success of the enterprise. At the heart of it is trust and integrity, and this is no different than any other franchise relationship, it's just that the stakes are higher and the distance is greater.

Eagle Eyes _____

A franchisor must be very careful when selecting its master franchisees. Although a master franchisee brings more to the table than an individual franchisee, the personal relationship between the master franchisee and the franchisor shouldn't be overlooked. The master franchisee should have personal connections not only with those people who can help him or her build the franchise within the country, but he or she should have a personal connection with those in the franchisor's organization. Chemistry is an intangible quality, but no good agreement can exist without it.

The master franchisee should have a sterling reputation, a thorough familiarity with the industry and with franchising as a business structure, and should have plenty of capital to fund the business. He or she should have connections to developers and those in government who can assist the franchise in setting up operations. They must also share the franchisor's goal of achieving disproportionate market share. The master franchisee who is chosen must have a three- to five-year development schedule that satisfies the franchisor. The master developer should also have a personal connection to the franchisor. Even if the master developer is a large institution, the relationship is developed between people, and they must trust each other and make decisions that have integrity.

Aviary Alert _____

Remember to be aware of cultural differences when dealing with your prospective master franchisees and other business associates. Every culture has its own expectations and standards; for example, you don't want to unintentionally offend someone who wants to be wined and dined while you're all business. For example, I was in Saudi Arabia in the early 1990s, and had a meeting scheduled with the sheik on Monday. I arrived on Monday morning and met with everybody but the sheik, it seemed. Finally, on Wednesday, I was allowed to see the sheik, but it wasn't a private meeting. His advisers were there, but also kids and grandchildren were running around. I asked him if we could speak in private, and he put his ear close to my mouth, indicating that this was as private as the meeting would be. Now, this isn't a typical business meeting in the United States, but in Saudi Arabia it is. If I had arrived Monday morning without plans to stick around, I would not have had that meeting. International business development is always full of interesting stories, and I can't stress enough how sensitive people should be in their business dealings with those from another culture.

You'll also need the right people in your own organization to devote their energies to building your international operations. They should be familiar with the business climate, legal issues, and culture of the targeted country, and be willing to work for you for the long term. Setting up these deals takes time—I've found it always takes longer than you think—and then they'll need to make sure that the new franchise system is operating as planned.

Locating the right market presents a variety of challenges. You'll need to target specific countries that will play into your overall strategy for growth. Moving into each country should make sense to your business; you can try a scattershot approach based on some interest detected here or there, but if it doesn't make sense from a business or operations standpoint, it's not worth doing. This requires a certain amount of discipline and restraint, but it's better to take this long-range strategic approach to building your international network.

The demand for your product or service in the host country is important to consider. While some people may be familiar with your brand thanks to traveling to the States, to many people your product or service may be completely unfamiliar. If it's too different from what people are used to, they may not want it. But, as more and more American businesses are building their operations overseas, and more international travelers are coming to the United States, more American brands will be recognized, easing your marketing efforts. Still, you'll need to know if your business will be accepted in your targeted countries. Marketing and business experts can help you test your brand and business concept.

Take a look at the political and economic conditions of your targeted countries. Are there enough people who can afford your product? Is the society politically and economically stable? Can you source some products locally? Are there excessive regulations placed on businesses in your industry? Must you modify your operations so much that you won't be able to do your business properly?

The accepted business practices of the country you're targeting are something to be aware of. Some practices may be perfectly fine in another country, but would be considered to be unethical in the United States. For example, some government officials may want to be paid for access or to approve your deal. Some of these practices may make you uncomfortable. Be true to yourself and know what your values are. In some cases, your deal will be dragged out or may be more expensive, but your actions may be the right thing for you and your organization.

Negotiating International Agreements

Not surprising, negotiating your agreements will require a certain amount of finesse and a lot of patience. Not only will your terms need to be clarified and agreed upon, but you'll also want to find the right people with whom to be associated.

Part of your mission will be to identify how your targeted countries regulate franchising in their borders. You'll need to adhere to their regulations and most likely offer a different type of disclosure document to your prospective franchisees. After all, you can't just send your regular UFOC to someone in another country—the numbers and information won't be relevant or useful to someone using a different currency in a vastly different real estate market. Therefore, your disclosure document will need to reflect conditions in your targeted country. Most developed or developing countries have trade associations like International Franchise Association (IFA), which can be helpful. They are listed on www.franchise.org.

Eagle Eyes

The U.S. State Department sponsors trade missions and provides a host of information on doing business abroad. You can find more information at www.state.gov. In addition, the U.S. Department of Commerce prepares Country Commercial Guides, which are prepared annually by U.S. embassies with the assistance of several U.S. government agencies. These reports present a comprehensive look at countries' commercial environments, using economic, political, and market analysis. You can find them at www.export.gov. The IFA also has information on how to establish a franchise business in other countries.

You also need to protect your trademark, logo, and other service marks, as well as your operating manual and other proprietary information. Copyright infringement is a serious concern, and you don't want to find that someone has taken over the essence of your brand without your permission. I can't stress enough the importance of protecting yourself. In some countries, there are first usage issues in certain cases; if another company conducts business with your products and services, your logo, and your business operations, they can demonstrate that they own your intellectual property. In these countries, it may be more difficult for you to win a case to get your intellectual property back.

> **Aviary Alert** _____
>
> Your legal papers must be in place when you begin franchising abroad—in some cases, you'll want to protect your trademark and logo before you begin working overseas. You'll need to work with experienced attorneys in the United States. The IFA membership includes several law firms with international franchising experience. During my career, I used the Chicago-based Piper Rudnick (now DLA Piper Rudnick Gray Cary after a recent merger) and felt they had the leading practice devoted to international franchising.

Your franchise agreements also will need to be modified so that they conform to local standards and are fair. Related to this is the amount that you'll charge your master franchisee and subfranchisees. These amounts probably will vary quite a bit from your domestic fees—along with the differences in currency and the cost-of-living standards elsewhere, the franchisees will be buying an almost tailor-made system for them. This can affect what you charge for the right to do business under your brand.

You'll need to understand which regulations affect your particular industry—especially those of you in the food service industry. Just as in the United States, you'll need to meet certain safety standards and nutritional guidelines. This also may affect your decision to export supplies or to source them locally.

Understanding Cultural Issues

Franchising is all about relationships—between the franchisor and franchisees and your customers or clients. You want to appeal to your customers, not offend them, so being culturally sensitive is absolutely required. Having a local master franchisee and subfranchisees will definitely help you find the right message and product mix for your location.

You probably will need to adapt your business to the needs of your market. For example, some American foods may be taboo in a different country, or all of the items on your full menu may not seem appetizing. You may not be able to serve alcohol in some cases—which, incidentally, gives coffee franchises an advantage.

You may need to change your message in your advertising if it doesn't make sense in another language. (This, too, could be offensive.) You'll need to project an image that fits your brand's concept but also is attractive to potential customers. In most cases, the franchisor will provide their domestic marketing material to the master franchisee. You have to be careful. The domestic franchisee pays into the ad fund, and may resent that you give it to the master franchisee. To make this more fair, you can ask the master franchisee to pay into the fund or you can make him or her a member of the domestic ad council. In addition to developing your ads and marketing materials, you'll have to work with local ad agencies in the other country or you can work with an American agency that has offices in your targeted country.

The way you run your business will be affected, too, since your franchisee's employees will be part of the culture as well. Business hours may shift, since some countries don't use a Monday through Friday work week. In the Tropics, many businesses are open in the evening, when it's cooler and people are more comfortable. You may shut down for a few hours during the workday, or you may have more—and different—national holidays.

But despite these modifications, franchises have an advantage regarding cultural issues. First, they can adapt to local conditions thanks to local ownership. Second, your franchise system won't be imposing its products and services on a foreign market; local owners will offer your brand's products and services to their communities.

Tied into this is the factor that, I believe, gives franchising the ultimate advantage: the dream. Americans are not the only ones who have the dream of owning and operating their own businesses. Millions of people around the world share this dream. They can fulfill it through franchising, and that's a powerful message to send across the globe.

Bringing a Foreign Franchise to the United States

American franchises aren't just reaching across the globe; foreign franchises are moving into the American market. Foreign franchises are drawn to the United States because of Americans' acceptance of franchising as a profitable method of doing business and the vast market that can be reached within one country. Foreign franchises may be more willing to do a joint venture with an American company, but they're also interested in working with a master franchisee. The United States is a huge market, and foreign franchisors can find various vehicles that will help them tap into it.

Foreign franchises are held to the same standards as American franchises. They must fit the American definition of a franchise and follow American laws. They have to offer a UFOC and register in the 14 states that require it. They attempt to find market advantages and build their brand, just like any other franchise.

International franchising is exhilarating but it has to be approached with the right mindset. It's definitely not an ego trip. It should be approached carefully, with due diligence. It will always cost you more time than you plan on spending—and it will always take you longer. It also will require more energy and money than you anticipate. But international expansion is worth the effort if you're willing to stay the course. There are great benefits.

The Least You Need to Know

◆ Franchisees that move into foreign countries should target their markets carefully and move into them strategically.

◆ The best arrangement is the master franchisee relationship, in which one franchisee is assigned the task of developing all franchisees within a country or region of a country.

◆ While the strength of domestic franchising is in its consistency, franchisors that move into other countries should be more flexible about their products, services, and brand representation.

◆ The State Department and IFA's global marketing department can be valuable resources for franchisors that want to expand abroad.

Chapter 22

Franchising Trends

In This Chapter

- ◆ Discovering areas for growth
- ◆ New franchisees
- ◆ Going global
- ◆ Owning more than one franchise
- ◆ Conducting business ethically
- ◆ Relationships, relationships, relationships

The power of franchising is due to the people involved in the franchising community. They come from all walks of life and have a variety of personal and professional experiences they can draw upon in a franchise business. This focus on people also makes franchising a very dynamic way of doing business. The human factor enables franchises to adapt to larger changes—in the economy—for example, but also create innovations, as well.

In this chapter, I touch on the trends in franchising, from the people who are being drawn to franchising to how franchising is developing around the globe. I also look at how the franchising community at large is coping with these changes and setting new standards for itself, mainly through self-regulation.

Trends in Franchising

The franchising way of doing business is growing, there's no doubt about that. I think it's because it's a win-win situation for those who want to be in business. For franchisors, franchisees provide the capital and manpower needed to grow the business. For franchisees, the franchisor provides a complete system of doing business, as well as brand recognition, training, and support. Plus, franchising supports the dream that so many of us share, the dream to own one's business. That's a powerful message, one more and more people are attracted to.

Franchising isn't an industry, it's a method of doing business. This type of business structure is found in almost any industry you can think of: lodging, quick-service restaurants, dry cleaners, business support services, florists, fitness centers, office tech support, and so on.

Some of the trends in franchising's growth match the growth in the U.S. economy as a whole. As more people are working at home, business support services are growing. This includes franchises that ship packages, offer technical support, create marketing materials, and do bookkeeping and accounting. As more people are purchasing their own homes, home inspection services, repair and remodeling companies, and cleaners will generate more business. As the job market remains in flux, franchised temporary help agencies will meet the needs of employers. If you can think of an emerging, potentially long-term trend that will affect a large portion of the American economy, you'll find a franchisor willing to move into and dominate that market segment.

Technology also plays an important role in franchising. Not only are tech-based franchises becoming more plentiful—and profitable—but technology is changing the way that franchisors do business. Some franchisors have highly developed communications systems that allow them to keep in touch with their franchisees and know quite a bit about how each unit is doing. Technology also gives franchisors more training alternatives. Although websites and conference calls should never replace a personal training session, they can supplement initial training programs and help franchisees be aware of changes in products and services at any time.

Who Are the New Franchisees?

Franchising is becoming a more attractive business vehicle for a variety of people, and this diversity is strengthening the franchising community.

Women franchisees are becoming more common. Working with data provided by the U.S. Bureau of the Census, the Center for Women's Business Research found that as of 2004, there are an estimated 10.6 million privately held U.S. firms that are 50 percent or more women-owned, accounting for nearly half (47.7 percent) of all privately held firms in the country. These firms generate $2.46 trillion in sales and employ 19.1 million people nationwide. The largest share of these firms is in the service sector; however, the greatest growth in the number of women business owners can be seen in the construction sector.

Many of these women business owners are franchisees. Women franchisors are also becoming more common, too, such as JoAnne Shaw of The Coffee Beanery. Women also are becoming more involved at the top levels of franchisors' organizational headquarters as well.

Franchising Eagles

Its name may be humble—Two Men and a Truck—and its concept may be simple—move the contents of its customers' homes and businesses—but this franchise system shouldn't be underestimated. Two Men and a Truck International, Inc., began in 1985 with the two college student founders and a pickup truck. It made history as the first and local moving franchise in the United States when it began franchising in 1989. Mary Ellen Sheets, mother of the two founders, created a midlife career change when her sons graduated and she took over the business and franchised it. Her founder sons are now back in the business. In 1998, it established its own training center, the Stick Men University, which simulates the challenges its employees face, such as moving a piano and navigating stairways. As of 2004, it had 139 locations operating more than 880 trucks. And here's an interesting fact: women and husband-and-wife teams operate more than half of the company's franchises.

The International Franchise Association (IFA) is striving to meet the needs of women in franchising and to welcome new women to the community. It has developed the Women's Franchise Committee as a resource for women seeking career-growth opportunities in franchising. It also provides international network opportunities, an annual meeting, and monthly phone conferences.

Minorities are finding that franchising presents opportunities as well. Franchising allows someone to become a business owner—but it also provides training, financing, and ongoing support that many minority entrepreneurs lack. To help meet this need, the IFA has established its Minorities in Franchising Committee. The mission of this committee is to increase the number and success of minorities in franchising, including franchisors, franchisees, suppliers, and employees.

Veterans, too, are being welcomed into the franchising community thanks to the IFA's VetFran program, which not only helps veterans connect with franchisors but also helps to finance their ventures. I'm a great supporter of veterans' involvement in franchising, because they are able to follow a system, hang in there when times get tough, and can lead others with authority.

The changes in the economy are bringing new people to franchising. Those who have been downsized find they can use their skills and business connections in the variety of industries served by franchising. Franchising also provides a measure of stability and security that many who have been downsized are seeking. With their franchisor's support, these people can create a second career that's as fulfilling, or even more fulfilling, than their first.

People who aren't quite ready to retire but are at a turning point in their careers are drawn to franchising as well. While some employers may not want to hire an older worker, these workers can become great franchisees before retiring full-time. They can make a 10-year commitment to a franchise system, at which point they can sell their business or pass it on to one of their sons or daughters. In some cases, they can tap into their 401(k) or IRA to help fund their franchise. There are abundant examples in franchising of people collecting social security who in fact come out of retirement to develop a franchise. It may be for the cash flow, but more often it's to restore a meaningful purpose for their life.

This diversity of the franchisee community ensures that it will continue to thrive. Franchises come in all shapes and sizes and aim to meet a host of different consumer needs. The franchise community needs franchisees with diverse skill sets and ties to communities in all parts of the country. In fact, just about anyone who is willing to work hard, has a thirst for knowledge, and lives up to high standards can find a place in the franchising community.

International Growth and Globalization

As the global village becomes more of a reality and provides opportunities where few previously existed, franchising has proved to be an effective vehicle for growth. More franchises are going global either because they've saturated the American market or because operating internationally gives them a competitive edge. Franchises have advantages over traditionally structured corporations. In fact, some companies that don't franchise within the United States are using the franchise system to fuel their international expansion.

American franchises will appeal to Americans abroad, many of whom are looking for a familiar brand—whether it's hamburgers or hotels—and want the standards that they're used to. For example, franchised American business such as Mail Boxes Etc. provides the same services in Asia as they do in Oregon. Some of the franchise's functions are tailored to local needs, but the business is essentially the same, with the same reliability and accountability, no matter where it's located.

As more people from around the world visit America, either for business or pleasure, American brands are recognized by people around the globe. When a franchise brand is developed in another country, it's recognized by those who have already heard about it, and perhaps patronized it, in the States.

As I explained in Chapter 21, I believe that the master franchise system is the best, most efficient way to franchise outside of this country. In this arrangement, the franchisor grants one master franchise license, or perhaps more, depending on the country's size and market, for the development of the franchise system within that territory. The master franchisee must have a lot of connections, since he or she or it, in the case of an institution, will need to select sites, deal with local laws and regulations, choose subfranchisees, and market the brand to an entirely new community. The master franchisee also helps the franchisor adapt its products or services to the local market so that it appeals to customers, and doesn't offend them.

Eagle Eyes

You can find a list of IFA member franchisors who offer international opportunities on the IFA website at www.franchise.org. Some of these franchisors include Baskin-Robbins, Burger King, McDonald's, The Coffee Beanery, Jani-King International, Sanford Rose Associates, Ben & Jerry's, The UPS Store, Applebee's, Big Apple Bagels, Dry Clean USA, Sona MedSpa, and many more.

But franchising isn't a one-way street. An increasing number of foreign franchisors are bringing their systems to the United States. And why not? The American market is a huge one and Americans are familiar with franchising as a way of doing business. But once foreign franchisors are operating in the States, they're treated like any other franchisor and must follow national and state regulations placed on franchises.

Multiple-Unit Ownership

Another trend in franchising is the movement toward multiple-unit ownership. In this situation, a franchisee owns more than one franchise unit, either by acquiring them singly from sibling franchisees, or by developing an area as an area franchisee who builds up a territory according to a schedule set by the franchisor. In some cases, a franchisee will buy a block of franchises from another franchisee, increasing his or her holdings considerably. This strategy, in fact, is how Russ Umphenour, who was profiled in Chapter 18, built his company, RTM.

In many ways, this trend is due to the maturity of some franchise systems. A franchisee in a well-developed system may not have much room to grow; the territory in his system will be saturated by sibling franchisees. To grow, become more efficient, and profitable, the franchisee buys other units in his or her system. When the franchisee has two or more units, this minisystem can consolidate back-office functions, have more purchasing power with suppliers and vendors, and gain more benefits from advertising and marketing efforts.

In response, franchisors are offering training for multiple-unit franchisees. These franchisors have found that a different skill set is needed to keep these units functioning at top speed. So even though these franchisees may have years of experience within the system, they'll still benefit from training. As I've said before, the franchisor's training program should be ongoing, not just a quick session conducted before a franchise's doors are opened for business.

Self-Regulation

In the early years, franchising had a troubling reputation. Thanks to the great opportunities presented by franchising, some people abused their franchisees' trust and ran less-than-reputable systems.

Fortunately, franchising has matured and the franchising community now sets the standard for integrity. Some of this has to do with national and local regulations; the Federal Trade Commission now requires that franchisors provide extensive disclosure documents to prospective franchisees so that they may go into business with their eyes wide open. Some states require franchisors to register with a state agency, and may even have more stringent regulations on the franchisors that operate within their jurisdictions.

The franchising community is working toward elevating its reputation as well, through self-regulation. This trend toward self-regulation is meant to complement the federal and state regulations on franchising. An important part of this trend is the IFA, which has set up various programs to ensure that its members treat their franchisees, suppliers, and customers ethically. This helps protect those who do business with IFA members; they know that IFA members must live up to certain standards of conduct.

One component of the IFA's self-regulation program is its Code of Ethics. Each member must abide by this code, which provides guidelines for doing business. Those who don't live up to it face losing their IFA membership, which would be a great loss. The IFA also has set up an ombudsman program, which helps its members resolve conflicts with the help of the neutral party.

Individual franchisors provide self-regulation in a sense, too. Franchisees must adhere to certain standards of business and conduct, or they will be taken to task by the franchisor. After all, the franchisor wants each unit in its system to operate at peak performance, and franchisees who can't achieve this will drag down the brand. This affects not only the franchisor, but also sibling franchisees that work so hard to provide top-notch service. In addition, many franchisors have dedicated staff members that work on franchisee issues, so that problems can be solved internally. In this way, each franchisor ensures that its franchisees are building the brand, not tearing it down.

Relationship Management

As I've explained many times throughout this book, franchising is all about relationships. These relationships can be challenging at times, but they are the lifeblood of the system. After all, the franchisor contracts with people to own and operate franchises within its system, and these franchisees will be forging relationships with customers and clients within their territory. This personal connection is integral to the success of each franchise organization.

Like I said, these relationships can be challenging at times, but this often happens when the franchisor and franchisee have a zero-sum, us-versus-them attitude that puts franchisors and franchisees in competition with each other. With this attitude, franchisees often feel that they're solely responsible for their success and that the franchisor is out to profit off of the franchisee's hard work while giving nothing in return. Franchisors with this conflict-laden attitude feel that franchisees are nothing but problems and refuse to be grateful for all that the franchisor does for them.

But there's another way of looking at the franchisor-franchisee relationship. In this alternative, more positive view, the franchise system is seen as being built on mutual gain, trust, and integrity. In this view, what's good for the franchisor is good for the franchisees within the system. And, what's more, what's good for a franchisee is good for not only the franchisor, but for the system as a whole.

Definitions

A franchisee advisory council (FAC) is an organized group of franchisees that provide input on the franchisor's strategy and other issues within their franchise system. These councils give franchisees more of a voice within their system, but they rarely set policy.

Many franchisors know their franchisees may resent playing by the rules or making out that royalty check, and they set out to earn their franchisees' trust. They do this by being fair in their business dealings, providing complete training and support, and listening to their franchisees' insights. Many franchisors have set up *franchisee advisory councils (FAC)*, which help the franchisor understand the issues that franchisees face and need help with. Many franchisors also have created ombudsman positions within their organizations, which helps resolve conflicts between the franchisor and franchisee.

However, none of these efforts would mean anything if the relationship lacks trust. Trust requires a sincere effort on the part of the franchisor and franchisees. They must try to see each other's point of view. Franchisees must trust that their franchisor will make decisions that will benefit the system as a whole, in the long term, even when those decisions seem baffling at first. And franchisors must trust that their franchisees are representing the brand as the franchisor wishes them to, even when they aren't in close contact and can't evaluate every operation in the system. This mutual trust can elevate a struggling system into a well-run one, one that benefits everyone involved both professionally and personally.

This attention to relationships was the single most important ingredient that precipitated the growth of the entire franchising segment. Franchisees and franchisors that failed to remember this did so at their own misfortune. The good news is that it appears all of franchising is returning to its roots and is focusing on relationships.

The Least You Need to Know

- Developing franchise markets include office-support services, home repair and maintenance services, and anything to do with technology.

- Women, minorities, veterans, those who have been downsized, and not-quite-ready-to-retire workers are becoming more involved in franchising.

- Due to the maturity of many franchise systems within the United States, multiple-unit ownership is becoming more common.

- Attention to the personal relationships that make up each franchise system supports the growth of franchising.

Getting Advice from Others

In This Chapter

- ◆ Listening to franchisors
- ◆ Learning from franchisees
- ◆ Key pointers from industry professionals
- ◆ Making franchising work for you

In this book, I've given you all sorts of advice about how to get involved in franchising and what it can do for you. But you don't have to take my word for it. Millions of people make up the franchising community, and they are the lifeblood of the system. These people come from all walks of life, are employed in a variety of industries, and have found that franchising fits their way of life.

In this chapter, you'll hear from some of these people. They include franchisors and franchisees, as well as an academic, the chairman of one of the nation's most influential business magazines, and the director of the Federal Trade Commission (FTC). These folks are all consummate professionals, friends, and heroes in the world of franchising. It is a profound privilege to be able to share their thoughts with you.

Hearing from Franchisors

Franchising as a whole has matured into a profitable, well-respected, widespread business model that is accepted not only in the United States, but around the world. But I always think it's helpful to hear how successful franchisors built their companies. Believe me, there is a lot of work, and prayer that goes on behind the scenes of a new franchisor's operations. Although franchising can reduce one's risk in developing a business, it doesn't eliminate the risk altogether. Success is not guaranteed, which we sometimes forget when thinking about businesses that are at the forefront of their industry.

The Visionary

JoAnne Shaw, the co-founder of The Coffee Beanery, shared with me the story of how she and her husband, Julius, developed their gourmet coffee outlet:

> Sitting across from the banker, we nervously waited for him to finish his review of our business plan. He leaned back and put his feet on the desk, crossed his arms and said, "You have champagne taste on a beer budget. I recommend you find another mall." The problem was we had already signed a lease with this mall for 10 years at a cost of $180,000. Another problem was that this was the third bank we met with for a loan to open our first store. At that point, our only option was to continue to present to new banks until we found one that would work with us. Four banks later, we finally heard a yes, but it would require Small Business Administration (SBA) approval and doing a business plan in the SBA format.

> The two weeks it took for me to write that business plan in the SBA format on paper by hand in pencil using a calculator (we didn't have computers in 1975) were probably the best two weeks I spent preparing for the business we were about to build. I learned so many things that were needed to make the business survive and ultimately thrive. Nine months later, after many bumps and bruises during the construction phase, we opened our first Coffee Beanery.

> The early to mid-'70s were called 'the Pepsi Generation.' Coffee, at least good coffee, was nowhere to be found. What was available was freeze-dried and instant as well as some very low-quality cans of major brand coffees. It probably wasn't the best time to open in a regional mall with a concept that never existed.

> Our store wasn't an instant success. I remember the first day we opened the store, my husband, Julius, totaled the sales for the day and looked at me and said, 'If

this is all the business we are going to do we are in deep trouble.' I was determined and said that his full-time job in the insurance field would pay our personal bills, I wouldn't take a salary, and we would manage.

We did. Over the first nine years in business, we opened eight corporate stores, all in malls, all financed on a wing and a prayer. As I look back today I still don't know how we managed to finance those stores. Some of the financing was very creative. Using "leasing money" for everything we could, including the storefront gates and water heaters. And, of course, I still didn't get a salary. In fact, my services were rented for several years before I ever received a real paycheck.

In 1985, we began franchising. My dream had always been, and still continues to be, to help others get in business. Franchising is a business unto itself. It required a different set of skills and knowledge that we didn't have when we started franchising. The first year we sold two franchises to a young man who was a franchisee of Presidents Tuxedo. Thank God he was wonderful to work with and helped us muddle through the first few years.

The second year, we sold one franchise—and we were off to a quick start on a fast track. Actually, our slow growth in the first few years probably allowed us to stay in business. We were learning as much about franchising as our franchisees were learning about the specialty coffee business.

The Inventor Entrepreneur

Richard Rennick was a policeman, but before that, he worked for his father, a plumber. The lessons he learned while working for his father played a large part of his later success, as the head of American Leak Detection, which has more than 300 franchises around the world. Rennick is a former IFA Entrepreneur of the Year, and he's a widely respected franchisor who gives back to the community. But his success came after a lot of hard work and more than a little ingenuity. When I asked him about his early years in business, he had this to say:

> Growing up in a family plumbing company, as a teenager my job was to go to homes and buildings with concrete foundations to look for 'hidden water leaks' coming through those foundations. I was given a couple of heavy hammers and coal chisels to break up concrete here and there in an effort to locate the leaking pipe.

> It was then that I realized the opportunity to establish a company using some type of electronic devices to ferret out hidden leaks. This was not an easy task as

in the late fifties and very early sixties; nothing was available for me to use to locate these hidden leaks. After several years of trial and error, I came upon an electronics engineer who took the chance with me to begin the process of building equipment to help in the locating of hidden pipes, leaks, and so on.

By June 1974, American Leak Detection was born. As we proceeded to alert the insurance industry, the building/plumbing industry and the pool service industry, our fledgling company grew. By December 1984 we sold our first franchise and now have only a very few locations left in North America but the rest of the world is available for this unique and very narrow niche "high tech" service.

When I began the process of awarding franchises, my dream was merely to become a success in this new enterprise. After a few years of attending the 'school of hard knocks' I quickly became skilled in learning that being in business came with a lot of luck coupled with hard work while learning how to build relationships. The biggest dream I have achieved is all about people and helping them to achieve their own dreams. As Ralph Waldo Emerson put those words so eloquently, "Success is what one does for one's fellow man".

The Humble Leader

Ken Walker, the CEO of Meineke Mufflers, shared this advice about the role of an executive in a franchise company. "Those traits your parents taught you—integrity, honor, work ethics, loyalty—are the cornerstones of an individual's success at work," he explained. "The culture the CEO establishes of any company will shine through to the customers. You spend more time with those folks you work with than your family, so hiring people you genuinely like is important if you are to enjoy your life. Ego from anyone in a business hurts much more than it helps. No business has the right to exist based upon what it has done in the past. Success is always based upon today's accomplishments. (Just look at the great brands of the past that are gone today). I believe 99 percent of employees want to do the right things, want to please, want to work hard, want to be loyal. One of the CEO's jobs is to create an environment that lets people know how you define success so that the team can find a way to reach that success."

Finally, he added, "My spouse has been one of my biggest assets in business. Her listening, counsel, courage, and support as we have gone from turnaround to turnaround were a significant reason each was successful."

The Influential Executive

U. Gary Charlwood is another successful franchisor who has touched many lives. Based in Canada, Charlwood is chairman of the board and chief executive officer of Uniglobe Travel (International) Inc., a large corporate-focused franchise travel agency network with 800 locations and 3,000 travel professionals around the globe, including the United States, Canada, the United Kingdom, Belgium, Holland, Germany, Italy, Japan, Southern Africa, the Middle East, and India. Charlwood, as a master licensee, is also co-founder, owner, and chairman of the board of Century 21 Real Estate (Canada) Ltd. with 325 locations and 5,000 salespeople spread across the country. The franchise real estate sales organization has sold more than 1.1 million properties in Canada. He is also a former chairman of the International Franchise Association.

When I asked Gary about his years in franchising, the material success didn't come to his mind. Instead, the personal aspect meant the most to him. "What I find to be most rewarding is when people come up to me and say, 'Do you have any idea the impact you've had on people's lives?'," he said.

To me, that attitude is the sign of a great franchisor, and an attitude that everyone in the franchising community should share.

Observations from Franchisees

Some of the most astute observations about franchising come from those who are on the front lines of the franchise: the franchisee.

The Cookie Man

Doc Cohen has become a successful franchisee who operates a number of Great American Cookie Company outlets, and his story highlights the many changes the franchising community has experienced. Read this story about the good old days, the 1970s, when franchising was gaining in strength but wasn't quite a fully mature way to do business:

> In 1977, I was vice president of what I thought was a successful drugstore chain in Los Angeles. I arrived at the office one day, learned that we were not so successful, and became a very early example of corporate downsizing. Of course in those days, we just called it getting fired. Desperate to find a way to put food on the table, I decided to look into a new concept that my sister had been telling

me about for several months. Great American Cookie Company had opened their first store in a mall in Atlanta, selling fresh-baked chocolate chip cookies. At 25 cents a cookie, they had to sell a bunch of cookies to pay the rent in a regional mall, so I was skeptical that this concept would succeed.

There was no FTC rule in 1977 so when I met with Arthur Karp and Michael Coles, the founders of the company, I was given a glowing report of how much money I could make in the cookie business. I left their offices dreaming of rolling in dough and soon agreed to become a franchisee. To illustrate just how naive I was, I never saw the franchisor's financial statement, never talked to other franchisees in the system (there were only two and both failed in their first year), never saw any store projections, and I had no experience in the snack-food business. At least I had the good sense to engage the services of a top-notch franchise attorney and a very good financial consultant, both of whom helped to steer me in the right direction.

After spending much time searching out a location close to home in the Los Angeles area, I learned that California had a franchise disclosure law and that Great American Cookie Company had not registered to sell franchises in the state. That was a major disappointment, but I was determined to be in the cookie business and accepted the franchisor's offer to take a location in the new Acadiana Mall in Lafayette, Louisiana. At the time, and being from California, I had thought that Louisiana was a suburb of New Orleans. Such a sheltered life I was living. And so I was off to be a cookie magnate in a city that I had never heard of, never visited, and about which I knew absolutely nothing, and in a mall with a name that I could not pronounce. What a brilliant businessman I was!

Lafayette turned out to be a great city with the most wonderful people who fell in love with our product. The store was to become the highest volume store in the Great American Cookie system, and thanks to help from many people, I went on to open 35 locations in seven states over 25 years.

The Accountant Who Became a Frachisor

Bill Hall has a career as an entrepreneur for more than 30 years. A CPA by training, Bill has been a multiple-unit franchisee of Dairy Queen and Church's Chicken, with over 80 units at one time. In addition to Bill's franchisee experience, he has owned and operated community banks in Texas, independent restaurant concepts, a nationwide transportation company, and real estate investments. He has also been very active in the IFA, was a member of the Small Business Advisory Council to the Financial Accounting Standards Board (FASB), and has served as the president for multiple terms of the Texas Dairy Queen Operators' Council, representing more than 800 Dairy Queen Restaurants in Texas.

To prospective franchisees, Bill had the following advice:

◆ Obtain and maintain core competency in your field. Many people do not understand the complexity and risks of owning your own business.

◆ Take advantage of educational and training opportunities offered by franchisors, conferences, trade associations, higher learning institutions, and others to constantly improve your knowledge of your business.

Bob's first six years out of college, he worked as a CPA for a national public accounting firm. He devoted many extra hours to become a good accountant and businessman. That foundation of working and learning allowed him to be self-employed for the remainder of his business career. Over the years, Bob continued to learn and keep current in operations, marketing, accounting, administration, and other areas that impact his business. The knowledge to make good business decisions does not come automatically. He says:

> The effort to be competent, while not assuring you of making the right decision every time, will greatly increase your odds of success. In addition, when you hear the words 'unit economics,' pay attention! That means do whatever it takes to be successful at the individual unit level. Whether you operate 1 or 100 units, each should be successful on its own, as that is the lifeblood of your business. Don't let lower-performing units drag down the higher ones. Do something about the losers by either bringing them up to an acceptable level or consider divesting or closing them. In my view, all overhead of your company, including your compensation, should be allocated to the individual units so that you understand exactly how much cash flow the individual unit is producing for your company. When it comes time to obtain financing or sell your company, one of first questions of a lender or buyer will relate to the *unit economics*. So why not run your business by focusing on unit economics every day?

Definitions

The financial information about each franchise's profitability is called **unit economics**, and it helps franchisees—even those who own multiple units—pay attention to the details of running their business.

Sage Advice from Industry Professionals

In addition to those who operate franchise businesses day in and day out, a number of remarkable professionals make up the franchising community.

The Director at the FTC

One of these remarkable individuals is Eileen Harrington, the director of marketing practices at the FTC. Harrington has worked on franchising issues since 1987 and has seen integrity of the business improve:

> When I first came to franchising, there was a decidedly adversarial edge to the relationship between franchisors and franchisees …. There was not, in my experience, an understanding by either party that the success of one was completely dependent upon the success of the other. I have come to see franchising as one of the most interdependent forms of business relationship, and when that is realized, both in the terms of the agreement but more importantly in the way the relationship is lived out, there seems to be a far greater chance that all will succeed.

> The International Franchise Association has undergone over a decade of fundamental change and has come to embody that understanding of interdependence. From an organization perceived to be hostile to the interests of franchisees, it has evolved to include franchisee interests in all of its affairs. Of course, one reason for this may be that many franchisees are larger than many franchisors, but I think the reason goes deeper than that. Behind Don DeBolt's astute leadership, I think the association really has come to 'get it,' and its realignment speaks volumes to a fundamental shift in understanding.

> As franchising has become more transparent and inclusive of the interests of all parties, it's not surprising to find fewer complaints about deception and fraud, and less need for the federal government to step in with enforcement actions. In addition, the industry itself has developed significant self-regulatory policies, and they are enforced.

> And finally, the IFA runs an excellent compliance training program for all of its members, and a special program for franchisors who violate the FTC's Franchise Rule in ways that cause no economic harm to franchisees. We sometimes refer such violators to this program in lieu of a formal enforcement action, when we believe that the franchisor erred out of ignorance and caused no harm by its violation.

As franchising has matured and become such a significant method for business expansion around the world, it is gratifying to have watched here in the United States the planting of the seeds that now have grown into an industry that has at its core real integrity.

The Franchisee Turned Franchisor

Steven Siegel is another great person to turn to for advice because he has experience as a franchisor and a franchisee. He is currently a director and chairman of KaBloom Ltd. and KaBloom Franchise Corp. Steve was, until July 2004, a partner and director of Watermark Donut Company, a Dunkin' Donuts franchisee, operating approximately 40 Dunkin' Donuts franchise outlets in the Northeast. He also previously served as the chairman of the IFA—the first franchisee to serve as chair—and was the chairman of the Franchisee Advisory Council of the IFA, chairman of the IFA's Standards Committee and vice chairman of the Franchise Relations Committee, and the president of the Dunkin' Donuts Independent Franchise Owners Association.

Steve shared his advice with me:

> Be intellectually curious. Know what you know and, more importantly, what you don't know. Don't be afraid to ask. Don't be afraid to test—in fact, franchising is all about testing. When I was a Dunkin' Donuts franchisee and I saw our competition selling fresh bagels while ours were frozen and of inferior quality, I asked Dunkin' and received permission to test fresh ones. Today, Dunkin' Donuts is the largest seller of fresh bagels in the world.

> Franchising is all about entrepreneurship. Franchise meetings bring a wealth of knowledge, experience, and information together in one place. Share experiences and ask questions. I have never returned from a franchise meeting without at least one piece of information that is useful in my business.

Lastly, he added a few more bits of advice:

> Do the right thing. Communicate, communicate, communicate. Don't be afraid to take risks—just be sure that they are calculated risks. Build an organization. Don't forget to dream. Treat everyone (including customers, employees, franchisees, vendors, and others you encounter) fairly and as you would want them to treat you. Give back to the community—they deserve it. Finally, remember that nothing good comes easily. There is no substitute for hard work.

The Legal Advisor

No industry can grow and prosper without sage legal advice, and throughout the years, Lewis Rudnick has helped the franchising community become the powerful—and respected—force that it is today. Rudnick is a partner in the Chicago office of DLA Piper Rudnick Gray Cary US LLP, Chicago, Illinois. He is counsel to the International Franchise Association and has played a prominent role in the shaping of franchise laws and regulations. He explained how he got started in franchising law this way:

> I started my career as a lawyer in 1964 at the Chicago law firm of Rudnick & Wolfe. The firm represented a number of trade associations, one of which was the International Franchise Association (IFA), a small association of franchising companies that the firm had organized in 1960. There was no recognized franchise law at that time. Franchisors developed and operated their franchise networks subject to trademark law (primarily the Federal Trademark statute), antitrust law (primarily federal law), and the principles of contract law (primarily state law). Rudnick & Wolfe prepared periodic newsletters for the IFA and organized an annual legal symposium for its members and their counsel, tasks that soon became my responsibility. In the 1960's, federal antitrust law had a significantly greater impact of franchise relationships than it does currently. Several troublesome decisions of the United States Supreme Court and lower federal courts were of concern to franchisors and their lawyers and were the principal topics of the IFA newsletters and legal symposiums during the 1960s.

> Toward the end of that decade, franchising was beginning to attract attention in the business press and in state legislatures and administrative offices. The ranks of franchisors had grown rapidly from 1950 to 1965 and a fair number of the companies offering franchises were not well capitalized (relying on initial franchise and territorial rights fees for day to day operating capital), were offering franchises for unsound business models, had no plans or abilities to train and assist franchisees to succeed, or whose franchise programs had all of these characteristics. The inevitable shakeout occurred in the late 1960s and was well covered by the business and general press. The result was the development of state laws regulating the offer and sale of franchises. Starting in California in 1970 and ending in New York in 1980, fifteen states enacted some form of regulation of the offer and sale of franchises.

> In the 1970s, the Federal Trade Commission began a procedure to develop a trade regulation rule to regulate the offer and sale of franchises and business

opportunities. The IFA had its hands full during this period to ensure that the regulation of franchising did not cripple it as an effective business and legal relationship. As IFA counsel responsible for state regulation, my first assignment was to represent the interests of franchisors in the development of the California Franchise Law, a project undertaken by the California Corporations Commissioner and Attorney General.

Support for full disclosure has remained a principal government relations policy of the IFA and has generally placed the IFA in a good position to convince the federal and state governments that this was the only type of regulation that was needed. I believed, and continue to believe, that the full disclosure environment in which franchisors have operated for the past three decades has greatly strengthened franchising for the benefit of both franchisors and franchisees.

The Serial Franchise Owner

Serial entrepreneur Peter Shea knows franchising from the inside out. As former owner of Stained Glass Overlay, he grew the specialty glass franchise company from 10 franchises into 400 in 29 countries. And as owner of *Entrepreneur* magazine for nearly 20 years, he has overseen the publication's growth to a circulation of 575,000 and a readership of over two million a month. *Entrepreneur* and its website, Entrepreneur.com, have educated millions of readers about the opportunities and benefits franchising can offer to those seeking to achieve the American dream.

The first key to success as a franchisee, Shea says, is realizing you are independent—but not completely so. 'You're buying into a system, and you have to be willing to work within the system,' he explained. That's why he believes the most successful franchisees are those with middle-management experience. In fact, if you're too entrepreneurial, Shea said, a franchise may not be a good fit, since 'true entrepreneurs want to tinker and change the way things are done.'

The second key to success is matching your interests to the appropriate franchise system. 'If you're interested in car mechanics, for example, buying a sandwich franchise might not be the best idea,' he said. 'Look at your own interests and align your franchise choice with those.'

The third key, Shea advised, is due diligence. 'Call franchisees in the system and talk to them; meet with the executives and principals of the franchisor and make sure you can work with them.' You'll be working with these people regularly, so make sure you'll enjoy doing so.

Finding your franchise match is the first part of the equation, but not the last. 'Buying a franchise doesn't guarantee success,' says Shea. 'It takes hard work—often 24/7—until your business is off the ground. But with hard work and reasonable intelligence, you can make it a success.'

What advice does Shea have for those seeking to franchise their businesses? First, be aware that it's a whole new ball game. 'You may have a system you've developed for running your business, but being a franchisor is completely different. You're dealing with people looking to you to help them to succeed. More than employees, you now have partners.' To ensure your success as well as theirs, Shea said, be sure you're financially capable of doing all the things necessary to sell franchises and to help them thrive.

The IFA's President

Matthew Shay, who succeeded DeBolt as president of IFA, had this to say:

> During my life as a member of this wonderful franchise community, I've seen many exemplars of the best and brightest in franchising, which includes risk-taking entrepreneurs, visionaries, and savvy businessmen and women. Two of them in particular helped me get started, gave me sound advice when I needed it (and frequently when I didn't recognize that I needed it), and have helped me achieve my dreams.

> The first is the late Cliff Raber, the longtime head of the McDonald's Corporation government relations team, an IFA board member for many years, and recipient of the IFA Honorary Life Member Award for his contributions and achievement in protecting and promoting franchising in federal and state legislatures. Cliff introduced me to the IFA, encouraged me to consider moving from Columbus, Ohio, to Washington to work at IFA, and gave me guidance and counsel when IFA and franchising faced serious legislative challenges and threats in the 1990s. I'm still very proud that since joining the IFA in 1993, we successfully defended the franchise community from serious legislative threats in dozens of state legislatures and have a record of 31-0 against those proposals. Cliff just instilled this sense of success in everyone who worked with him—he just refused to consider defeat an option, and that's something I'll never forget.

> The second is IFA's longtime president, my mentor, predecessor, friend and colleague, Don DeBolt. Don's legacy here at IFA, and his lasting impression on me,

will be that of someone who when faced with a challenge or an opportunity, simply asked, 'What's the right thing to do?' In the answer to that question frequently lies the solution to any problem and certainly provides the appropriate framework for making any decision, great or small. Don's moral courage, his vision of what could be rather than what is, and his willingness to trust and believe in people has affected me in a lasting and profound way. He believes that it is an honor and a privilege to serve the franchise community and he has shared his passion and enthusiasm for this community in a very contagious way. He's helped me get started on the next great journey and adventure of my life, and for that I am eternally grateful. I couldn't have asked for a better teacher than Don.

The ServiceMaster CEO

Michael Isakson is another individual who has experience in all aspects of franchising. He began working at a ServiceMaster part-time while he was in high school, and then bought his own franchise in Bismark, North Dakota. He's been with ServiceMaster ever since, and now serves as president and chief operating officer of ServiceMaster Clean and Furniture Medic. He also was elected to the board of directors of the IFA in March 1999, and serves on the IFA Executive Committee.

When I asked him for advice on franchising, here's what he had to say:

> Advice from others has been a key factor in my success. Role models and mentors in my life have inspired me to seek them out and gain advice from them. As a high school and college student, I was privileged to be acquainted with a local ServiceMaster franchisee whose business and personal life were conducted in a manner that was attractive to me. My admiration for this man caused me to want to learn more about what made him so unique.

> When I was in a career change and was thinking about the advantages of owning my own business, I sought his advice because I knew that Dave had been very successful. My ServiceMaster career and my career in franchising started as a result of getting advice from Dave. He counseled me and helped me understand the benefits, the risks, and the opportunities for development as a part of a franchise organization. Dave's advice made all the difference in the world, and has given me and my family tremendous happiness.

The Academic Franchisee

Cheryl R. Babcock, CFE, is the founding director of the International Institute for Franchise Education in the H. Wayne Huizenga School of Business and Entrepreneurship at Nova Southeastern University. Her long involvement in franchising is an unusual one—she has experience as an academic as well as a franchisee.

My journey into franchising began in 1987 when I was a student in a franchising class at the University of Nebraska in Lincoln, Nebraska. I was just completing my undergraduate degree, and my professor offered me a graduate assistantship to study franchising and to help create the International Center for Franchise Studies. This was the first university program in the United States devoted to researching and teaching franchising. We held the inaugural International Society of Franchising Conference to encourage professors from throughout the world to pursue research initiatives in franchising, and to this day the Society holds an annual research conference and has members from over 20 countries. However, I felt that to truly understand franchising, some real-world, hands-on experience was needed. In 1988, I met Fred DeLuca, the co-founder of Subway Sandwiches & Salads, at an IFA annual convention and soon thereafter became a Subway franchisee and field representative.

I've found that franchising works because it is based on trust. The franchise system needs to have a strong culture that is based on shared values and a core purpose. It is important for each party in the franchise relationship to have the other's best interest at heart, to work toward common goals, and to minimize divergent interests. Franchising is an interdependent relationship that requires collaboration from both parties.

Franchising as a Way of Life

No matter how one is involved in franchising—as a franchisor, franchisee, employee, or supplier—each person realizes that franchising is more than just a business model—it's a way of life. I believe that franchising is so powerful because it allows people to own their own business but be connected to others who are on the same path. This reliance on relationships is franchising's strength, one that I hope each person is aware of and grateful for. There's something incredible about knowing that another person shares your experiences and understands what you are going through.

"I believe in franchising as a strategy to grow the business," said Shaw of The Coffee Beanery. "It can and will win over corporate-owned stores because franchisees are passionate about their businesses. They have a vested interest in making it successful and can be the ambassador to the local community. One of our first consultants taught us what should have been obvious—that in the franchise relationship between franchisor and franchisee no one entity is more important than the other. Working together we can grow the brand and the value of every store."

Cheryl Babcock had this to say: "Franchising is constantly evolving and providing opportunities for successful franchisors and franchisees. Whether you are a franchisor or a franchisee, you will be responsible for driving the success of your franchise system and leading it into the future. In order to take on the twenty-first-century franchise challenges, consider aspiring to the following ideals: strive to expand knowledge and awareness of best practices in ethical franchising; recognize that you are part of a broader community; build a strong team, and encourage team members to participate to the best of his or her abilities; respect the dignity of your workforce and create a working environment that maximizes their opportunities for growth and development; learn from your mistakes; and strive to lead a balanced and integrated life."

"I can't tell you how rewarding it is to see folks succeed who opened a Meineke," Ken Walker told me. "Sam Meineke believed his job was to help new franchisees become millionaires. I am a little different. I believe my job is help them become successful however they define success, which may be as much about lifestyle and family time as it is about money (although I do believe financial success is imperative to happiness)."

"The best advice to be successful is to work hard and do not give up," Bill Hall explained. "I heard someone give a definition of an entrepreneur as 'someone willing to work 16 hours a day for himself, so he can avoid working eight hours a day for someone else.' There is a lot of truth to that. Over the years, I have not always made the right decisions and I have had my share of failures. In the end by working hard and staying positive and focused on the problems a resolution can be found. As my longtime bank partner Ed Luskey said, 'Work hard and you might get lucky.' I sure got lucky and I hope you do, too."

"Franchising is a great way to do business," Doc Cohen of the Great American Cookie Company said. "Knowing what I know today, would I do it again? Without hesitation."

There is very little left to be said after hearing from such heroes and stars as these. I have loved franchising as a way of life precisely because it is so relationally intense.

Franchising is about people pursuing their dreams and making them come true in a community of help and assistance. It is about people helping people and leaving legacies and positively impacting the lives of others.

It is often said that the business of America is business. That may be true, but I believe the soul of business is the business of the soul and that is about the human heart. That is the heart of the franchising concept—changing hearts one person at a time all over the world. Do you have a dream? Then the world of franchising may be for you.

The Least You Need to Know

◆ Franchising is a great way to grow a business.

◆ Franchising is constantly changing and providing new opportunities for entrepreneurs.

◆ Relationships are important to the franchising business.

Appendix A

Glossary

advertising   The vehicles through which a marketing message is conveyed—through print ads, for example, or via billboards.

area franchisee   A franchisee that has exclusive rights to build multiple units in a specific territory.

attitude   A complex mental state involving beliefs, feelings, values, and dispositions to act in certain ways.

brother or sister franchisee   Other franchisees in your franchise system.

business-format franchise   The right to use a brand name and distribute a product plus the operating systems needed to execute the local business.

business opportunity (biz op)   An idea, product, or service that is being offered for sale that will help someone start his or her own business.

business services   An up-and-coming industry; this sector includes everything from photocopying services to package delivery—anything that helps a business continue to run.

co-branding   Sometimes known as piggyback franchising; offering two or more franchise brands under the same roof.

churning   When a franchise of a system is turned over repeatedly so that the franchisor can make money off the sales.

company-owned outlet   Many franchisors own and operate individual units in addition to supporting franchisees in their franchise system.

continuing education unit (CEU)   A nationally recognized method of quantifying the time spent in the classroom during professional development and training activities.

conversion franchisee   An independent business owner who joins a franchise system and adopts the franchise name and method of operation.

corporation   In a corporation, the owners have limited liability, shares of stock are issued, and the entity exists separate from its owners.

cross-training   Training employees in a number of tasks, including those outside of their job description.

exclusive territory   The area in which you, and only you, will have the right to represent your franchise brand.

Federal Trade Commission   The federal agency that regulates the franchise sales and disclosure process.

franchise   A right granted to others by a company to use the company's name and business model to provide products or services.

franchise fee   The nonrefundable purchase of the franchisor's format or business system, and the right to use the franchisor's name for a given amount of time and to receive ongoing assistance.

franchisee   The businessperson or entity who buys the right to sell the product or services of another company.

franchisee advisory council   An advisory committee made up of franchisees within a franchisor's organization.

franchisor   The company that sells the right to offer its product or service to a businessperson.

integrity   Steadfast adherence to a strict moral or ethical code to achieve unity or completeness.

inventory   The goods you hold before you sell them.

license   Permission granted to engage in a particular business activity, usually in exchange for a payment or royalty.

limited liability company   A business entity in which the officers or members are not personally liable for debts and other liabilities—the company is.

liquid assets   Cash on hand.

management information systems   A computer system designed to help managers plan and direct business and organizational operations.

marketing   A company's overall strategy for building its brand.

marketing campaign or plan   A specific strategy meant to identify and convey a message to a targeted market segment. It looks at present activities and the competitive environment.

master franchisee   A franchisee who has exclusive rights to build multiple units in a specific territory and usually does so by selling units to individual subfranchisees.

multilevel marketing programs (MLM)   Often confused with a pyramid scheme, this is a direct-sale business that includes "uplines" and "downlines." Each level buys or sells products to the next higher or lower level.

ongoing support   Assistance provided to up-and-running franchisees to help trouble-shoot, disseminate information about new products and services, and tweak procedures.

partnership   An unincorporated entity that has two or more people who conduct business for mutual benefit.

product-distribution franchise   The right to use a brand name and distribute a product, usually not requiring a specific operating system.

promotions   Temporary sales, offers, or incentives that encourage customers to buy one's products.

proprietary information   Confidential information that was developed by the company for use by the company and only by the company. This can include trade secrets, financial information, product designs, client lists, computer programs, and the operating manual.

quick-service restaurants   This sector encompasses fast-food restaurants and fast-casual restaurants.

registration states   The 14 states that have their own rules and regulations for the offer and sale of franchises within their borders.

renewal fee   If, at the end of the term of the franchise agreement, a franchisee wishes to sign a new agreement, a renewal fee is paid to the franchisor.

retrofranchising   When a franchisor sells a company-owned unit to a franchisee.

right of first refusal   The right the franchisor has to match an existing offer a franchisee may have received for the sale of his or her business and also to approve or reject a potential buyer as a franchisee within the system.

royalty payments   Payment made to some franchisors (usually a percentage of the franchisee's total revenue) during the duration of the term of the franchise agreement.

sales plan   Identifies the product to be sold to the identified market, how it will be sold, and where. This plan is developed after determining one's market.

servant leadership   True leadership; having others' best interests at heart and being willing to do more for them and serve them.

sole proprietorship   One person funds and runs the business and assumes all responsibility and liability.

subfranchisee   A franchisee that buys a unit from a master franchisee, and not the franchisor.

supplier   The companies that will provide you with your supplies or services required to operate the franchise.

supplies   The items you'll need to run your business, including the products you'll sell and items that are part of the structure, such as shelves, computers, and so on.

synergistic   Working together; used especially by groups as subsidiaries of a corporation, cooperating for an enhanced effect or cross-selling each other's products or services.

territory   The area in which you will conduct your business; usually this is defined geographically.

training   The ongoing instruction provided to new and existing franchisees, especially when new products or procedures are introduced.

transfer fee   If a franchisee wishes to sell his or her unit to a new owner, this fee is paid to the franchisor.

transfer rights   The franchisee's right to sell the unit to another person with the approval of the franchisor.

turnkey operation   A business that is already operating and is to be turned over to a new owner. This can be a franchise, but it doesn't have to be one.

Uniform Franchise Offering Circular (UFOC)   The extensive disclosure document a franchisor must present to any potential franchisee, the content of which is mandated by certain states and the Federal Trade Commission.

working capital   The amount of money needed to fund a business until it begins generating income. This is usually an estimated amount.

Appendix

Resources

To help you begin your search for the right franchise opportunity for you, here is a list of basic resources.

Better Business Bureau
The Council of Better Business Bureaus
4200 Wilson Blvd., Suite 800
Arlington, VA 22203-1838
703-276-0100
www.bbb.org

Entrepreneur Magazine
www.entrepreneur.com

Export.gov (the United States government portal to exporting and trade services)
1-800-USA-TRADE
www.export.gov

Federal Trade Commission
600 Pennsylvania Ave., NW
Washington, D.C. 20580
202-326-2222
www.ftc.gov

Fortune Magazine
www.fortune.com/fortune

IFA Educational Foundation
1350 New York Ave., NW, Suite 900
Washington, D.C. 20005
202-628-8000
www.franchise.org/edufound/edufound.asp

International Franchise Association
1350 New York Ave., NW, Suite 900
Washington, D.C. 20005-4709
202-628-8000
ifa@franchise.org
www.franchise.org

National Restaurant Association
1200 17th St., NW
Washington, D.C. 20036
202-331-5900
www.restaurant.org

Startup Journal
The Wall Street Journal Center for Entrepreneurs
www.startupjournal.com

U.S. Chamber of Commerce
1615 H St., NW
Washington, D.C. 20062-2000
Main Number: 202-659-6000
Customer Service: 1-800-638-6582
www.uschamber.com

U.S. Department of State
2201 C St., NW
Washington, D.C. 20520
Main Switchboard: 202-647-4000
TDD: 1-800-877-8339 (Federal Relay Service)
www.state.gov

U.S. Small Business Administration
409 Third St., SW
Washington, D.C. 20416
1-800-U-ASK-SBA
www.sba.gov

USA Today
www.usatoday.com

World Franchise Council
1350 New York Ave., NW, Suite 900
Washington, D.C. 20005-4709
202-628-8000
www.worldfranchisecouncil.org

Federal Trade Commission's Consumer Guide to Buying a Franchise

Buying a franchise is investing in your future. Because the International Franchise Association wants tomorrow's business owners to make educated decisions about their futures, it provides the following information from the Federal Trade Commission's (FTC) "Consumer Guide to Buying a Franchise." The IFA recommends enlisting the help of an attorney, business consultant, and accountant when investigating franchise systems before investing.

Note: The FTC "Consumer Guide to Buying a Franchise" is reprinted in IFA's *Franchise Opportunities Guide*, a directory of nearly 1,000 franchise companies that provides information to educate prospective franchisees. News media representatives may get a free copy of the guide by sending a request on company letterhead or by contacting IFA Media Relations, 202-628-8000. Visit IFA's website at www.franchise.org.

Introduction to the Guide

Many people dream of being an entrepreneur. By purchasing a franchise, you can sell goods and services that have instant name recognition and can obtain training and ongoing support to help you succeed. But be cautious. Like any investment, purchasing a franchise does not guarantee success.

To help you evaluate whether owning a franchise is right for you, the following information will help you understand your obligations as a franchise owner, how to shop for franchise opportunities, and how to ask the right questions before you invest.

The Benefits and Responsibilities of Franchise Ownership

A franchise typically enables you, the investor or "franchisee," to operate a business. By paying a franchise fee, which may cost several thousand dollars, you are given a format or system developed by the company ("franchisor"), the right to use the franchisor's name for a limited time, and assistance. For example, the franchisor may help you find a location for your outlet; provide initial training and an operating manual; and advise you on management, marketing, or personnel. Some franchisors offer ongoing support such as monthly newsletters, a toll free 800 telephone number for technical assistance, and periodic workshops or seminars.

While buying a franchise may reduce your investment risk by enabling you to associate with an established company, it can be costly. You also may be required to relinquish significant control over your business, while taking on contractual obligations with the franchisor. Following is an outline of several components of a typical franchise system. Consider each carefully.

I. The Cost

In exchange for obtaining the right to use the franchisor's name and its assistance, you may pay some or all of the fees discussed in the following sections.

Initial Franchise Fee and Other Expenses

Your initial franchise fee, which may be nonrefundable, may cost several thousand to several hundred thousand dollars. You may also incur significant costs to rent, build, and equip an outlet and to purchase initial inventory. Other costs include operating licenses and insurance. You also may be required to pay a "grand opening" fee to the franchisor to promote your new outlet.

Continuing Royalty Payments

You may have to pay the franchisor royalties based on a percentage of your weekly or monthly gross income. You often must pay royalties even if your outlet has not earned significant income during that time. In addition, royalties usually are paid for the right to use the franchisor's name. So even if the franchisor fails to provide promised support services, you still may have to pay royalties for the duration of your franchise agreement.

Advertising Fees

You may have to pay into an advertising fund. Some portion of the advertising fees may go for national advertising or to attract new franchise owners, but not to target your particular outlet.

II. Controls

To ensure uniformity, franchisors typically control how franchisees conduct business. These controls may significantly restrict your ability to exercise your own business judgment. The following sections are typical examples of such controls.

Site Approval

Many franchisors pre-approve sites for outlets. This may increase the likelihood that your outlet will attract customers. The franchisor, however, may not approve the site you want.

Design or Appearance Standards

Franchisors may impose design or appearance standards to ensure customers receive the same quality of goods and services in each outlet. Some franchisors require periodic renovations or seasonal design changes. Complying with these standards may increase your costs.

Restrictions on Goods and Services Offered for Sale

Franchisors may restrict the goods and services offered for sale. For example, as a restaurant franchise owner, you may not be able to add to your menu popular items or delete items that are unpopular. Similarly, as an automobile transmission repair franchise owner, you might not be able to perform other types of automotive work, such as brake or electrical system repairs.

Restrictions on Method of Operation

Franchisors may require you to operate in a particular manner, during certain hours, use only pre-approved signs, employee uniforms, and advertisements, or abide by certain accounting or bookkeeping procedures. These restrictions may impede you from operating your outlet as you deem best. The franchisor also may require you to purchase supplies only from an approved supplier, even if you can buy similar goods elsewhere at a lower cost.

Restrictions of Sales Area

Franchisors may limit your business to a specific territory. While these territorial restrictions may ensure that other franchisees will not compete with you for the same customers, they could impede your ability to open additional outlets or move to a more profitable location.

III. Terminations and Renewal

You can lose the right to your franchise if you breach the franchise contract. In addition, the franchise contract is for a limited time; there is no guarantee that you will be able to renew it.

Franchise Terminations

A franchisor can end your franchise agreement if, for example, you fail to pay royalties or abide by performance standards and sales restrictions. If your franchise is terminated, you may lose your investment.

Renewals

Franchise agreements typically run for 15 to 20 years. After that time, the franchisor may decline to renew your contract. Also be aware that renewals need not provide the original terms and conditions. The franchisor may raise the royalty payments, or impose new design standards and sales restrictions. Your previous territory may be reduced, possibly resulting in more competition from company-owned outlets or other franchisees.

IV. Before Selecting a Franchise System

Before investing in a particular franchise system, carefully consider how much money you have to invest, your abilities, and your goals. The checklists in the following sections may help you make your decision.

Your Investment

- How much money do you have to invest?

- How much money can you afford to lose?

- Will you purchase the franchise by yourself or with partners?

- Will you need financing and, if so, where can you obtain it?

- Do you have a favorable credit rating?

- Do you have savings or additional income to live on while starting your franchise?

Your Abilities

- Does the franchise require technical experience or relevant education, such as auto repair, home and office decorating, or tax preparation?

- What skills do you have?

- Do you have computer, bookkeeping, or other technical skills?

- What specialized knowledge or talents can you bring to a business?

- Have you ever owned or managed a business?

Your Goals

- What are your goals?

- Do you require a specific level of annual income?

- Are you interested in pursuing a particular field?

- Are you interested in retail sales or performing a service?

- How many hours are you willing to work?

- Do you want to operate the business yourself or hire a manager?

- Will franchise ownership be your primary source of income or supplement your current income?

- Would you be happy operating the business for the next 20 years?

- Would you like to own several outlets or only one?

Selecting a Franchise

Like any other investment, purchasing a franchise is a risk. When selecting a franchise, carefully consider a number of factors, such as the demand for the products or services, likely competition, the franchisor's background, and the level of support you will receive.

Demand

Is there a demand for the franchisor's products or services in your community? Is the demand seasonal? For example, lawn and garden care or swimming pool maintenance may be profitable only in the spring or summer. Is there likely to be a continuing demand for the products or services in the future? Is the demand likely to be temporary, such as selling a fad food item? Does the product or service generate repeat business?

Competition

What is the level of competition, nationally and in your community? How many franchised and company-owned outlets does the franchisor have in your area? How many competing companies sell the same or similar products or services? Are these competing companies well established, with wide name recognition in your community? Do they offer the same goods and services at the same or lower price?

Your Ability to Operate a Business

Sometimes, franchise systems fail. Will you be able to operate your outlet even if the franchisor goes out of business? Will you need the franchisor's ongoing training, advertising, or other assistance to succeed? Will you have access to the same or other suppliers? Could you conduct the business alone if you must lay off personnel to cut costs?

Name Recognition

A primary reason for purchasing a franchise is the right to associate with the company's name. The more recognized the name, the more likely it will draw customers who know its products or services. Therefore, before purchasing a franchise, consider ...

 ◆ The company's name and how widely recognized it is;

 ◆ If it has a registered trademark;

 ◆ How long the franchisor has been in operation;

- If the company has a reputation for quality products or services; and

- If consumers have filed complaints against the franchise with the Better Business Bureau or a local consumer protection agency.

Training and Support

Another reason for purchasing a franchise is to obtain support from the franchisor. What training and ongoing support does the franchisor provide? How does their training compare with the training for typical workers in the industry? Could you compete with others who have more formal training? What backgrounds do the current franchise owners have? Do they have prior technical backgrounds or special training that helps them succeed? Do you have a similar background?

Franchisor's Experience

Many franchisors operate well-established companies with years of experience both in selling goods or services and in managing a franchise system. Some franchisors started by operating their own business. There is no guarantee, however, that a successful entrepreneur can successfully manage a franchise system. Carefully consider how long the franchisor has managed a franchise system. Do you feel comfortable with the franchisor's expertise? If franchisors have little experience in managing a chain of franchises, their promises of guidance, training, and other support may be unreliable.

Growth

A growing franchise system increases the franchisor's name recognition and may enable you to attract customers. Growth alone does not ensure successful franchisees; a company that grows too quickly may not be able to support its franchisees with all the promised support services. Make sure the franchisor has sufficient financial assets and staff to support the franchisees.

Shopping at a Franchise Exposition

Attending a franchise exposition allows you to view and compare a variety of franchise possibilities. Keep in mind that exhibitors at the exposition primarily want to sell their franchise systems. Be cautious of salespersons who are interested in selling a franchise that you are not interested in. Before you attend, research what type of franchise best suits your investment limitations, experience, and goals. When you attend, comparison shop for the opportunity that best suits your needs and ask questions.

Know How Much You Can Invest

An exhibitor may tell you how much you can afford to invest or that you can't afford to pass up this opportunity. Before beginning to explore investment options, consider the amount you feel comfortable investing and the maximum amount you can afford.

Know What Type of Business Is Right for You

An exhibitor may attempt to convince you that an opportunity is perfect for you. Only you can make that determination. Consider the industry that interests you before selecting a specific franchise system. Ask yourself the following questions: Have you considered working in that industry before? Can you see yourself engaged in that line of work for the next twenty years? Do you have the necessary background or skills? If the industry does not appeal to you or you are not suited to work in that industry, do not allow an exhibitor to convince you otherwise. Spend your time focusing on those industries that offer a more realistic opportunity.

Comparison Shop

Visit several franchise exhibitors engaged in the type of industry that appeals to you. Listen to the exhibitors' presentations and discussions with other interested consumers. Get answers to the following questions: How long has the franchisor been in business? How many franchised outlets currently exist? Where are they located? How much is the initial franchise fee and any additional start-up costs? Are there any continuing royalty payments? How much? What management, technical and ongoing assistance does the franchisor offer? What controls does the franchisor impose?

Exhibitors may offer you prizes, free samples, or free dinners if you attend a promotional meeting later that day or over the next week to discuss the franchise in greater detail. Do not feel compelled to attend. Rather, consider these meetings as one way to acquire more information and to ask additional questions. Be prepared to walk away from any promotion if the franchise does not suit your needs.

Get Substantiation for Any Earnings Representations

Some franchisors may tell you how much you can earn if you invest in their franchise system or how current franchisees in their system are performing. Be careful. The FTC requires that franchisors who make such claims provide you with written substantiation. Make sure you ask for and obtain written substantiation for any income projections, or income or profit claims. If the franchisor does not have the required substantiation, or refuses to provide it to you, consider its claims to be suspect.

Take Notes

It may be difficult to remember each franchise exhibit. Bring a pad and pen to take notes. Get promotional literature that you can review. Take the exhibitors' business cards so you can contact them later with any additional questions.

Avoid High-Pressure Sales Tactics

You may be told that the franchisor's offering is limited, that there is only one territory left, or that this is a one-time reduced franchise sales price. Do not feel pressured to make any commitment. Legitimate franchisors expect you to comparison shop and to investigate their offering. A good deal today should be available tomorrow.

Study the Franchisor's Offering

Do not sign any contract or make any payment until you have the opportunity to investigate the franchisor's offering thoroughly. As will be explained further in the next section, the FTC's Franchise Rule requires the franchisor to provide you with a disclosure document containing important information about the franchise system. Study the disclosure document. Take time to speak with current and former franchisees about their experiences. Because investing in a franchise can entail a significant investment, you should have an attorney review the disclosure document and franchise contract and have an accountant review the company's financial disclosures.

Investigate Franchise Offerings

Before investing in any franchise system, be sure to get a copy of the franchisor's disclosure document. Sometimes this document is called a Franchise Offering Circular. Under the FTC's Franchise Rule, you must receive the document at least 10 business days before you are asked to sign any contract or pay any money to the franchisor. You should read the entire disclosure document. Make sure you understand all of the provisions. The following sections will help you to understand key provisions of typical disclosure documents. It also will help you ask questions about the disclosures. Get a clarification or answer to your concerns before you invest.

Business Background

The disclosure document identifies the executives of the franchise system and describes their prior experience. Consider not only their general business background, but their experience in managing a franchise system. Also consider how long they have been with the company. Investing with an inexperienced franchisor may be riskier than investing with an experienced one.

Litigation History

The disclosure document helps you assess the background of the franchisor and its executives by requiring the disclosure of prior litigation. The disclosure document tells you if the franchisor, or any of its executive officers, has been convicted of felonies involving, for example, fraud, any violation of franchise law or unfair or deceptive practices law, or are subject to any state or federal injunctions involving similar misconduct. It also will tell you if the franchisor, or any of its executives, has been held liable or settled a civil action involving the franchise relationship. A number of claims against the franchisor may indicate that it has not performed according to its agreements, or, at the very least, that franchisees have been dissatisfied with the franchisor's performance.

Opportunities Guide

Accounting/Tax Services

EXPRESSTAX
1-888-417-4461

Fiducial Franchises, Inc.
1-800-323-9000

H&R Block Tax Services, Inc.
1-800-869-9220

Instant Tax Services Corp.
1-888-870-1040

Jackson Hewitt Tax Service
1-800-475-2904

Liberty Tax Service
1-800-790-3863

Padgett Business Services USA, Inc.
1-800-323-7292

United Financial Services Group
1-800-626-0787

Advertising/Direct Mail

Billboard Connection
1-866-257-6025

Discovery Map International, LLC
1-877-820-7827

Money Mailer, LLC
1-800-819-9422

Profit-Tell International, Inc.
1-888-366-4653

SuperCoups
1-800-626-2620

Valpak Direct Marketing Systems, Inc.
1-800-237-6266

Auto & Truck Rentals

Payless Car Rental
1-800-729-5255

Automotive Products and Services

All Tune and Lube
1-800-935-8863

Alloy Wheel Repair Specialists, Inc.
770-903-1236

Alta Mere Window Tinting and Auto Alarms
1-800-581-8468

Altracolor Systems
1-800-727-6567

Altratouch Systems
1-800-678-5220

Autobacs Seven Company, Ltd.
81-03-3454-4105

Automotive Art
246-430-7056

AutoPlus Limited
965-434-9612

AutoQual USA
1-800-940-9909

Big O Tires, Inc.
1-800-321-2446

CarX
1-800-359-2359

Color-Glo International
1-800-333-8523

Colors On Parade
843-347-8818

Cottman Transmission
1-800-394-6116

Creative Colors International, Inc.
1-800-933-2656

Dent Doctor
1-800-946-3368

Dr. Vinyl and Associates, Ltd.
1-800-836-2840

Express Oil Change
1-888-945-1771

Glass Doctor
1-800-490-7501

Ice Cold Air
727-726-2577

J.D. Byrider Systems, Inc.
1-800-947-4532

Jiffy Lube International, Inc.
1-800-252-0554

Lentz USA Service Centers
1-800-354-2131

MAACO Enterprises, Inc.
1-800-296-2226

Matco Tools
1-800-368-6651

Matrix System Automotive Finishes
1-800-735-0303

Meineke Car Care Centers
1-800-275-5200

Merlin Muffler & Brake
1-800-652-9900

Midas International Corporation
1-800-621-0144

Mighty Distributing System
1-800-829-3900

Milex Tune Up and Brake
1-800-581-8468

Miracle Auto Painting & Body Repair
510-887-2211

Moran Industries, Inc.
1-800-581-8468

Mr. Transmission
1-800-581-8468

Multistate Transmission
1-800-581-8468

Oil Can Henry's Quick Lube
1-800-765-6244

Precision Tune Auto Care
1-800-438-8863

Rapido Rabbit, LLC
1-877-232-0139

Rent A Tire, Inc.
817-335-1100

Snap-on-Tools Company
1-800-786-6600

Speedy Transmission Centers
1-800-336-0310

Spot-Not Car Washes
1-800-682-7629

Super Wash, Inc.
1-800-633-7625

Tuffy Auto Service Centers
1-800-228-8339

Tunex Automotive Specialists
1-800-448-8639

V-Kool Franchise International, Pte Ltd.
65-6774-7077

Ziebart International Corporation
1-800-877-1312

Batteries: Retail/Commerical

Batteries Plus
1-800-274-9155

Beverages

Caribou Coffee Company, Inc.
763-592-2200

Coffee Bean & Tea Leaf, The
310-237-2326

Coffee Beanery, Ltd., The
1-800-728-2326

Dunn Brothers Coffee Shops
612-334-9746

Froots Franchising Companies
1-877-376-6871

The Grape
404-497-0505

It's A Grind Coffee
562-594-5600

Jamaica Blue
61-02-9362-4313

Juice It Up Franchise Corp.
1-888-705-8423

Let's Make Wine
1-888-416-9755

Maui Wowi Fresh Hawaiian Blends
1-888-862-8555

Orange Julius of America
952-830-0200

Orange Julius of Canada Ltd.
416-639-1492

P. J.'s Coffee
504-454-9459

Planet Smoothie
404-442-8933

Tapioca Express, Inc.
1-888-887-1616

Vino 100
1-866-846-6425

Vintner's Cellar Franchising International Inc.
1-800-480-7417

Wine Not International
1-888-946-3668

WineStyles Inc.
1-866-424-9463

Business Brokers

Entrepreneur's Source, The
1-800-289-0086

Sunbelt Business Brokers Inc.
1-800-771-7866

VR Business Brokers
1-800-377-8722

Business Services

24seven Vending (US), Inc.
858-366-0580

ACTION International
1-888-483-2828

AHEAD Human Resources Franchise Corp.
1-877-485-5858

Allegra Print & Imaging
1-888-258-2730

AlphaGraphics Inc.
1-800-955-6246

Alternative Board TAB, The
1-800-727-0126

BEI Group Gmbh
49-911206000

Bevinco
1-888-238-4626

Brightscape Investment Centers
305-670-4880

City Wide Maintenance
1-866-887-4029

Concerto Networks, Inc.
1-866-551-4007

Crestcom International, Ltd.
1-888-273-7826

Dale Carnegie & Associates, Inc.
631-415-9300

DentalPeople
1-866-921-4995

Discount Imaging Franchise Corporation
1-800-987-8258

Entrepreneur's Source, The
1-800-289-0086

Expense Reduction Analysts USA
858-795-7400

Fastway Couriers
49-3419882

Fiducial Franchises, Inc.
1-800-323-9000

FiltaFry
1-866-513-4582

FocalPoint International, Inc.
1-877-433-6225

Geeks On Call
1-888-667-4577

Growth Coach
1-888-292-7992

HR First Contact
1-800-388-8827

Instant Imprints
1-800-542-3437

Intelligent Office, The
303-447-9000

Island Ink-Jet (R) Systems
1-877-446-5538

Mini-Tankers Canada LTD
604-513-0386

OnlyOne
1-866-887-4310

Profit-Tell International, Inc.
1-888-366-4653

Proforma
1-800-825-1525

ProSource Wholesale Floorcoverings
1-800-466-6984

QuikDrop
1-888-784-5266

Rapid Refill Ink International, LLC
541-431-4665

Renaissance Executive Forums
858-551-6600

Sandler Sales Institute
1-800-669-3537

SaveItNow! Franchising Systems LLC
1-888-668-9727

Screenz Computing Center
773-296-0300

Shop24 NV Belgium
32-14-259696

Snappy Auctions
615-463-7355

Soft-Temps
1-800-221-2880

Unishippers
1-800-999-8721

UPS Store, The
1-877-623-7253

VR Business Brokers
1-800-377-8722

We the People Legal Document Services
805-962-4100

Business/Management Consulting

ACTION International
1-888-483-2828

Brightscape Investment Centers
305-670-4880

City Wide Maintenance
1-866-887-4029

Expense Reduction Analysts USA
858-795-7400

FocalPoint International, Inc.
1-877-433-6225

Quantum Organization Limited
44-1453-794810

Renaissance Executive Forums
858-551-6600

Winfree Systems, Inc.
1-800-616-9260

Campgrounds

Leisure Systems, Inc.
1-800-626-3720

Check Cashing/Financial Service Center

ACE Cash Express, Inc.
1-800-713-3338

Cash America Pawn
1-800-645-3811

Cash Plus, Inc.
1-888-707-2274

Mr. Payroll
817-335-1100

United Financial Services Group
1-800-626-0787

Chemicals & Related Products

ChemStation
1-800-554-8265

Syngenta Pakistan Limited
92-21-231-4828

Children's Services

@WORK HelpingHands Services
1-800-383-0804

3D Memories
719-481-5710

Abrakadoodle
703-871-7356

Cartoon Cuts
1-800-791-2887

Children's Orchard, Inc.
1-800-999-5437

Children's Technology Workshop, The
416-425-2289

CHIP The Remarkable Child I.D. Program
1-866-244-7462

ComputerTots/Computer Explorers
1-888-638-8722

Drama Kids International, Inc.
1-877-543-7456

FasTracKids International Ltd.
1-888-576-6888

Goddard School, The
1-800-272-4901

Helen Doron Early English and MathJogs
386-760-9033

Huntington Learning Center, Inc.
1-800-653-8400

IDENT-A-Kid Services of America, Inc.
1-800-890-1000

Images 4 Kids
972-316-3500

JumpBunch, Inc.
1-866-826-5645

JW Tumbles
858-794-0484

Kid to Kid
1-888-543-2543

Kiddie Academy Domestic Franchising, LLC
1-800-554-3343

KidzArt
1-800-379-8302

Kinderdance
1-800-554-2334

KnowledgePoints Development Corp.
1-866-204-4220

Kumon Math & Reading Centers
1-866-633-0740

Little Gym International, Inc., The
1-888-228-2878

Little Scoops
845-365-4500

Mad Science
1-800-586-5231

Mathnasium Learning Centers
310-943-6100

McGruff Safe Kids Total Identification
System
1-888-209-4218

My Family CD
760-486-1506

My Gym Children's Fitness Centers
1-800-469-4967

Once Upon A Child
1-800-453-7750

Play Programs, Inc.
1-800-520-7529

Primrose School Franchising Company
1-800-291-2555

Pump It Up—The Inflatable Party Zone
1-866-325-9663

Rainbow Station
1-888-716-1717

Snip-Its
508-651-7052

Sports Section, Inc., The
1-866-877-4746

Theater Fun
1-800-586-5231

Tutor Time Learning Centers, LLC
1-866-244-5384

USA Baby
1-800-323-4108

Viva the Chef LLC
973-359-0600

Wee Watch
734-822-6800

Young Rembrandts Franchise, Inc.
1-866-300-6010

Clothing & Shoes

Athlete's Foot, The
1-800-524-6444

Educational Outfitters
1-877-814-1222

Furla
1-888-387-5287

JACADI
914-697-7684

Computer/Electronics/Internet Services

@Wireless
1-800-613-2355

Cartridge World
1-866-473-5623

CM IT Solutions
512-477-6667

Computer Renaissance
863-669-1155

Concerto Networks, Inc.
1-866-551-4007

easyInternetcafe Franchising, Inc.
212-981-3953

Expetec Technology Services
1-888-209-3951

Flicko's Franchise Corp., Inc.
1-866-354-2567

Friendly Computers
702-656-2780

Geeks On Call
1-888-667-4577

Island Ink-Jet (R) Systems
1-877-446-5538

Netspace (R)
1-800-638-7722

New Horizons Computer Learning
Centers, Inc.
714-940-8240

Nextwave Computers
1-877-734-5800

RadioShack
1-800-826-3905

Screenz Computing Center
773-296-0300

Soft-Temps
1-800-221-2880

TeamLogic IT
949-582-6300

Wireless Dimensions
1-888-809-4934

Wireless Toyz
248-426-8200

Wireless Zone
860-632-9494

Construction: Materials, Services & Remodeling

1st Propane Franchising, Inc.
1-877-977-6726

Aire Serv Heating and Air Conditioning,
Inc.
1-800-583-2662

B-Dry System, Inc.
1-800-321-0985

California Closet Company, Inc.
1-800-274-6754

Case Handyman Service
1-800-426-9434

Christmas Decor, Inc.
1-800-687-9551

Classic Handyman Company
1-888-578-3668

Closet & Storage Concepts
1-800-862-1919

Closets By Design
1-800-377-5737

Crack Team, The
314-426-0900

Cure Water Damage, The
206-547-7460

DreamMaker Bath & Kitchen
1-800-214-7189

DRY-B-LO Designer Deck Drain System
1-800-437-9256

EnergyCraft Systems, Inc.
1-800-350-0776

EPMARK, Inc.
1-800-783-3838

Floortastic
1-800-332-7397

Glass Doctor
1-800-490-7501

Granite Transformations
1-866-685-5300

Grout Doctor
1-877-476-8800

Handyman Connection
1-800-466-5530

Handyman Matters Franchise
Corporation
1-866-808-8401

HomePros Home Improvement
Specialists
812-473-1776

House Doctors Handyman Service
1-800-319-3359

Interior Door Replacement Company
650-965-4372

Jet-Black
1-888-538-2525

Kitchen Solvers
1-800-845-6779

Kitchen Tune-Up
1-800-333-6385

Lighthouse Landscape Lighting
1-888-531-5483

Luxury Franchise Corporation
1-800-354-2284

Mend-A-Bath International (Pty) Ltd
27-41-3978200

Metal Supermarkets International
1-888-807-8755

Mr. Appliance
1-800-207-8515

Mr. Electric
1-800-805-0575

Mr. Handyman
1-800-289-4600

Nite Lites
513-424-5510

Only Doors & Windows, Inc.
1-877-636-4639

Outdoor Lighting Perspectives
1-877-898-8808

Owens Corning Remodeling Systems,
LLC
419-248-8000

Paul Davis Restoration
1-800-722-1818

Perma-Glaze, Inc.
1-800-332-7397

Pirtek
1-888-774-7835

PremierGarage
1-866-483-4272

Puroclean
1-800-247-9047

ReCeil It Ceiling Restoration
1-800-234-5464

Screen Machine, The
1-877-505-1985

SealMaster
1-800-341-7325

Stained Glass Overlay
1-800-944-4746

Suburban Cylinder Express
1-866-218-7026

Superior Walls of America, Ltd.
1-800-452-9255

Systems Paving Franchising, Inc.
1-800-801-7283

Tiffany Marble Molds International Inc.
1-800-654-9093

Wood Re New
1-888-244-3303

Consumer Buying Services

UCC TotalHome
1-800-827-6400

Convenience Stores

7-Eleven, Inc.
1-800-255-0711

AmeriStop
859-781-3800

ampm Mini Market
1-800-322-2726

CoGo's Company
1-800-472-1481

FamilyMart Co., Ltd. Japan
81-3-3989-7755

Tedeschi Food Shops, Inc.
1-800-833-3724

TMC Franchise Corporation
1-800-813-7677

Cosmetics

Aloette Cosmetics, Inc.
1-800-256-3883

Contem 1g Franchising Ltda
55-11-36656500

FACES
905-760-0110

Glamour Secrets
1-866-713-7487

Merle Norman Cosmetics
1-800-421-6648

Natural Source USA, The
858-488-3609

Dating Services

Hand-In-Hand
44-207-3816521

It's Just Lunch
619-234-7200

Right One, The
1-800-348-3283

Together Dating Service
1-877-730-8866

Drug Stores

Farmacias Unidas, S.A.
58-61-976414

Medicap Pharmacies, Inc.
1-800-445-2244

Medicine Shoppe International, Inc.
1-800-325-1397

Educational Products & Services

Abrakadoodle
703-871-7356

BEI Group Gmbh
49-911206000

Berlitz Franchising Corporation
1-800-626-6419

Best Year Yet, LLC
970-544-4747

Cambridge Educational Centers
703-421-4300

CM IT Solutions
512-477-6667

ComputerTots/Computer Explorers
1-888-638-8722

Crestcom International, Ltd.
1-888-273-7826

Daekyo America, Inc (Western)
1-888-628-4776

Dale Carnegie & Associates, Inc.
631-415-9300

Direct English
44-20-8687-6104

Drama Kids International, Inc.
1-877-543-7456

E.nopi Math & Reading (Daekyo USA, Inc.)
1-888-835-1212

ELS Language Centers
1-800-468-8978

Entrepreneur's Source, The
1-800-289-0086

FasTracKids International Ltd.
1-888-576-6888

FastTrain Licensing Corp.
305-226-2800

Helen Doron Early English and MathJogs
49-175 5932899

Huntington Learning Center, Inc.
1-800-653-8400

JEI Learning Centers
1-877-534-6284

John Casablancas Modeling and Career Centers
636-536-6100

KANJUKU Co., Ltd.
81-6-6241-8123

KnowledgePoints Development Corp.
1-866-204-4220

Kumon Math & Reading Centers
1-866-633-0740

LearningRx
1-800-535-5441

Mad Science
1-800-586-5231

Mathnasium Learning Centers
310-943-6100

McGruff Safe Kids Total Identification System
1-888-209-4218

New Horizons Computer Learning Centers, Inc.
714-940-8240

Oxford Learning Centers
1-888-559-2212

Renaissance Executive Forums
858-551-6600

Sandler Sales Institute
1-800-669-3537

Sylvan Learning Center
1-800-284-8214

Theater Fun
1-800-586-5231

Tutor Time Learning Centers, LLC
1-866-244-5384

Wall Street Institute
410-843-8000

Winfree Systems, Inc.
1-800-616-9260

Employment Services

@WORK Medical Services
1-800-383-0804

@WORK Personnel Services, Inc.
1-800-233-6846

Accountants Inc.
1-800-491-9411

AHEAD Human Resources Franchise
Corp.
1-877-485-5858

CareersUSA
1-888-227-3377

Express Personnel Services
1-877-652-6400

Labor Finders
1-800-864-7749

Link Staffing Services
1-800-848-5465

Lloyd Personnel Systems, Inc
1-888-292-6678

Management Recruiters International,
Inc.
1-800-875-4000

PersoNet, Inc.
727-781-2983

Sales Consultants
1-800-875-4000

Sanford Rose Associates
1-800-731-7724

Snelling Personnel Services
1-800-766-5556

Spherion Corporation
1-800-388-7783

Talent Tree, Inc.
1-800-999-1515

Environmental Services

1-800-GOT-JUNK?
1-877-408-5865

Aire Serv Heating and Air Conditioning,
Inc.
1-800-583-2662

Duskin Co., Ltd.
81-6-6821-5002

Humitech Franchise Corporation
972-490-9393

Truly Nolen of America
1-800-458-3664

TurboHaul, LLC
301-931-6993

Financial Services

American Express Financial Advisors
612-671-3131

Brightscape Investment Centers
305-670-4880

Instant Tax Services Corp.
1-888-870-1040

Fireworks

Lantis Fireworks & Lasers
702-384-2595

Fitness

Bally Fitness Franchising, Inc.
1-800-410-2582

Blitz 20 Minute Total Fitness for Men, The
1-866-968-2548

Contours Express, Inc.
1-877-227-2282

Curves
1-800-848-1096

Cuts Fitness for Men
732-574-0999

Gold's Gym Franchising
1-800-457-5375

IM=X Pilates Studio
212-997-5550

LA Boxing Franchise Corporation
1-866-LABOXING

LA Shapes
1-888-258-7099

Liberty Fitness
1-888-521-2582

Velocity Sports Performance
1-866-955-0400

Florist Shops

1-800-FLOWERS
1-800-266-7697

Flowerama of America, Inc.
1-800-728-6004

KaBloom Franchising Corp.
781-935-6500

Food: Baked Goods/Donuts/Pastries

Atlanta Bread Company
1-800-398-3728

Auntie Anne's Hand-Rolled Soft Pretzels
717-442-4766

Big Apple Bagels
1-800-251-6101

Bruegger's Franchise Corporation
1-866-660-4104

Buttercup Bake Shop
212-350-9940

Cinnabon
1-800-227-8353

Cookies by Design/Cookie Bouquet
1-800-945-2665

Dunkin' Donuts
1-800-777-9983

Einstein/Noah Bagel Corp.
303-568-8026

Foodco Group Pty Ltd
61-02-9362-4313

Golden Krust Caribbean Bakery, Inc.
718-655-7878

Great American Cookie Inc.
1-800-343-5377

Honey Dew Donuts
781-849-3000

House of Donuts International
20(0)2 525 60 76-81

LaMar's Donuts
1-888-533-7489

Manhattan Bagel Company, Inc.
1-800-872-2243

Mrs. Fields Original Cookies, Inc.
1-800-343-5377

Muffin Break
61-02-9362-4313

Nestle Toll House Cafe by Chip
214-495-9533

New World Coffee
1-800-308-2457

Pretzel Time
1-800-343-5377

PretzelMaker, Inc.
1-800-343-5377

T. J. Cinnamons
1-800-487-2729

Tim Hortons
1-888-376-4835

Food: Candy/Popcorn/Snacks

Candy Bouquet
1-877-226-3901

Kilwin's Chocolates and Ice Cream
Franchise, Inc.
231-439-0972

Rocky Mountain Chocolate Factory
1-800-438-7623

Schakolad Chocolate Factory
407-248-6400

Food: Carribean

Golden Krust Caribbean Bakery, Inc.
718-655-7878

Food: Ice Cream/Yogurt

2 Scoops Cafe
407-381-0378

All American Deli & Ice Cream Shops
1-800-311-3930

American Dairy Queen Corporation
1-800-285-8515

Andy's Frozen Custard Franchising,
L.L.C.
417-881-3500

Baskin-Robbins
1-800-777-9983

Ben & Jerry's Franchising, Inc.
802-846-1500

Blue Sky Creamery
515-268-4336

Carvel Corporation
1-800-227-8353

Cold Stone Creamery, Inc.
480-348-1704

Cremalita
212-645-2000

Dippin' Dots Franchising, Inc.
270-575-6990

Friendly's Restaurants
1-800-576-8088

Haagen-Dazs Shoppe Company, Inc., The
1-800-793-6872

Happy & Healthy Products, Inc.
1-800-764-6114

Helados Bon C.X.A.
809-530-7901

Johnny Rockets Group, Inc., The
949-643-6119

Juice It Up Franchise Corp.
1-888-705-8423

La Paletera Franchise Systems, Inc.
1-866-621-6200

MaggieMoo's International, LLC
1-800-949-8114

Marble Slab Creamery, Inc.
713-780-3601

Maui Wowi Fresh Hawaiian Blends
1-888-862-8555

Morrone's Treat Centers
610-650-7726

Oberweis Franchise Systems, LLC
1-877-939-3900

Ralph's Famous Italian Ices Franchise
Corp.
718-448-0853

Rita's Ices, Cones, Shakes & Other Cool
Stuff
1-800-677-7482

Ritter's Frozen Custard
317-819-0700

Smoothie King
1-800-577-4200

TCBY Systems, LLC
1-800-343-5377

Uncle Louie G—Gourmet Italian Ices &
Ice Cream
718-677-9551

Food: Pizza

Boston's The Gourmet Pizza
1-866-277-8721

Chanticlear Pizza
768-862-2230

CiCi's Pizza
972-745-4200

Daddio's USA, Inc.
402-884-3300

Domino's Pizza
734-930-3030

Donatos Pizza, Inc.
1-800-366-2867

Eatza Pizza, Inc.
480-941-5200

Famous Famiglia
212-262-0970

Figaro's Italian Pizza, Inc.
1-888-344-2767

Hungry Howie's Pizza & Subs
1-800-624-8122

La Porchetta Pizza & Pasta Restaurants
61-3-94606700

LaRosa's Inc.
513-347-5660

Ledo Pizza System, Inc.
410-721-6887

Little Caesars
1-800-553-5776

Marco's Pizza
1-800-262-7267

Mazzio's Pizza
1-800-827-1910

Nick-N-Willy's World Famous Take-N-Bake Pizza
1-888-642-6945

NYPD Pizza
407-253-5000

Papa John's Pizza
502-261-7272

Papa Murphy's Take and Bake Pizza
1-800-257-7272

Peter Piper Pizza
1-800-899-3425

Pizza Hut, Inc.
972-338-6948

Pizza Inn, Inc.
1-800-284-3466

Pizza Schmizza
503-640-2328

Rocky Rococo Pan Style Pizza & Pasta
262-569-5580

Rotelli Pizza & Pasta
1-888-768-3554

Sarpinos Pizzeria International Inc.
250-881-8733

Shakey's Pizza
1-888-444-6686

Straw Hat Pizza
925-837-3400

Unos Restaurant Corporation
1-877-855-8667

Food: Restaurants

360-Degree Franchise Corporation
925-256-6300

A&W Restaurants, Inc.
859-543-6000

American Dairy Queen Corporation
1-800-285-8515

Applebee's International, Inc.
913-967-4000

Arby's, LLC
1-800-487-2729

Arthur Treacher's Fish and Chips
516-358-0600

Au Bon Pain
617-423-2100

Back Yard Burgers, Inc.
1-800-292-6939

Bain's Deli
1-800-205-6050

Baja Fresh Mexican Grill
1-877-225-2373

Baker Bros. American Deli
214-696-8780

Beef O'Brady's Family Sports Pubs
1-800-728-8878

Big Boy Restaurants International LLC
586-759-6000

Big City Burrito
303-781-4022

Blimpie Subs & Salads
1-800-447-6256

Bojangles' Restaurants, Inc.
1-800-366-9921

Boston Market
303-278-9500

Boston's The Gourmet Pizza
1-866-277-8721

Buffalo Wild Wings Grill & Bar
1-800-499-9586

Burger King Corporation
305-378-7011

Burger King Restaurants of Canada Inc.
416-626-7423

Camille's Sidewalk Cafe
1-800-230-7004

Captain D's
1-800-550-4877

Carl's Jr. Restaurants
1-866-253-7655

Charley's Grilled Subs
1-800-437-8325

Checkers Drive-In Restaurants, Inc.
813-283-7000

Cheeburger Cheeburger Restaurants, Inc.
1-800-487-6211

Chester's International, LLC
1-800-288-1555

Church's Chicken
1-800-639-3495

Cosi, Inc.
847-444-3200

Cousins Subs
1-800-238-9736

Coyote Canyon
620-669-9372

Crabby Bills
727-432-7430

Culver's
608-643-7980

Dairy Queen Canada Inc.
905-639-1492

D'Angelo Sandwich Shops
1-888-374-2830

Del Taco
1-800-628-1368

Denny's Inc.
1-800-304-0222

Dickey's Barbecue Restaurants, Inc.
972-248-9899

Doc Green's Gourmet Salads
404-442-8933

Donato Food Corporation
1-800-555-5726

Duke Sandwich Co.
1-877-308-2343

Dunkin' Brands, Inc.
781-737-3000

Earl of Sandwich
407-903-5701

Eatza Pizza, Inc.
480-941-5200

Einstein/Noah Bagel Corp.
303-568-8026

El Pollo Loco, Inc.
1-800-997-6556

El Taco Tote Franchise Systems, LTD.
915-838-6000

Elmer's Breakfast*Lunch*Dinner
1-800-325-5188

Famous Dave's
1-800-210-4040

Famous Sam's Inc.
602-902-0822

Farmer Boys Restaurants
951-275-9900

Fatburger Corporation
310-319-1850

Fazoli's Restaurants
859-268-1668

Firehouse Subs
904-886-8300

FoodNet
804-273-0600

Fresh City
781-453-0200

Friendly's Restaurants
1-800-576-8088

Fuddruckers EMA E.C.
966-2-6616601

Fuddruckers, Inc.
978-907-1300

George Webb Restaurants
262-970-0084

Gimme Sum Fresh Asian Grill
702-525-3070

Golden Corral Buffet & Grill
1-800-284-5673

Golden Krust Caribbean Bakery, Inc.
718-655-7878

Gorin's Famous Sandwiches
1-888-489-7277

Grandy's, Inc.
1-877-457-8145

Great American Steak and Buffet
Company
1-800-247-8325

Hardee's
1-866-253-7655

Hooters of America, Inc.
770-951-2040

Huddle House, Inc.
1-800-868-5700

International House of Pancakes
818-240-6055

Jack in the Box Inc.
858-571-2121

Jackson's All American Sports Grill
303-713-1700

Jason's Deli
409-832-5055

Jimmy John's Gourmet Sandwiches
1-800-546-6904

Jody Maroni's Sausage Kingdom
1-800-628-8364

Johnny Rockets Group, Inc., The
949-643-6119

Just Fresh Franchise Systems, Inc.
1-866-468-3935

KFC Corporation
502-874-8300

Krystal Company, The
1-800-458-5912

L&L Hawaiian Barbecue
808-951-9888

La Porchetta Pizza & Pasta Restaurants
61-3-94606700

La Salsa Fresh Mexican Grill
1-866-253-7655

LA Shish Franchising, LLC
313-441-2900

LaRosa's Inc.
513-347-5660

Lenny's Sub Shop
1-877-705-7827

Long John Silver's Restaurants, Inc.
859-543-6000

Made In Japan Teriyaki Experience
1-800-555-5726

Mama Fu's Noodle House
404-442-8933

Manchu Wok
561-798-7800

Maui Tacos
1-888-628-4822

McAlister's Deli
1-888-855-3354

McDonald's Corporation
630-623-5550

Melting Pot Restaurants Inc., The
1-800-783-0867

Moe's Southwest Grill
404-844-8335

Montana Mike's Steakhouse
620-669-9372

Mr. Goodcents Subs & Pastas
1-800-648-2368

Mrs. Vanelli's Fresh Italian Foods
514-336-8885

My Girlfriend's Kitchen
801-944-8900

National Sports Grill
949-225-5460

New York Subs Fresh Deli
1-800-285-7310

Nick-N-Willy's World Famous Take-N-
Bake Pizza
1-888-642-6945

Nothing But Noodles
480-513-7008

Oberweis Franchise Systems, LLC
1-877-939-3900

Outback Steakhouse International, L.P.
404-231-4329

Papa Murphy's Take and Bake Pizza
1-800-257-7272

Philly Connection, The
1-800-886-8826

Pollo Campero
502-333-7233

Popeyes Chicken & Biscuits
1-800-639-3780

Port of Subs, Inc.
1-800-245-0245

Prime Restaurants of Canada, Inc.
905-568-0000

Pudgie's Famous Chicken
1-800-783-4437

Qdoba Mexican Grill
720-898-2300

Quaker Steak & Lube
724-981-6571

Quizno's Sub
1-800-335-4782

R.J. Gator's
1-800-438-4286

Rally's
813-283-7000

Red Robin Gourmet Burgers
303-846-6000

Rocky Rococo Pan Style Pizza & Pasta
262-569-5580

Roy Rogers Franchise Company, LLC
301-695-5051

Ruby's Franchise Systems, Inc.
949-644-7829

Ruby Tuesday, Inc.
1-800-325-0755

Saladworks, Inc.
610-825-3080

Sbarro Inc.
1-800-766-4949

SFO Franchise Development
1-800-230-7202

Shoney's Restaurants
1-877-474-6693

Sicily's Italian Buffet
225-647-5847

Silver Mine Subs
970-266-2600

Sirloin Stockade
620-669-9372

Sizzler USA
818-662-9900

Skyline Chili, Inc.
1-800-443-4371

Sonic Drive-In
1-800-569-6656

Spicy Pickle Franchising, LLC
303-297-1902

Steak-Out Franchising, Inc.
1-877-878-3257

Subway World Headquarters
1-800-888-4848

Taco Bell Corporation
949-863-2810

Taco Del Mar
206-624-7060

TGI Friday's
1-800-374-3297

Tim Hortons
1-888-376-4835

Togo's Eatery
1-800-777-9983

Tony Roma's
1-800-286-7662

Wall Street Deli, Inc.
1-800-545-6944

Wendy's International, Inc.
1-800-443-7266

Western Sizzlin
1-800-247-8325

Whataburger, Inc.
1-877-551-0660

Williams Fried Chicken
214-371-1430

Wing Zone
1-877-333-9464

Wings Over
1-866-349-9464

WingStop Restaurants Inc.
972-686-6500

WOW Cafe & Wingery Franchising, LLC
985-875-1263

Yum! Brands, Inc.
502-874-8300

Zaxby's Franchising, Inc.
706-353-8107

ZOUP! Fresh Soup Co.
1-888-778-7687

Zyng Asian Grill
703-549-5332

Food: Specialty

24seven Vending (US), Inc.
858-366-0580

All American Deli & Ice Cream Shops
1-800-311-3930

Charley's Grilled Subs
1-800-437-8325

Coffee Bean & Tea Leaf, The
310-237-2326

Coffee Beanery, Ltd., The
1-800-728-2326

Daddio's USA, Inc.
402-884-3300

DogOut
1-800-794-0117

Dunn Brothers Coffee Shops
612-334-9746

Friendly's Restaurants
1-800-576-8088

Froots Franchising Companies
1-877-376-6871

Get Nuts
506-248-1313

Gloria Jean's Coffees
949-260-1600

Golden Krust Caribbean Bakery, Inc.
718-655-7878

Great Wraps!
1-888-489-7277

HoneyBaked Ham Co. and Cafe, The
1-866-968-7424

Hot Dog On A Stick
1-800-321-8400

It's A Grind Coffee
562-594-5600

Jamaica Blue
61-02-9362-4313

Juice It Up Franchise Corp.
1-888-705-8423

La Paletera Franchise Systems, Inc.
1-866-621-6200

Logan Farms Honey Glazed Hams
1-800-833-4267

Manhattan Bagel Company, Inc.
1-800-872-2243

My Girlfriend's Kitchen
801-944-8900

New World Coffee
1-800-308-2457

Orange Julius of America
952-830-0200

Orange Julius of Canada Ltd.
416-639-1492

P.J.'s Coffee
504-454-9459

Philly Connection, The
1-800-886-8826

Planet Smoothie
404-442-8933

Rita's Ices, Cones, Shakes & Other Cool Stuff
1-800-677-7482

Robeks Franchise Corporation
310-727-0500

Subway World Headquarters
1-800-888-4848

Tapioca Express, Inc.
1-888-887-1616

Tim Hortons
1-888-376-4835

Totally Low Carb Stores Inc.
1-800-631-2272

Tropical Smoothie Cafe
1-888-292-2522

WineStyles Inc.
1-866-424-9463

Wing Zone
1-877-333-9464

Woody's Chicago Style
1-877-469-6639

WOW Cafe & Wingery Franchising, LLC
985-875-1263

ZOUP! Fresh Soup Co.
1-888-778-7687

Franchise Consulting

Entrepreneur's Source, The
1-800-289-0086

Golf Equipment, Products & Services

Bogart Golf
904-274-0203

GOLF USA Inc.
1-800-488-1107

Pro Golf Discount
1-800-521-6388

Greeting Cards

Cardsmart Retail Corporation
1-877-227-3762

Hair Salons & Services

Beauty Brands Salon Spa Superstore
1-888-725-6608

Beautyfirst
316-529-1430

Cartoon Cuts
1-800-791-2887

City Looks
952-947-7000

Cost Cutters
1-888-888-7008

Fantastic Sams
978-232-5600

First Choice Haircutters
1-800-617-3961

Great Clips, Inc.
1-800-947-1143

Hair Club for Men and Women
1-800-251-2658

Hair Cuttery
1-877-876-7400

Hair Saloon For Men
1-877-576-7300

Jon'Ric International Medical, Dental &
Day Spas
1-877-4-JONRIC

Lemon Tree Family Hair Salon, The
516-735-2828

Marsha Scott's Hair Loss Clinic For
Women
1-800-625-4247

Pro-Cuts
952-947-7000

Snip-Its
508-651-7052

Sport Clips
1-800-872-4247

Supercuts
1-888-888-7008

Health Aids & Services

Aloette Cosmetics, Inc.
1-800-256-3883

AristoCare
1-866-731-2273

Atir Natural Nail Care Clinic
757-258-0696

Blitz 20 Minute Total Fitness for Men, The
1-866-968-2548

ComForcare Senior Services
1-800-886-4044

Foot Solutions
1-866-338-2597

Gold's Gym Franchising
1-800-457-5375

Home Care Assistance
650-462-6900

Home Helpers
1-800-216-4196

Home Instead Senior Care
1-888-484-5759

Ideal Image
1-866-774-3325

Jon'Ric International Medical, Dental &
Day Spas
1-877-4-JONRIC

Medihealth Solutions
1-888-595-9244

Natural Source USA, The
858-488-3609

Health Aids & Services

Planet Beach Franchising Corporation
1-888-290-8266

Positive Changes Hypnosis
1-800-880-0436

Radiance Medspa
1-866-963-3772

Relax The Back Corporation
562-860-1019

Right At Home, Inc.
1-877-697-7537

Sleek MedSpa
781-237-4819

Sona MedSpa
615-591-5040

Women's Health Boutique
1-888-280-2053

Woodhouse Day Spa, The
1-877-570-7772

Home Furnishings: Retail, Sale & Rental

Aaron's Sales & Leasing
1-866-756-3339

Big Picture Framing
1-800-315-0024

Blind Guy, Inc., The
208-777-1545

Blind Man of America
1-800-547-9889

ColorTyme Rent To Own
1-800-411-8963

Deck The Walls, Inc.
1-800-543-3325

Decor & You, Inc.
1-800-477-3326

DOTI Design Stores
1-888-382-7488

FastFrame U.S.A Inc.
1-800-333-3225

Floor Coverings International
1-800-955-4324

Floortastic
1-800-332-7397

Framing & Art Centre
1-800-563-7263

Furniture Medic L.P.
1-800-877-9933

Gotcha Covered Blinds
1-877-777-2544

Great Frame Up, The
1-800-543-3325

INTERIORS by Decorating Den
1-877-918-1500

Nationwide Floor & Window Coverings
1-800-366-8088

Norwalk—The Furniture Idea
419-744-3200

Slumberland Furniture
1-888-482-7500

Stained Glass Overlay
1-800-944-4746

Stone Mountain/GCO Flooring Outlets
1-800-466-6984

UCC TotalHome
1-800-827-6400

Verlo Mattress Factory Stores, LLC
1-800-229-8957

Home Inspection/Radon Detection

AmeriSpec Home Inspection Service
1-800-426-2270

A-Pro Home Inspection Services
1-800-793-2776

HomeTeam Inspection Service, Inc., The
1-800-598-5297

HouseMaster
1-800-526-3939

Inspect-It 1st Franchising Corp.
1-800-510-9100

Pillar To Post—Professional Home Inspection
1-877-963-3129

ProSpection, LLC
1-866-328-7720

World Inspection Network: Home Inspection Service
1-800-967-8127

Hotels & Motels

Abbington Franchising, Inc.
1-866-461-3945

America's Best Inns & Suites
404-321-4045

AmericInn
952-294-5000

AmeriSuites
1-888-778-3111

Choice Hotels International, Inc.
1-800-547-0007

Clarion Inns, Hotels, Suites, Resorts
1-800-547-0007

Comfort Suites
1-800-547-0007

Country Inns & Suites by Carlson, Inc.
1-800-336-3301

Courtyard By Marriott
301-380-3000

Days Inn Worldwide Inc.
1-800-952-3297

Doubletree
1-800-286-0645

Econo Lodges of America, Inc.
1-800-547-0007

Embassy Suites Hotels
1-800-286-0645

Fairfield Inns by Marriott
301-380-7658

Hampton Inn/Hampton Inn & Suites
1-800-286-0645

Hawthorn Suites
404-321-4045

Hilton
1-800-286-0645

Hilton Garden Inn
1-800-286-0645

Homewood Suites by Hilton
1-800-286-0645

Howard Johnson Franchise Canada Inc.
1-800-249-4656

Howard Johnson International, Inc.
1-800-932-4656

InterContinental Hotels Group
770-604-2000

Knights Inn
1-800-932-3300

Knights Inn Franchise Canada Inc.
1-800-249-4656

MainStay Suites
1-800-547-0007

Microtel Inns & Suites
404-321-4645

Motel 6 Operating L.P.
1-888-668-3503

Park Inn
1-800-336-3301

Park Plaza
1-800-336-3301

Quality Inn, Quality Suites, Quality Inn & Suites
1-800-547-0007

Radisson Hotels & Resorts
1-800-336-3301

Ramada Franchise Canada Inc.
1-800-249-4656

Ramada Franchise Systems, Inc.
1-800-758-8999

Red Roof Inns, Inc.
1-888-842-2942

Regent International Hotels
1-800-336-3301

Residence Inn by Marriott
301-380-3000

Rodeway Inns
1-800-547-0007

Sleep Inn and Sleep Inn & Suites
1-800-547-0007

SpringHill Suites By Marriott
301-380-7658

Starwood Hotels & Resorts Worldwide, Inc.
770-857-2000

Studio 6
1-888-842-2942

Super 8 Motels, Inc.
1-800-889-8847

TownePlace Suites of Marriott
301-380-3000

Travelodge Hotels, Inc.
973-428-9700

Villager Lodge and Premier
1-800-694-6428

Villager Lodge Franchise Canada Inc.
1-800-249-4656

Wellesley Inns & Suites Franchising, Inc.
1-888-778-3111

Wingate Inns
1-800-567-4283

Insurance

Brooke Franchise Corporation
1-800-642-1872

FED-USA, Inc.
1-888-440-6875

Janitorial Services

1-800-DRYCARPET Carpet Cleaning
1-888-379-2277

BuildingStars, Inc.
314-991-3356

Chem-Dry Carpet & Upholstery
Cleaning
1-877-307-8233

Coverall Cleaning Concepts
1-800-537-3371

Duraclean International, Inc.
1-800-251-7070

Heits Building Services, Inc.
201-288-7708

Jani-King International, Inc.
1-800-552-5264

Maids To Order, Inc.
1-800-701-6243

OpenWorks
1-800-777-6736

ServeCorp International
1-800-513-5100

ServiceMaster Clean
1-800-255-9687

Vanguard Cleaning Systems, Inc.
1-800-564-6422

Jewelry

Fast-Fix Jewelry Repairs
1-800-359-0407

Hannoush Jewelers
1-888-325-3935

Laundry & Dry Cleaning

1-800-DryClean, LLC
1-866-822-6115

Dryclean U.S.A.
1-800-746-4583

Martinizing Dry Cleaning
1-800-827-0345

OXXO Care Cleaners
954-927-7410

Lawn, Garden & Agricultural

Border Magic, LLC
1-877-893-2954

DRY-B-LO Designer Deck Drain System
1-800-437-9256

Lawn Doctor
1-800-452-9637

Nutrilawn, Inc.
1-800-396-6096

Outdoor Lighting Perspectives
1-877-898-8808

Spring-Green Lawn Care Corp.
1-800-435-4051

TruGreen—Chemlawn
901-681-2008

U.S. Lawns, Inc.
1-800-875-2967

Maid & Personal Services

Cleaning Authority, The
1-877-504-6221

Home Cleaning Centers of America, Inc.
1-800-767-1118

Maid Brigade
1-800-722-6243

Maid to Perfection Corporation
1-800-648-6243

MaidPro
1-888-624-3776

MAIDS International, Inc., THE
1-800-843-6243

Maids To Order, Inc.
1-800-701-6243

Merry Maids, L.P.
1-800-798-8000

Molly Maid
1-800-665-5962

1-800-DRYCARPET Carpet Cleaning
1-888-379-2277

1-800-GOT-JUNK?
1-877-408-5865

Maintenance Services

AeroWest Services
1-888-663-6726

Aire Serv Heating and Air Conditioning, Inc.
1-800-583-2662

American Leak Detection
1-800-755-6697

Bonus Building Care
1-800-931-1102

BuildingStars, Inc.
314-991-3356

Cannon Hygiene International
44-1524-60894

CertiRestore
1-888-502-3784

CIM Commercial Industrial Mold USA, Inc.
561-844-3800

City Wide Maintenance
1-866-887-4029

Cleaning Authority, The
1-877-504-6221

COIT Services, Inc.
1-800-243-8797

Coustic-Glo International
1-800-333-8523

Coverall Cleaning Concepts
1-800-537-3371

Cure Water Damage, The
206-547-7460

Dublcheck Limited
01-244-550150

Duraclean International, Inc.
1-800-251-7070

Dwyer Group, The
1-800-490-7501

Fish Window Cleaning Services, Inc.
1-877-707-3474

Furniture Medic L.P.
1-800-877-9933

Grout Doctor
1-877-476-8800

Heits Building Services, Inc.
201-288-7708

Jani-King International, Inc.
1-800-552-5264

Maids To Order, Inc.
1-800-701-6243

MilliCare Commercial Carpet Care
1-877-812-8803

Mint Condition Franchising, Inc.
803-548-6121

Mr. Rooter Plumbing
1-800-298-6855

Omni-Kleen
44-1443-237800

OpenWorks
1-800-777-6736

Oven Clean Ltd.
44-753-890606

Precision Door Service, Inc.
321-433-3494

ProSource Wholesale Floorcoverings
1-800-466-6984

Puroclean
1-800-247-9047

Rainbow International Restoration &
Cleaning
1-800-583-9100

ReCeil It Ceiling Restoration
1-800-234-5464

Renovation Professionals
1-800-400-6455

Roto-Rooter Corporation
515-223-1343

Sears Carpet & Upholstery Care, Inc.
1-800-586-1603

ServiceMaster Clean
1-800-255-9687

Sparkle Wash
1-800-321-0770

Stanley Steemer International, Inc.
614-764-2007

Steamatic, Inc.
1-800-527-1295

Swisher Hygiene Franchise Corp.
1-800-444-4138

TurboHaul, LLC
301-931-6993

Valcourt Building Services, L.C.
703-294-6202

Vanguard Cleaning Systems, Inc.
1-800-564-6422

Window Genie
1-800-700-0022

Marine Services

Super Clean Yacht Service Franchising,
Inc.
949-646-2990

MedSpas

Jon'Ric International Medical, Dental &
Day Spas
1-877-4-JONRIC

Radiance Medspa
1-866-963-3772

Sleek MedSpa
781-237-4819

Sona MedSpa
615-591-5040

Metal

Metal Supermarkets International
1-888-807-8755

Online Auction Consignment

QuikDrop
1-888-784-5266

Snappy Auctions
615-463-7355

Optical Aids & Services

BEI Franchising, Inc.
1-866-765-2740

Pearle Vision
1-800-282-3931

Sterling Optical
1-800-856-9664

Package Preparation/Shipment/ Mail Service

AIM Mail Centers
1-800-669-4246

Craters & Freighters
1-800-949-9931

Navis Pack and Ship Centers
1-866-738-6820

Pak Mail Centers of America, Inc.
1-800-838-2821

Parcel Plus
1-888-280-2053

Postal Connections
1-800-767-8257

PostalAnnex+
1-800-456-1525

PostNet Postal & Business Services
1-800-841-7171

Sunshine Pack and Ship
1-877-751-1513

TNT China
86-21-5352-4688

Unishippers
1-800-999-8721

UPS Store, The
1-877-623-7253

Worldwide Express
1-800-758-7447

Painting Services

CertaPro Painters
1-800-452-3782

College Pro Painters (US) Ltd.
519-964-3107

Paralegal Services

Sign Here
1-888-299-6076

We the People Legal Document Services
805-962-4100

Payroll Services

Fiducial Franchises, Inc.
1-800-323-9000

Mr. Payroll
817-335-1100

Pest Control Services

MosquitoNix Franchise Systems, Ltd.
1-866-934-2002

Pestmaster Franchise Network
1-800-525-8866

Terminix
1-800-654-7848

Truly Nolen of America
1-800-458-3664

Pet Sales, Supplies & Services

Aussie Pet Mobile
1-888-677-7387

Banfield, The Pet Hospital
1-800-838-6738

Bark Busters
1-877-280-7100

Camp Bow Wow/Digs! for Dogs
1-866-821-0409

Interquest Detection Canines
1-800-481-7768

Photography & Supplies

Glamour Shots
1-800-336-4550

Grins 2 Go
858-558-4948

Images 4 Kids
972-316-3500

MotoPhoto
1-800-733-6686

Pre-Employment Screening Services

HR First Contact
1-800-388-8827

Pressure Washing & Restoration

Perma-Glaze, Inc.
1-800-332-7397

Sparkle Wash
1-800-321-0770

Printing/Photocopying Services

Allegra Print & Imaging
1-888-258-2730

AlphaGraphics Inc.
1-800-955-6246

American Wholesale Thermographers
1-888-280-2053

Business Cards Tomorrow, Inc.
1-800-627-9998

Cartridge World
1-866-473-5623

Copy Club
1-888-280-2053

Island Ink-Jet (R) Systems
1-877-446-5538

Kwik Kopy Business Centers
1-800-746-9498

Minuteman Press International, Inc.
1-800-645-3006

PIP Printing & Document Services
1-800-894-7498

Rapid Refill Ink International, LLC
541-431-4665

Sir Speedy, Inc.
1-800-854-3321

Publications

Discovery Map International, LLC
1-877-820-7827

Franchise Development Services Ltd.
44-1603-620301

Homes & Land Publishing, Ltd.
1-800-726-6683

Real Estate Services

AVALAR
1-800-801-4030

Century 21 Real Estate Corporation
1-800-826-8083

Coldwell Banker Commercial
1-800-222-2162

Coldwell Banker Real Estate Corporation
973-496-5705

Crye-Leike Franchises, Inc.
1-866-603-2470

EPMARK, Inc.
1-800-783-3838

ERA Franchise Systems, Inc.
1-800-869-1260

GMAC Home Services
1-800-274-7661

HomeVestors of America
1-888-495-5220

Integra Realty Resources
212-255-7858

RE/MAX International
1-800-525-7452

Showhomes of America
251-432-2310

Recreation: Equipment & Supplies

Crown Trophy
1-800-583-8228

GOLF USA Inc.
1-800-488-1107

Herman's Direct, Inc.
1-888-853-3200

PODS
1-888-776-7637

Pro Golf Discount
1-800-521-6388

Scooter Planet
702-869-0099

Super Kick International, Inc.
770-390-9399

Volvo Construction Equipment Rents, Inc.
828-650-2000

Recreation: Exercise/Sports/Products

American Poolplayers Association
1-800-372-2536

Bally Fitness Franchising, Inc.
1-800-410-2582

Bogart Golf
904-274-0203

Contours Express, Inc.
1-877-227-2282

Curves
1-800-848-1096

Gold's Gym Franchising
1-800-457-5375

Herman's Direct, Inc.
1-888-853-3200

i9 Sports
813-662-6773

IM=X Pilates Studio
212-997-5550

LA Boxing Franchise Corporation
1-866-LABOXING

Mile High Karate, LLC
303-740-9467

Parmasters Indoor Golf Training Centers, Inc.
1-800-663-2331

Personal Best Karate
508-285-5425

Reality Sports Entertainment, Inc.
1-866-232-5023

Sports Section, Inc., The
1-866-877-4746

Velocity Sports Performance
1-866-955-0400

Woodhouse Day Spa, The
1-877-570-7772

Retail Stores: Specialty

@Wireless
1-800-613-2355

1st Propane Franchising, Inc.
1-877-977-6726

Air Traffic—Games of Skill
1-888-292-5558

Athlete's Foot, The
1-800-524-6444

Batteries Plus
1-800-274-9155

Beauty Brands Salon Spa Superstore
1-888-725-6608

BEI Franchising, Inc.
1-866-765-2740

Big Picture Framing
1-800-315-0024

Build-A-Bear Workshop
314-423-8000

Cardsmart Retail Corporation
1-877-227-3762

Cartridge World
1-866-473-5623

Children's Orchard, Inc.
1-800-999-5437

Coffee Beanery, Ltd., The
1-800-728-2326

Cookies by Design/Cookie Bouquet
1-800-945-2665

Deck The Walls, Inc.
1-800-543-3325

Dollar Discount
1-800-227-5314

DOTI Design Stores
1-888-382-7488

DVDPlay
408-395-1727

Edible Arrangements
1-888-727-4258

EmbroidMe
1-800-727-6720

FASTFRAME USA INC.
1-800-333-3225

Framing & Art Centre
1-800-563-7263

Furla
1-888-387-5287

Glamour Secrets
1-866-713-7487

The Grape
404-497-0505

Great Canadian Dollar Store (1993) Ltd.
1-877-388-0123

Great Frame Up, The
1-800-543-3325

HobbyTown USA
1-800-858-7370

HomeTown Hearth & Grill
1-888-298-0031

Incredibly Edible Delites, Inc.
1-866-203-7848

Instant Imprints
1-800-542-3437

Island Ink-Jet (R) Systems
1-877-446-5538

Just-A-Buck
1-800-332-2229

Kid to Kid
1-888-543-2543

Learning Express Toys
1-800-924-2296

Let's Make Wine
1-888-416-9755

Max Muscle
1-800-530-3539

Music Go Round
1-800-269-4076

Natural Source USA, The
858-488-3609

Once Upon A Child
1-800-453-7750

Palm Beach Tan
972-931-6595

Parable
1-800-366-6031

Party City Corporation
1-800-883-2100

Pinch A Penny, Inc.
727-531-8913

Planet Beach Franchising Corporation
1-888-290-8266

Plato's Closet
1-800-269-4081

Play It Again Sports
1-800-453-7754

PrePlayed
1-866-640-7529

Pump It Up—The Inflatable Party Zone
1-866-325-9663

Purified Water To Go
1-800-976-9283

QuikDrop
1-888-784-5266

Rapid Refill Ink International, LLC
541-431-4665

Relax The Back Corporation
562-860-1019

Slumberland Furniture
1-888-482-7500

Snappy Auctions
615-463-7355

Tinder Box International
1-800-846-3372

Totally Low Carb Stores Inc.
1-800-631-2272

Verlo Mattress Factory Stores, LLC
1-800-229-8957

Vino 100
1-866-846-6425

Vintner's Cellar Franchising International Inc.
1-800-480-7417

We the People Legal Document Services
805-962-4100

Wild Bird Centers of America, Inc.
1-800-945-3247

Wild Birds Unlimited, Inc.
1-888-730-7108

WineStyles Inc.
1-866-424-9463

Wireless Dimensions
1-888-809-4934

Wireless Toyz
248-426-8200

Wireless Zone
860-632-9494

Security Systems

Sonitrol Corporation
1-800-328-5607

Senior Care

@WORK HelpingHands Services
1-800-383-0804

Abbington Franchising, Inc.
1-866-461-3945

AristoCare
1-866-731-2273

ComForcare Senior Services
1-800-886-4044

Comfort Keepers
1-800-387-2415

GRISWOLD SPECIAL CARE
1-888-777-7630

Home Care Assistance
650-462-6900

Home Helpers
1-800-216-4196

Home Instead Senior Care
1-888-484-5759

Right At Home, Inc.
1-877-697-7537

Sarah Adult Day Services, Inc.
1-800-472-5544

Sarah Adult Day Services, Inc.
1-800-472-5544

Senior Living Communities

Abbington Franchising, Inc.
1-866-461-3945

Sign Products & Services

FastFrame U.S.A. Inc.
1-800-333-3225

FastSigns
1-800-827-7446

Have Signs Will Travel
631-218-6801

Instant Imprints
1-800-542-3437

SIGN*A*RAMA
1-800-286-8671

Signs By Tomorrow
1-800-765-7446

Signs Now Corporation
1-800-356-3373

Tanning Centers

Hollywood Tans
856-914-9090

Palm Beach Tan
972-931-6595

Planet Beach Franchising Corporation
1-888-290-8266

Tan Company, The
1-888-688-8222

Tropi Tan Franchising
1-866-818-1826

Telecommunication Services

@Wireless
1-800-613-2355

Concerto Networks, Inc.
1-866-551-4007

easyInternetcafe Franchising, Inc.
212-981-3953

OnlyOne
1-866-887-4310

SaveItNow! Franchising Systems LLC
1-888-668-9727

Wireless Dimensions
1-888-809-4934

Wireless Toyz
248-426-8200

Wireless Zone
860-632-9494

Tools & Hardware

Matco Tools
1-800-368-6651

Snap-on-Tools Company
1-800-786-6600

Transportation Services

Fastway Couriers
49-3419882

SaveItNow! Franchising Systems LLC
1-888-668-9727

TravelCenters of America, Inc.
440-808-9100

Two Men And A Truck International, Inc.
1-800-345-1070

Unishippers
1-800-999-8721

Travel Agents

Carlson Wagonlit Travel Associates, Inc.
1-800-678-8241

Cruise Holidays
763-212-1359

CruiseOne
1-800-892-3928

Travel Lines Express
561-482-9557

Uniglobe Travel (International) Inc.
1-800-863-1606

Vending

24seven Vending (US), Inc.
858-366-0580

Video/Audio Sales & Rentals

Blockbuster, Inc.
214-854-3000

Bogart Golf
904-274-0203

DVDPlay
408-395-1727

Flicko's Franchise Corp., Inc.
1-866-354-2567

Vitamin & Mineral Stores

Positive Changes Hypnosis
1-800-880-0436

Water Conditioning

Culligan International
847-205-6000

Purified Water To Go
1-800-976-9283

Rainsoft Water Treatment Systems
1-800-724-6763

Weight Control

Jenny Craig International, Inc.
760-696-4000

LA Weight Loss Centers
1-888-258-7099

Lite For Life
650-941-3200

Positive Changes Hypnosis
1-800-880-0436

International Franchise Association Code of Ethics

Preface

The International Franchise Association Code of Ethics is intended to establish a framework for the implementation of best practices in the franchise relationships of IFA members. The Code represents the ideals to which all IFA members agree to subscribe in their franchise relationships. The Code is one component of the IFA's self-regulation program, which also includes the IFA Ombudsman and revisions to the IFA bylaws that will streamline the enforcement mechanism for the Code. The Code is not intended to anticipate the solution to every challenge that may arise in a franchise relationship, but rather to provide a set of core values that are the basis for the resolution of the challenges that may arise in franchise relationships. Also the Code is not intended to establish standards to be applied by third parties, such as the courts, but to create a framework under which IFA and its members will govern themselves. The IFA's members believe that adherence to the values expressed in the IFA Code will result in healthy, productive and mutually beneficial franchise relationships. The Code, like franchising, is dynamic and may be revised to reflect the most current developments in structuring and maintaining franchise relationships.

Trust, Truth, and Honesty

Foundations of Franchising

Every franchise relationship is founded on the mutual commitment of both parties to fulfill their obligations under the franchise agreement. Each party will fulfill its obligations, will act consistent with the interests of the brand and will not act so as to harm the brand and system. This willing interdependence between franchisors and franchisees, and the trust and honesty upon which it is founded, has made franchising a worldwide success as a strategy for business growth.

Honesty embodies openness, candor and truthfulness. Franchisees and franchisors commit to sharing ideas and information and to face challenges in clear and direct terms. IFA members will be sincere in word, act and character—reputable and without deception.

The public image and reputation of the franchise system is one of its most valuable and enduring assets. A positive image and reputation will create value for franchisors and franchisees, attract investment in existing and new outlets from franchisees and from new franchise operators, help capture additional market share and enhance consumer loyalty and satisfaction. This can be achieved with trust, truth and honesty between franchisors and franchisees.

Mutual Respect and Reward

Winning Together, As a Team

The success of franchise systems depends upon both franchisors and franchisees attaining their goals. The IFA's members believe that franchisors cannot be successful unless their franchisees are also successful, and conversely, that franchisees will not succeed unless their franchisor is also successful. IFA members believe that a franchise system should be committed to help its franchisees succeed, and that such efforts are likely to create value for the system and attract new investment in the system.

IFA's members are committed to showing respect and consideration for each other and to those with whom they do business. Mutual respect includes recognizing and honoring extraordinary achievement and exemplary commitment to the system. IFA members believe that franchisors and franchisees share the responsibility for improving their franchise system in a manner that rewards both franchisors and franchisees.

Open and Frequent Communication

Successful Franchise Systems Thrive on It

IFA's members believe that franchising is a unique form of business relationship. Nowhere else in the world does there exist a business relationship that embodies such a significant degree of mutual interdependence. IFA members believe that to be successful, this unique relationship requires continual and effective communication between franchisees and franchisors.

IFA's members recognize that misunderstanding and loss of trust and consensus on the direction of a franchise system can develop when franchisors and franchisees fail to communicate effectively. Effective communication requires openness, candor and trust and is an integral component of a successful franchise system. Effective communication is an essential predicate for consensus and collaboration, the resolution of differences, progress and innovation.

To foster franchising as a unique and enormously successful relationship, IFA's members commit to establishing and maintaining programs that promote effective communication within franchise systems. These programs should be widely publicized within systems, available to all members of the franchise system and should facilitate frequent dialogue within franchise systems. IFA members are encouraged to also utilize the IFA Ombudsman to assist in enhancing communication and collaboration about issues affecting the franchise system.

Obey the Law

A Responsibility to Preserve the Promise of Franchising

IFA's members enthusiastically support full compliance with, and vigorous enforcement of, all applicable federal and state franchise regulations. This commitment is fundamental to enhancing and safeguarding the business environment for franchising. IFA's members believe that the information provided during the presale disclosure process is the cornerstone of a positive business climate for franchising, and is the basis for successful and mutually beneficial franchise relationships.

Conflict Resolution

IFA's members are realistic about franchise relationships, and recognize that from time to time disputes will arise in those relationships. IFA's members are committed to the amicable and prompt resolution of these disputes. IFA members believe that franchise systems should establish a method for internal dispute resolution and should publicize and encourage use of such dispute resolution mechanisms. For these reasons, the IFA has created the IFA Ombudsman program, an independent third-party who can assist franchisors and franchisees by facilitating dialogue to avoid disputes and to work together to resolve disputes. The IFA also strongly recommends the use of the National Franchise Mediation Program (NFMP) when a more structured mediation service is needed to help resolve differences.

Support of IFA and the Member Code of Ethics

Franchisees and franchisors have a responsibility to voice their concerns and offer suggestions on how the Code and the International Franchise Association can best meet the needs of its members. Franchisors and franchisees commit to supporting and promoting the initiatives of the IFA and advocating adherence to the letter and spirit of the Member Code of Ethics. Members who feel that another member has violated the Code in their U.S. operations may file a formal written complaint with the President of the IFA. For more information, contact the IFA at 202-628-8000 or visit our website at www. franchise.org.

Index